NON SANZ DROICT.

The Comedie of Errors.

Actus primus, Scena prima.

Decorative headband and title of the first printed version of
The Comedy of Errors, 1623.

William Shakespeare

The Comedy of Errors

With New and Updated
Critical Essays
and a Revised Bibliography

Edited by Harry Levin

THE SIGNET CLASSIC SHAKESPEARE
General Editor: Sylvan Barnet

SIGNET CLASSIC
Published by New American Library, a division of
Penguin Putnam Inc., 375 Hudson Street, New York, New York 10014, U.S.A.
Penguin Books Ltd, 80 Strand, London WC2R 0RL, England
Penguin Books Australia Ltd, Ringwood, Victoria, Australia
Penguin Books Canada Ltd, 10 Alcorn Avenue, Toronto, Ontario, Canada M4V 3B2
Penguin Books (N.Z.) Ltd, 182–190 Wairau Road, Auckland 10, New Zealand

Penguin Books Ltd, Registered Offices:
Harmondsworth, Middlesex, England

Published by Signet Classic, an imprint of New American Library,
a member of Penguin Putnam Inc.

First Signet Classic Printing (Second Revised Edition), June 2002
10 9 8 7 6 5 4 3 2 1

Contents

Shakespeare: An Overview

Biographical Sketch

Between the record of his baptism in Stratford on 26 April 1564 and the record of his burial in Stratford on 25 April 1616, some forty official documents name Shakespeare, and many others name his parents, his children, and his grandchildren. Further, there are at least fifty literary references to him in the works of his contemporaries. More facts are known about William Shakespeare than about any other playwright of the period except Ben Jonson. The facts should, however, be distinguished from the legends. The latter, inevitably more engaging and better known, tell us that the Stratford boy killed a calf in high style, poached deer and rabbits, and was forced to flee to London, where he held horses outside a playhouse. These traditions are only traditions; they may be true, but no evidence supports them, and it is well to stick to the facts.

Mary Arden, the dramatist's mother, was the daughter of a substantial landowner; about 1557 she married John Shakespeare, a tanner, glove-maker, and trader in wool, grain, and other farm commodities. In 1557 John Shakespeare was a member of the council (the governing body of Stratford), in 1558 a constable of the borough, in 1561 one of the two town chamberlains, in 1565 an alderman (entitling him to the appellation of "Mr."), in 1568 high bailiff— the town's highest political office, equivalent to mayor. After 1577, for an unknown reason he drops out of local politics. What *is* known is that he had to mortgage his wife's property, and that he was involved in serious litigation.

The birthday of William Shakespeare, the third child and the eldest son of this locally prominent man, is unrecorded, but the Stratford parish register records that the infant was baptized on 26 April 1564. (It is quite possible that he was born on 23 April, but this date has probably been assigned by tradition because it is the date on which, fifty-two years later, he died, and perhaps because it is the feast day of St. George, patron saint of England.) The attendance records of the Stratford grammar school of the period are not extant, but it is reasonable to assume that the son of a prominent local official attended the free school—it had been established for the purpose of educating males precisely of his class—and received substantial training in Latin. The masters of the school from Shakespeare's seventh to fifteenth years held Oxford degrees; the Elizabethan curriculum excluded mathematics and the natural sciences but taught a good deal of Latin rhetoric, logic, and literature, including plays by Plautus, Terence, and Seneca.

On 27 November 1582 a marriage license was issued for the marriage of Shakespeare and Anne Hathaway, eight years his senior. The couple had a daughter, Susanna, in May 1583. Perhaps the marriage was necessary, but perhaps the couple had earlier engaged, in the presence of witnesses, in a formal "troth plight" which would render their children legitimate even if no further ceremony were performed. In February 1585, Anne Hathaway bore Shakespeare twins, Hamnet and Judith.

That Shakespeare was born is excellent; that he married and had children is pleasant; but that we know nothing about his departure from Stratford to London or about the beginning of his theatrical career is lamentable and must be admitted. We would gladly sacrifice details about his children's baptism for details about his earliest days in the theater. Perhaps the poaching episode is true (but it is first reported almost a century after Shakespeare's death), or perhaps he left Stratford to be a schoolmaster, as another tradition holds; perhaps he was moved (like Petruchio in *The Taming of the Shrew*) by

> Such wind as scatters young men through the world,
> To seek their fortunes farther than at home
> Where small experience grows.   (1.2.49–51)

In 1592, thanks to the cantankerousness of Robert Greene, we have our first reference, a snarling one, to Shakespeare as an actor and playwright. Greene, a graduate of St. John's College, Cambridge, had become a playwright and a pamphleteer in London, and in one of his pamphlets he warns three university-educated playwrights against an actor who has presumed to turn playwright:

> There is an upstart crow, beautified with our feathers, that with his *tiger's heart wrapped in a player's hide* supposes he is as well able to bombast out a blank verse as the best of you, and being an absolute Johannes-factotum [i.e., jack-of-all-trades] is in his own conceit the only Shake-scene in a country.

The reference to the player, as well as the allusion to Aesop's crow (who strutted in borrowed plumage, as an actor struts in fine words not his own), makes it clear that by this date Shakespeare had both acted and written. That Shakespeare is meant is indicated not only by *Shake-scene* but also by the parody of a line from one of Shakespeare's plays, *3 Henry VI*: "O, tiger's heart wrapped in a woman's hide" (1.4.137). If in 1592 Shakespeare was prominent enough to be attacked by an envious dramatist, he probably had served an apprenticeship in the theater for at least a few years.

In any case, although there are no extant references to Shakespeare between the record of the baptism of his twins in 1585 and Greene's hostile comment about "Shake-scene" in 1592, it is evident that during some of these "dark years" or "lost years" Shakespeare had acted and written. There are a number of subsequent references to him as an actor. Documents indicate that in 1598 he is a "principal comedian," in 1603 a "principal tragedian," in 1608 he is one of the "men players." (We do not have, however, any solid information about which roles he may have played; later traditions say he played Adam in *As You Like It* and the ghost in *Hamlet*, but nothing supports the assertions. Probably his role as dramatist came to supersede his role as actor.) The profession of actor was not for a gentleman, and it occasionally drew the scorn of university men like Greene who resented writing speeches for persons less educated than themselves, but it was respectable enough; players, if prosperous, were in effect members of the bourgeoisie, and there is nothing to suggest that Stratford considered William Shakespeare less than a solid citizen. When, in 1596, the Shakespeares were granted a coat of arms—i.e., the right to be considered gentlemen—the grant was made to Shakespeare's father, but probably William Shakespeare had arranged the matter on his own behalf. In subsequent transactions he is occasionally styled a gentleman.

Although in 1593 and 1594 Shakespeare published two narrative poems dedicated to the Earl of Southampton, *Venus and Adonis* and *The Rape of Lucrece*, and may well have written most or all of his sonnets in the middle nineties, Shakespeare's literary activity seems to have been almost entirely devoted to the theater. (It may be significant that the two narrative poems were written in years when the plague closed the theaters for several months.) In 1594 he was a charter member of a theatrical company called the Chamberlain's Men, which in 1603 became the royal company, the King's Men, making Shakespeare the king's playwright. Until he retired to Stratford (about 1611, apparently), he was with this remarkably stable company. From 1599 the company acted primarily at the Globe theater, in which Shakespeare held a one-tenth interest. Other Elizabethan dramatists are known to have acted, but no other is known also to have been entitled to a share of the profits.

Shakespeare's first eight published plays did not have his name on them, but this is not remarkable; the most popular play of the period, Thomas Kyd's *The Spanish Tragedy*, went through many editions without naming Kyd, and Kyd's authorship is known only because a book on the profession of acting happens to quote (and attribute to Kyd) some lines on the interest of Roman emperors in the drama. What is remarkable is that after 1598 Shakespeare's name commonly appears on printed plays—some of which are not his. Presumably his name was a drawing card, and publishers used it to attract potential buyers. Another indication of his popularity comes from Francis Meres, author of *Palladis Tamia: Wit's Treasury* (1598). In this anthology of snippets accompanied by an essay on literature, many playwrights are mentioned, but Shakespeare's name occurs more often than any other, and Shakespeare is the only play-wright whose plays are listed.

From his acting, his play writing, and his share in a playhouse, Shakespeare seems to have made considerable money. He put it to work, making substantial investments in Stratford real estate. As early as 1597 he bought New Place, the second-largest house in Stratford. His family moved in soon afterward, and the house remained in the family until a granddaughter died in 1670. When Shakespeare made his will in 1616, less than a month before he died, he sought to leave his property intact to his descendants. Of small bequests to relatives and to friends (including three actors, Richard Burbage, John Heminges, and Henry Condell), that to his wife of the second-best bed has provoked the most comment. It has sometimes been taken as a sign of an unhappy marriage (other supposed signs are the apparently hasty marriage, his wife's seniority of eight years, and his residence in London without his family). Perhaps the second-best bed was the bed the couple had slept in, the best bed being reserved for visitors. In any case, had Shakespeare not excepted it, the bed would have gone (with the rest of his household possessions) to his daughter and her husband.

On 25 April 1616 Shakespeare was buried within the chancel of the church at Stratford. An unattractive monument to his memory, placed on a wall near the grave, says that he died on 23 April. Over the grave itself are the lines, perhaps by Shakespeare, that (more than his literary fame) have kept his bones undisturbed in the crowded burial ground where old bones were often dislodged to make way for new:

> Good friend, for Jesus' sake forbear
> To dig the dust enclosed here.
> Blessed be the man that spares these stones
> And cursed be he that moves my bones.

A Note on the Anti-Stratfordians, Especially Baconians and Oxfordians

Not until 1769—more than a hundred and fifty years after Shakespeare's death—is there any record of anyone expressing doubt about Shakespeare's authorship of the plays and poems. In 1769, however, Herbert Lawrence nominated Francis Bacon (1561–1626) in *The Life and Adventures of Common Sense*. Since then, at least two dozen other nominees have been offered, including Christopher Marlowe, Sir Walter Raleigh, Queen Elizabeth I, and Edward de Vere, 17th earl of Oxford. The impulse behind all anti-Stratfordian movements is the scarcely concealed snobbish opinion that "the man from Stratford" simply could not have written the plays because he was a country fellow without a university education and without access to high society. Anyone, the argument goes, who used so many legal terms, medical terms, nautical terms, and so forth, and who showed some familiarity with classical writing, must have attended a university, and anyone who knew so much about courtly elegance and courtly deceit must himself have moved among courtiers. The plays do indeed reveal an author whose interests were exceptionally broad, but specialists in any given field—law, medicine, arms and armor, and so on—soon find that the plays do not reveal deep knowledge in specialized matters; indeed, the playwright often gets technical details wrong.

The claim on behalf of Bacon, forgotten almost as soon as it was put forth in 1769, was independently reasserted by Joseph C. Hart in 1848. In 1856 it was reaffirmed by W. H. Smith in a book, and also by Delia Bacon in an article; in 1857 Delia Bacon published a book, arguing that Francis Bacon had directed a group of intellectuals who wrote the plays.

Francis Bacon's claim has largely faded, perhaps because it was advanced with such evident craziness by Ignatius Donnelly, who in *The Great Cryptogram* (1888) claimed to break a code in the plays that proved Bacon had written not only the plays attributed to Shakespeare but also other Renaissance works, for instance the plays of Christopher Marlowe and the essays of Montaigne.

Consider the last two lines of the Epilogue in *The Tempest*:

As you from crimes would pardoned be,
Let your indulgence set me free.

What was Shakespeare—sorry, Francis Bacon, Baron Verulam—*really* saying in these two lines? According to Baconians, the lines are an anagram reading, "Tempest of Francis Bacon, Lord Verulam; do ye ne'er divulge me, ye words." Ingenious, and it is a pity that in the quotation the letter *a* appears only twice in the cryptogram, whereas in the deciphered message it appears three times. Oh, no problem; just alter "Verulam" to "Verul'm" and it works out very nicely.

Most people understand that with sufficient ingenuity one can torture any text and find in it what one wishes. For instance: Did Shakespeare have a hand in the King James Version of the Bible? It was nearing completion in 1610, when Shakespeare was forty-six years old. If you look at the 46th Psalm and count forward for forty-six words, you will find the word *shake*. Now if you go to the end of the psalm and count backward forty-six words, you will find the word *spear*. Clear evidence, according to some, that Shakespeare slyly left his mark in the book.

Bacon's candidacy has largely been replaced in the twentieth century by the candidacy of Edward de Vere (1550–1604), 17th earl of Oxford. The basic ideas behind the Oxford theory, advanced at greatest length by Dorothy and Charlton Ogburn in *This Star of England* (1952, rev. 1955), a book of 1297 pages, and by Charlton Ogburn in *The Mysterious William Shakespeare* (1984), a book of 892 pages, are these: (1) The man from Stratford could not possibly have had the mental equipment and the experience to have written the plays—only a courtier could have written them; (2) Oxford had the requisite background (social position, education, years at Queen Elizabeth's court); (3) Oxford did not wish his authorship to be known for two basic reasons: writing for the public theater was a vulgar pursuit, and the plays show so much courtly and royal disreputable behavior that they would have compromised Oxford's position at court. Oxfordians offer countless details to support the claim. For example, Hamlet's phrase "that ever I was born to set it right" (1.5.89) barely conceals "E. Ver, I was born to set it right," an unambiguous announcement of de Vere's authorship, according to *This Star of England* (p. 654). A second example: Consider Ben

Jonson's poem entitled "To the Memory of My Beloved Master William Shakespeare," prefixed to the first collected edition of Shakespeare's plays in 1623. According to Oxfordians, when Jonson in this poem speaks of the author of the plays as the "swan of Avon," he is alluding not to William Shakespeare, who was born and died in Stratford-on-Avon and who throughout his adult life owned property there; rather, he is alluding to Oxford, who, the Ogburns say, used "William Shakespeare" as his pen name, and whose manor at Bilton was on the Avon River. Oxfordians do not offer any evidence that Oxford took a pen name, and they seem unconcerned that Oxford sold the manor in 1581, forty-two years before Jonson wrote his poem. Surely a reference to the Shakespeare who was born in Stratford, who had returned to Stratford, and who had died there only seven years before Jonson wrote the poem is more plausible. And exactly why Jonson, who elsewhere also spoke of Shakespeare as a playwright, and why Heminges and Condell, who had acted with Shakespeare for about twenty years, should speak of Shakespeare as the author in their dedication in the 1623 volume of collected plays is never adequately explained by Oxfordians. Either Jonson, Heminges and Condell, and numerous others were in on the conspiracy, or they were all duped—equally unlikely alternatives. Another difficulty in the Oxford theory is that Oxford died in 1604, and some of the plays are clearly indebted to works and events later than 1604. Among the Oxfordian responses are: At his death Oxford left some plays, and in later years these were touched up by hacks, who added the material that points to later dates. *The Tempest*, almost universally regarded as one of Shakespeare's greatest plays and pretty clearly dated to 1611, does indeed date from a period after the death of Oxford, but it is a crude piece of work that should not be included in the canon of works by Oxford.

The anti-Stratfordians, in addition to assuming that the author must have been a man of rank and a university man, usually assume two conspiracies: (1) a conspiracy in Elizabethan and Jacobean times, in which a surprisingly large number of persons connected with the theater knew that the actor Shakespeare did not write the plays attributed to him but for some reason or other pretended that he did; (2) a conspiracy of today's Stratfordians, the professors who teach Shakespeare in the colleges and universities, who are said to have a vested interest in preserving Shakespeare as the author of the plays they teach. In fact, (1) it is inconceivable that the secret of Shakespeare's non-authorship could have been preserved by all of the people who supposedly were in on the conspiracy, and (2) academic fame awaits any scholar today who can disprove Shakespeare's authorship.

The Stratfordian case is convincing not only because hundreds or even thousands of anti-Stratford arguments—of the sort that say "ever I was born" has the secret double meaning "E. Ver, I was born"—add up to nothing at all but also because irrefutable evidence connects the man from Stratford with the London theater and with the authorship of particular plays. The anti-Stratfordians do not seem to understand that it is not enough to dismiss the Stratford case by saying that a fellow from the provinces simply couldn't have written the plays. Nor do they understand that it is not enough to dismiss all of the evidence connecting Shakespeare with the plays by asserting that it is perjured.

The Shakespeare Canon

We return to William Shakespeare. Thirty-seven plays as well as some nondramatic poems are generally held to constitute the Shakespeare canon, the body of authentic works. The exact dates of composition of most of the works are highly uncertain, but evidence of a starting point and/or of a final limiting point often provides a framework for informed guessing. For example, *Richard II* cannot be earlier than 1595, the publication date of some material to which it is indebted; *The Merchant of Venice* cannot be later than 1598, the year Francis Meres mentioned it. Sometimes arguments for a date hang on an alleged topical allusion, such as the lines about the unseasonable weather in *A Midsummer Night's Dream*, 2.1.81–117, but such an allusion, if indeed it is an allusion to an event in the real world, can be variously interpreted, and in any case there is always the possibility that a topical allusion was inserted years later, to bring the play up to date. (The issue of alterations in a text between the time that Shakespeare drafted it and the time that it was printed—alterations due to censorship or playhouse practice or Shakespeare's own second thoughts—will be discussed in "The Play Text as a Collaboration" later in this overview.) Dates are often attributed on the basis of style, and although conjectures about style usually rest on other conjectures (such as Shakespeare's development as a playwright, or the appropriateness of lines to character), sooner or later one must rely on one's literary sense. There is no documentary proof, for example, that *Othello* is not as early as *Romeo and Juliet*, but one feels that *Othello* is a later, more mature work, and because the first record of its performance is 1604, one is glad enough to set its composition at that date and not push it back into Shakespeare's early years. (*Romeo and Juliet* was first published in 1597, but evidence suggests that it was written a little earlier.) The following chronology, then, is indebted not only to facts but also to informed guesswork and sensitivity. The dates, necessarily imprecise for some works, indicate something like a scholarly consensus concerning the time of original composition. Some plays show evidence of later revision.

Plays. The first collected edition of Shakespeare, published in 1623, included thirty-six plays. These are all accepted as Shakespeare's, though for one of them, *Henry VIII*, he is thought to have had a collaborator. A thirty-seventh play, *Pericles*, published in 1609 and attributed to Shakespeare on the title page, is also widely accepted as being partly by Shakespeare even though it is not included in the 1623 volume. Still another play not in the 1623 volume, *The Two Noble Kinsmen*, was first published in 1634, with a title page attributing it to John Fletcher and Shakespeare. Probably most students of the subject now believe that Shakespeare did indeed have a hand in it. Of the remaining plays attributed at one time or another to Shakespeare, only one, *Edward III*, anonymously published in 1596, is now regarded by some scholars as a serious candidate. The prevailing opinion, however, is that this rather simpleminded play is not Shakespeare's; at most he may have revised some passages, chiefly scenes with the Countess of

Salisbury. We include *The Two Noble Kinsmen* but do not include *Edward III* in the following list.

1588–94	*The Comedy of Errors*
1588–94	*Love's Labor's Lost*
1589–91	*2 Henry VI*
1590–91	*3 Henry VI*
1589–92	*1 Henry VI*
1592–93	*Richard III*
1589–94	*Titus Andronicus*
1593–94	*The Taming of the Shrew*
1592–94	*The Two Gentlemen of Verona*
1594–96	*Romeo and Juliet*
1595	*Richard II*
1595–96	*A Midsummer Night's Dream*
1596–97	*King John*
1594–96	*The Merchant of Venice*
1596–97	*1 Henry IV*
1597	*The Merry Wives of Windsor*
1597–98	*2 Henry IV*
1598–99	*Much Ado About Nothing*
1598–99	*Henry V*
1599	*Julius Caesar*
1599–1600	*As You Like It*
1599–1600	*Twelfth Night*
1600–1601	*Hamlet*
1601–1602	*Troilus and Cressida*
1602–1604	*All's Well That Ends Well*
1603–1604	*Othello*
1604	*Measure for Measure*
1605–1606	*King Lear*
1605–1606	*Macbeth*
1606–1607	*Antony and Cleopatra*
1605–1608	*Timon of Athens*
1607–1608	*Coriolanus*
1607–1608	*Pericles*
1609–10	*Cymbeline*
1610–11	*The Winter's Tale*
1611	*The Tempest*

1612–13	*Henry VIII*
1613	*The Two Noble Kinsmen*

Poems. In 1989 Donald W. Foster published a book in which he argued that "A Funeral Elegy for Master William Peter," published in 1612, ascribed only to the initials W.S., *may* be by Shakespeare. Foster later published an article in a scholarly journal, *PMLA* 111 (1996), in which he asserted the claim more positively. The evidence begins with the initials, and includes the fact that the publisher and the printer of the elegy had published Shakespeare's *Sonnets* in 1609. But such facts add up to rather little, especially because no one has found any connection between Shakespeare and William Peter (an Oxford graduate about whom little is known, who was murdered at the age of twenty-nine). The argument is based chiefly on statistical examinations of word patterns, which are said to correlate with Shakespeare's known work. Despite such correlations, however, many readers feel that the poem does not sound like Shakespeare. True, Shakespeare has a great range of styles, but his work is consistently imaginative and interesting. Many readers find neither of these qualities in "A Funeral Elegy."

1592–93	*Venus and Adonis*
1593–94	*The Rape of Lucrece*
1593–1600	*Sonnets*
1600–1601	*The Phoenix and the Turtle*

Shakespeare's English

1. Spelling and Pronunciation. From the philologist's point of view, Shakespeare's English is modern English. It requires footnotes, but the inexperienced reader can comprehend substantial passages with very little help, whereas for the same reader Chaucer's Middle English is a foreign language. By the beginning of the fifteenth century the chief grammatical changes in English had taken place, and the final unaccented -*e* of Middle English had been lost (though it survives even today in spelling, as in *name*); during the fifteenth century the dialect of London, the commercial and political center, gradually displaced the provincial dialects, at least in writing; by the end of the century, printing had helped to regularize and stabilize the language, especially spelling. Elizabethan spelling may seem erratic to us (there were dozens of spellings of *Shakespeare*, and a simple word like *been* was also spelled *beene* and *bin*), but it had much in common with our spelling. Elizabethan spelling was conservative in that for the most part it reflected an older pronunciation (Middle English) rather than the sound of the language as it was then spoken, just as our spelling continues to reflect medieval pronunciation—most obviously in the now silent but formerly pronounced letters in a word such as *knight*. Elizabethan pronunciation, though not identical with ours, was much closer to ours than to that of the Middle Ages. Incidentally, though no one can be certain about what Elizabethan English sounded like, specialists tend to believe it was rather like the speech of a modern stage Irishman (*time* apparently was pronounced *toime*, *old* pronounced *awld*, *day* pronounced *die*, and *join* pronounced *jine*) and not at all like the Oxford speech that most of us think it was.

An awareness of the difference between our pronunciation and Shakespeare's is crucial in three areas—in accent, or number of syllables (many metrically regular lines may look irregular to us); in rhymes (which may not look like rhymes); and in puns (which may not look like puns). Examples will be useful. Some words that were at least on occasion stressed differently from today are *aspèct*, *còmplete*, *fòrlorn*, *revènue*, and *sepùlcher*. Words that sometimes had an additional syllable are *emp[e]ress*, *Hen[e]ry*, *mon[e]th*, and *villain* (three syllables, *vil-lay-in*). An additional syllable is often found in possessives, like *moon*'s (pronounced *moones*) and in words ending in *-tion* or *-sion*. Words that had one less syllable than they now have are *needle* (pronounced *neel*) and *violet* (pronounced *vilet*). Among rhymes now lost are *one* with *loan*, *love* with *prove*, *beast* with *jest*, *eat* with *great*. (In reading, trust your sense of metrics and your ear, more than your eye.) An example of a pun that has become obliterated by a change in pronunciation is Falstaff's reply to Prince Hal's "Come, tell us your

reason" in *1 Henry IV*: "Give you a reason on compulsion?
If reasons were as plentiful as blackberries, I would give no
man a reason upon compulsion, I" (2.4.237–40). The *ea* in
reason was pronounced rather like a long *a,* like the *ai* in
raisin, hence the comparison with blackberries.

Puns are not merely attempts to be funny; like metaphors
they often involve bringing into a meaningful relationship
areas of experience normally seen as remote. In *2 Henry IV,*
when Feeble is conscripted, he stoically says, "I care not. A
man can die but once. We owe God a death" (3.2.242–43),
punning on *debt,* which was the way *death* was pronounced.
Here an enormously significant fact of life is put into simple
commercial imagery, suggesting its commonplace quality.
Shakespeare used the same pun earlier in *1 Henry IV,* when
Prince Hal says to Falstaff, "Why, thou owest God a death,"
and Falstaff replies, " 'Tis not due yet: I would be loath
to pay him before his day. What need I be so forward with
him that calls not on me?" (5.1.126–29).

Sometimes the puns reveal a delightful playfulness;
sometimes they reveal aggressiveness, as when, replying to
Claudius's "But now, my cousin Hamlet, and my son,"
Hamlet says, "A little more than kin, and less than kind!"
(1.2.64–65). These are Hamlet's first words in the play, and
we already hear him warring verbally against Claudius.
Hamlet's "less than kind" probably means (1) Hamlet is not
of Claudius's family or nature, *kind* having the sense it still
has in our word *mankind*; (2) Hamlet is not kindly (affec-
tionately) disposed toward Claudius; (3) Claudius is not
naturally (but rather unnaturally, in a legal sense incestu-
ously) Hamlet's father. The puns evidently were not put in
as sops to the groundlings; they are an important way of
communicating a complex meaning.

2. *Vocabulary.* A conspicuous difficulty in reading Shakespeare is rooted in the fact that some of his words are no
longer in common use—for example, words concerned with
armor, astrology, clothing, coinage, hawking, horsemanship, law, medicine, sailing, and war. Shakespeare had a
large vocabulary—something near thirty thousand words—
but it was not so much a vocabulary of big words as a
vocabulary drawn from a wide range of life, and it is partly

his ability to call upon a great body of concrete language that gives his plays the sense of being in close contact with life. When the right word did not already exist, he made it up. Among words thought to be his coinages are *accommodation, all-knowing, amazement, bare-faced, countless, dexterously, dislocate, dwindle, fancy-free, frugal, indistinguishable, lackluster, laughable, overawe, premeditated, sea change, star-crossed*. Among those that have not survived are the verb *convive*, meaning to feast together, and *smilet*, a little smile.

Less overtly troublesome than the technical words but more treacherous are the words that seem readily intelligible to us but whose Elizabethan meanings differ from their modern ones. When Horatio describes the Ghost as an "erring spirit," he is saying not that the ghost has sinned or made an error but that it is wandering. Here is a short list of some of the most common words in Shakespeare's plays that often (but not always) have a meaning other than their most usual modern meaning:

'a	he
abuse	deceive
accident	occurrence
advertise	inform
an, and	if
annoy	harm
appeal	accuse
artificial	skillful
brave	fine, splendid
censure	opinion
cheer	(1) face (2) frame of mind
chorus	a single person who comments on the events
closet	small private room
competitor	partner
conceit	idea, imagination
cousin	kinsman
cunning	skillful
disaster	evil astrological influence
doom	judgment
entertain	receive into service

envy	malice
event	outcome
excrement	outgrowth (of hair)
fact	evil deed
fancy	(1) love (2) imagination
fell	cruel
fellow	(1) companion (2) low person (often an insulting term if addressed to someone of approximately equal rank)
fond	foolish
free	(1) innocent (2) generous
glass	mirror
hap, haply	chance, by chance
head	army
humor	(1) mood (2) bodily fluid thought to control one's psychology
imp	child
intelligence	news
kind	natural, acting according to nature
let	hinder
lewd	base
mere(ly)	utter(ly)
modern	commonplace
natural	a fool, an idiot
naughty	(1) wicked (2) worthless
next	nearest
nice	(1) trivial (2) fussy
noise	music
policy	(1) prudence (2) stratagem
presently	immediately
prevent	anticipate
proper	handsome
prove	test
quick	alive
sad	serious
saw	proverb
secure	without care, incautious
silly	innocent

sensible	capable of being perceived by the senses
shrewd	sharp
so	provided that
starve	die
still	always
success	that which follows
tall	brave
tell	count
tonight	last night
wanton	playful, careless
watch	keep awake
will	lust
wink	close both eyes
wit	mind, intelligence

All glosses, of course, are mere approximations; sometimes one of Shakespeare's words may hover between an older meaning and a modern one, and as we have seen, his words often have multiple meanings.

3. Grammar. A few matters of grammar may be surveyed, though it should be noted at the outset that Shakespeare sometimes made up his own grammar. As E.A. Abbott says in *A Shakespearian Grammar,* "Almost any part of speech can be used as any other part of speech": a noun as a verb ("he childed as I fathered"); a verb as a noun ("She hath made compare"); or an adverb as an adjective ("a seldom pleasure"). There are hundreds, perhaps thousands, of such instances in the plays, many of which at first glance would not seem at all irregular and would trouble only a pedant. Here are a few broad matters.

Nouns: The Elizabethans thought the *-s* genitive ending for nouns (as in *man's*) derived from *his*; thus the line " 'gainst the count his galleys I did some service," for "the count's galleys."

Adjectives: By Shakespeare's time adjectives had lost the endings that once indicated gender, number, and case. About the only difference between Shakespeare's adjectives and ours is the use of the now redundant *more* or *most* with the comparative ("some more fitter place") or superlative

("This was the most unkindest cut of all"). Like double comparatives and double superlatives, double negatives were acceptable; Mercutio "will not budge for no man's pleasure."

Pronouns: The greatest change was in pronouns. In Middle English *thou, thy,* and *thee* were used among familiars and in speaking to children and inferiors; *ye, your,* and *you* were used in speaking to superiors (servants to masters, nobles to the king) or to equals with whom the speaker was not familiar. Increasingly the "polite" forms were used in all direct address, regardless of rank, and the accusative *you* displaced the nominative *ye.* Shakespeare sometimes uses *ye* instead of *you,* but even in Shakespeare's day *ye* was archaic, and it occurs mostly in rhetorical appeals.

Thou, thy, and *thee* were not completely displaced, however, and Shakespeare occasionally makes significant use of them, sometimes to connote familiarity or intimacy and sometimes to connote contempt. In *Twelfth Night* Sir Toby advises Sir Andrew to insult Cesario by addressing him as *thou:* "If thou thou'st him some thrice, it shall not be amiss" (3.2.46–47). In *Othello* when Brabantio is addressing an unidentified voice in the dark he says, "What are you?" (1.1.91), but when the voice identifies itself as the foolish suitor Roderigo, Brabantio uses the contemptuous form, saying, "I have charged thee not to haunt about my doors" (93). He uses this form for a while, but later in the scene, when he comes to regard Roderigo as an ally, he shifts back to the polite *you,* beginning in line 163, "What said she to you?" and on to the end of the scene. For reasons not yet satisfactorily explained, Elizabethans used *thou* in addresses to God—"O God, thy arm was here," the king says in *Henry V* (4.8.108)—and to supernatural characters such as ghosts and witches. A subtle variation occurs in *Hamlet.* When Hamlet first talks with the Ghost in 1.5, he uses *thou,* but when he sees the Ghost in his mother's room, in 3.4, he uses *you,* presumably because he is now convinced that the Ghost is not a counterfeit but is his father.

Perhaps the most unusual use of pronouns, from our point of view, is the neuter singular. In place of our *its, his* was often used, as in "How far that little candle throws *his* beams." But the use of a masculine pronoun for a neuter noun came to seem unnatural, and so *it* was used for the possessive as well as the nominative: "The hedge-sparrow fed the cuckoo so long / That it had it head bit off by it young." In the late sixteenth century the possessive form *its* developed, apparently by analogy with the -*s* ending used to indicate a genitive noun, as in *book*'s, but *its* was not yet common usage in Shakespeare's day. He seems to have used *its* only ten times, mostly in his later plays. Other usages, such as "you have seen Cassio and she together" or the substitution of *who* for *whom,* cause little problem even when noticed.

Verbs, Adverbs, and Prepositions: Verbs cause almost no difficulty: The third person singular present form commonly ends in -*s,* as in modern English (e.g., "He blesses"), but sometimes in -*eth* (Portia explains to Shylock that mercy "blesseth him that gives and him that takes"). Broadly speaking, the -*eth* ending was old-fashioned or dignified or "literary" rather than colloquial, except for the words *doth, hath,* and *saith.* The -*eth* ending (regularly used in the King James Bible, 1611) is very rare in Shakespeare's dramatic prose, though not surprisingly it occurs twice in the rather formal prose summary of the narrative poem *Lucrece.* Sometimes a plural subject, especially if it has collective force, takes a verb ending in -*s,* as in "My old bones aches." Some of our strong or irregular preterites (such as *broke*) have a different form in Shakespeare (*brake*); some verbs that now have a weak or regular preterite (such as *helped*) in Shakespeare have a strong or irregular preterite (*holp*). Some adverbs that today end in -*ly* were not inflected: "grievous sick," "wondrous strange." Finally, prepositions often are not the ones we expect: "We are such stuff as dreams are made on," "I have a king here to my flatterer."

Again, none of the differences (except meanings that have substantially changed or been lost) will cause much difficulty. But it must be confessed that for some elliptical passages there is no widespread agreement on meaning. Wise editors resist saying more than they know, and when they are uncertain they add a question mark to their gloss.

Shakespeare's Theater

In Shakespeare's infancy, Elizabethan actors performed wherever they could—in great halls, at court, in the courtyards of inns. These venues implied not only different audiences but also different playing conditions. The innyards must have made rather unsatisfactory theaters: on some days they were unavailable because carters bringing goods to London used them as depots; when available, they had to be rented from the innkeeper. In 1567, presumably to avoid such difficulties, and also to avoid regulation by the Common Council of London, which was not well disposed toward theatricals, one John Brayne, brother-in-law of the carpenter turned actor James Burbage, built the Red Lion in an eastern suburb of London. We know nothing about its shape or its capacity; we can say only that it may have been the first building in Europe constructed for the purpose of giving plays since the end of antiquity, a thousand years earlier. Even after the building of the Red Lion theatrical activity continued in London in makeshift circumstances, in marketplaces and inns, and always uneasily. In 1574 the Common Council required that plays and playing places in London be licensed because

> sundry great disorders and inconveniences have been found to ensue to this city by the inordinate haunting of great multitudes of people, specially youth, to plays, interludes, and shows, namely occasion of frays and quarrels, evil practices of incontinency in great inns having chambers and secret places adjoining to their open stages and galleries.

The Common Council ordered that innkeepers who wished licenses to hold performance put up a bond and make contributions to the poor.

The requirement that plays and innyard theaters be licensed, along with the other drawbacks of playing at inns and presumably along with the success of the Red Lion, led James Burbage to rent a plot of land northeast of the city walls, on property outside the jurisdiction of the city. Here he built England's second playhouse, called simply the Theatre. About all that is known of its construction is that it was wood. It soon had imitators, the most famous being the Globe (1599), essentially an amphitheater built across the Thames (again outside the city's jurisdiction), constructed with timbers of the Theatre, which had been dismantled when Burbage's lease ran out.

Admission to the theater was one penny, which allowed spectators to stand at the sides and front of the stage that jutted into the yard. An additional penny bought a seat in a covered part of the theater, and a third penny bought a more comfortable seat and a better location. It is notoriously difficult to translate prices into today's money, since some things that are inexpensive today would have been expensive in the past and vice versa—a pipeful of tobacco (imported, of course) cost a lot of money, about three pennies, and an orange (also imported) cost two or three times what a chicken cost—but perhaps we can get some idea of the low cost of the penny admission when we realize that a penny could also buy a pot of ale. An unskilled laborer made about five or sixpence a day, an artisan about twelve pence a day, and the hired actors (as opposed to the sharers in the company, such as Shakespeare) made about ten pence a performance. A printed play cost five or sixpence. Of course a visit to the theater (like a visit to a baseball game today) usually cost more than the admission since the spectator probably would also buy food and drink. Still, the low entrance fee meant that the theater was available to all except the very poorest people, rather as movies and most athletic events are today. Evidence indicates that the audience ranged from apprentices who somehow managed to scrape together the minimum entrance fee and to escape from their masters for a few hours, to prosperous members of the middle class and aristocrats who paid the additional fee for admission to the galleries. The exact proportion of men to women cannot be determined, but women of all classes certainly were present. Theaters were open every afternoon but Sundays for much of the year, except in times of plague, when they were closed because of fear of infection. By the way, no evidence suggests the presence of toilet facilities. Presumably the patrons relieved themselves by making a quick trip to the fields surrounding the playhouses.

There are four important sources of information about the

structure of Elizabethan public playhouses—drawings, a contract, recent excavations, and stage directions in the plays. Of drawings, only the so-called de Witt drawing (c. 1596) of the Swan—really his friend Aernout van Buchell's copy of Johannes de Witt's drawing—is of much significance. The drawing, the only extant representation of the interior of an Elizabethan theater, shows an amphitheater of three tiers, with a stage jutting from a wall into the yard or

Johannes de Witt, a Continental visitor to London, made a drawing of the Swan theater in about the year 1596. The original drawing is lost; this is Aernout van Buchell's copy of it.

center of the building. The tiers are roofed, and part of the stage is covered by a roof that projects from the rear and is supported at its front on two posts, but the groundlings, who paid a penny to stand in front of the stage or at its sides, were exposed to the sky. (Performances in such a playhouse were held only in the daytime; artificial illumination was not used.) At the rear of the stage are two massive doors; above the stage is a gallery.

The second major source of information, the contract for the Fortune (built in 1600), specifies that although the Globe (built in 1599) is to be the model, the Fortune is to be square, eighty feet outside and fifty-five inside. The stage is to be forty-three feet broad, and is to extend into the middle of the yard, i.e., it is twenty-seven and a half feet deep.

The third source of information, the 1989 excavations of the Rose (built in 1587), indicate that the Rose was fourteen-sided, about seventy-two feet in diameter with an inner yard almost fifty feet in diameter. The stage at the Rose was about sixteen feet deep, thirty-seven feet wide at the rear, and twenty-seven feet wide downstage. The relatively small dimensions and the tapering stage, in contrast to the rectangular stage in the Swan drawing, surprised theater historians and have made them more cautious in generalizing about the Elizabethan theater. Excavations at the Globe have not yielded much information, though some historians believe that the fragmentary evidence suggests a larger theater, perhaps one hundred feet in diameter.

From the fourth chief source, stage directions in the plays, one learns that entrance to the stage was by the doors at the rear (*"Enter one citizen at one door, and another at the other"*). A curtain hanging across the doorway—or a curtain hanging between the two doorways—could provide a place where a character could conceal himself, as Polonius does, when he wishes to overhear the conversation between Hamlet and Gertrude. Similarly, withdrawing a curtain from the doorway could "discover" (reveal) a character or two. Such discovery scenes are very rare in Elizabethan drama, but a good example occurs in *The Tempest* (5.1.171), where a stage direction tells us, *"Here Prospero discovers Ferdinand and Miranda playing at chess."* There was also some sort of playing space "aloft" or "above" to represent, for instance, the top of a city's walls or a room above the street. Doubtless each theater had its own peculiarities, but perhaps we can talk about a "typical" Elizabethan theater if we realize that no theater need exactly fit the description, just as no mother is the average mother with 2.7 children.

This hypothetical theater is wooden, round, or polygonal (in *Henry V* Shakespeare calls it a "wooden *O*") capable of holding some eight hundred spectators who stood in the yard around the projecting elevated stage—these spectators were the "groundlings"—and some fifteen hundred additional spectators who sat in the three roofed galleries. The stage, protected by a "shadow" or "heavens" or roof, is entered from two doors; behind the doors is the "tiring house" (attiring house, i.e., dressing room), and above the stage is some sort of gallery that may sometimes hold spectators but can be used (for example) as the bedroom from which Romeo—according to a stage direction in one text—"goeth down." Some evidence suggests that a throne can be lowered onto the platform stage, perhaps from the "shadow"; certainly characters can descend from the stage through a trap or traps into the cellar or "hell." Sometimes this space beneath the stage accommodates a sound-effects man or musician (in *Antony and Cleopatra* "*music of the hautboys* [oboes] *is under the stage*") or an actor (in *Hamlet* the "*Ghost cries under the stage*"). Most characters simply walk on and off through the doors, but because there is no curtain in front of the platform, corpses will have to be carried off (Hamlet obligingly clears the stage of Polonius's corpse, when he says, "I'll lug the guts into the neighbor room"). Other characters may have fallen at the rear, where a curtain on a doorway could be drawn to conceal them.

Such may have been the "public theater," so called because its inexpensive admission made it available to a wide range of the populace. Another kind of theater has been called the "private theater" because its much greater admission charge (sixpence versus the penny for general admission at the public theater) limited its audience to the wealthy or the prodigal. The private theater was basically a large room, entirely roofed and therefore artificially illuminated, with a stage at one end. The theaters thus were distinct in two ways: One was essentially an amphitheater that catered to the general public; the other was a hall that catered to the wealthy. In 1576 a hall theater was established in Blackfriars, a Dominican priory in London that had been suppressed in 1538 and confiscated by the Crown and thus was not under the city's jurisdiction. All the actors in this Blackfriars theater were boys about eight to thirteen years old (in the public theaters similar boys played female parts; a boy Lady Macbeth played to a man Macbeth). Near the end of this section on Shakespeare's theater we will talk at some length about possible implications in this convention of using boys to play female roles, but for the moment we should say that it doubtless accounts for the relative lack of female roles in Elizabethan drama. Thus, in *A Midsummer Night's Dream*, out of twenty-one named roles, only four are female; in *Hamlet*, out of twenty-four, only two (Gertrude and Ophelia) are female. Many of Shakespeare's characters have fathers but no mothers—for instance, King Lear's daughters. We need not bring in Freud to explain the disparity; a dramatic company had only a few boys in it.

To return to the private theaters, in some of which all of the performers were children—the "eyrie of . . . little eyases" (nest of unfledged hawks—2.2.347–48) which Rosencrantz mentions when he and Guildenstern talk with Hamlet. The theater in Blackfriars had a precarious existence, and ceased operations in 1584. In 1596 James Burbage, who had already made theatrical history by building the Theatre, began to construct a second Blackfriars theater. He died in 1597, and for several years this second Blackfriars theater was used by a troupe of boys, but in 1608 two of Burbage's sons and five other actors (including Shakespeare) became joint operators of the theater, using it in the winter when the open-air Globe was unsuitable. Perhaps such a smaller theater, roofed, artificially illuminated, and with a tradition of a wealthy audience, exerted an influence in Shakespeare's late plays.

Performances in the private theaters may well have had intermissions during which music was played, but in the public theaters the action was probably uninterrupted, flowing from scene to scene almost without a break. Actors would enter, speak, exit, and others would immediately enter and establish (if necessary) the new locale by a few properties and by words and gestures. To indicate that the scene took place at night, a player or two would carry a torch. Here are some samples of Shakespeare establishing the scene:

> This is Illyria, lady.   (*Twelfth Night,* 1.2.2)

> Well, this is the Forest of Arden.   (*As You Like It,* 2.4.14)

> This castle has a pleasant seat; the air
> Nimbly and sweetly recommends itself
> Unto our gentle senses.   (*Macbeth,* 1.6.1–3)

> The west yet glimmers with some streaks of day.
>   (*Macbeth,* 3.3.5)

Sometimes a speech will go far beyond evoking the minimal setting of place and time, and will, so to speak, evoke the social world in which the characters move. For instance, early in the first scene of *The Merchant of Venice* Salerio suggests an explanation for Antonio's melancholy. (In the following passage, *pageants* are decorated wagons, floats, and *cursy* is the verb "to curtsy," or "to bow.")

> Your mind is tossing on the ocean,
> There where your argosies with portly sail—
> Like signiors and rich burghers on the flood,
> Or as it were the pageants of the sea—
> Do overpeer the petty traffickers
> That cursy to them, do them reverence,
> As they fly by them with their woven wings.   (1.1.8–14)

Late in the nineteenth century, when Henry Irving produced the play with elaborate illusionistic sets, the first scene showed a ship moored in the harbor, with fruit vendors and dock laborers, in an effort to evoke the bustling and exotic life of Venice. But Shakespeare's words give us this exotic, rich world of commerce in his highly descriptive language when Salerio speaks of "argosies with portly sail" that fly with "woven wings"; equally important, through Salerio Shakespeare conveys a sense of the orderly, hierarchical society in which the lesser ships, "the petty traffickers," curtsy and thereby "do . . . reverence" to their superiors, the merchant prince's ships, which are "Like signiors and rich burghers."

On the other hand, it is a mistake to think that except for verbal pictures the Elizabethan stage was bare. Although Shakespeare's Chorus in *Henry V* calls the stage an "unworthy scaffold" (Prologue 1.10) and urges the spectators to "eke out our performance with your mind" (Prologue 3.35), there was considerable spectacle. The last act of *Macbeth,* for instance, has five stage directions calling for *"drum and colors,"* and another sort of appeal to the eye is indicated by the stage direction *"Enter Macduff, with Macbeth's head."* Some scenery and properties may have been substantial; doubtless a throne was used, but the pillars supporting the roof would have served for the trees on which Orlando pins his poems in *As You Like It.*

Having talked about the public theater—"this wooden *O*"—at some length, we should mention again that Shakespeare's plays were performed also in other locales. Alvin Kernan, in *Shakespeare, the King's Playwright: Theater in the Stuart Court 1603–1613* (1995) points out that "several of [Shakespeare's] plays contain brief theatrical performances, set always in a court or some noble house. When Shakespeare portrayed a theater, he did not, except for the choruses in *Henry V*, imagine a public theater" (p. 195). (Examples include episodes in *The Taming of the Shrew*, *A Midsummer Night's Dream*, *Hamlet*, and *The Tempest*.)

A Note on the Use of Boy Actors in Female Roles

Until fairly recently, scholars were content to mention that the convention existed; they sometimes also mentioned that it continued the medieval practice of using males in female roles, and that other theaters, notably in ancient Greece and in China and Japan, also used males in female roles. (In classical Noh drama in Japan, males still play the female roles.) Prudery may have been at the root of the academic failure to talk much about the use of boy actors, or maybe there really is not much more to say than that it was a convention of a male-centered culture (Stephen Green-

blatt's view, in *Shakespearean Negotiations* [1988]). Further, the very nature of a convention is that it is not thought
about: Hamlet is a Dane and Julius Caesar is a Roman, but
in Shakespeare's plays they speak English, and we in the
audience never give this odd fact a thought. Similarly, a
character may speak in the presence of others and we understand, again without thinking about it, that he or she is not
heard by the figures on the stage (the aside); a character
alone on the stage may speak (the soliloquy), and we do
not take the character to be unhinged; in a realistic (box)
set, the fourth wall, which allows us to see what is going on,
is miraculously missing. The no-nonsense view, then, is
that the boy actor was an accepted convention, accepted
unthinkingly—just as today we know that Kenneth Branagh
is not Hamlet, Al Pacino is not Richard III, and Denzel Washington is not the Prince of Aragon. In this view, the audience
takes the performer for the role, and that is that; such is the
argument we now make for race-free casting, in which
African-Americans and Asians can play roles of persons
who lived in medieval Denmark and ancient Rome. But
gender perhaps is different, at least today. It is a matter of
abundant academic study: The Elizabethan theater is now
sometimes called a transvestite theater, and we hear much
about cross-dressing.

   Shakespeare himself in a very few passages calls attention
to the use of boys in female roles. At the end of *As You Like
It* the boy who played Rosalind addresses the audience, and
says, "O men, . . . if I were a woman, I would kiss as many
of you as had beards that pleased me." But this is in the Epilogue; the plot is over, and the actor is stepping out of the
play and into the audience's everyday world. A second reference to the practice of boys playing female roles occurs in
Antony and Cleopatra, when Cleopatra imagines that she
and Antony will be the subject of crude plays, her role being
performed by a boy:

> The quick comedians
> Extemporally will stage us, and present
> Our Alexandrian revels: Antony
> Shall be brought drunken forth, and I shall see
> Some squeaking Cleopatra boy my greatness.   (5.2.216–20)

In a few other passages, Shakespeare is more indirect. For instance, in *Twelfth Night* Viola, played of course by a boy, disguises herself as a young man and seeks service in the house of a lord. She enlists the help of a Captain, and (by way of explaining away her voice and her beardlessness) says,

> I'll serve this duke
> Thou shalt present me as an eunuch to him.   (1.2.55–56)

In *Hamlet*, when the players arrive in 2.2, Hamlet jokes with the boy who plays a female role. The boy has grown since Hamlet last saw him: "By'r Lady, your ladyship is nearer to heaven than when I saw you last by the altitude of a chopine" (a lady's thick-soled shoe). He goes on: "Pray God your voice . . . be not cracked" (434–38).

Exactly how sexual, how erotic, this material was and is, is now much disputed. Again, the use of boys may have been unnoticed, or rather not thought about—an unexamined convention—by most or all spectators most of the time, perhaps *all* of the time, except when Shakespeare calls the convention to the attention of the audience, as in the passages just quoted. Still, an occasional bit seems to invite erotic thoughts. The clearest example is the name that Rosalind takes in *As You Like It*, Ganymede—the beautiful youth whom Zeus abducted. Did boys dressed to play female roles carry homoerotic appeal for straight men (Lisa Jardine's view, in *Still Harping on Daughters* [1983]), or for gay men, or for some or all women in the audience? Further, when the boy actor played a woman who (for the purposes of the plot) disguised herself as a male, as Rosalind, Viola, and Portia do—so we get a boy playing a woman playing a man—what sort of appeal was generated, and for what sort of spectator?

Some scholars have argued that the convention empowered women by letting female characters display a freedom unavailable in Renaissance patriarchal society; the convention, it is said, undermined rigid gender distinctions. In this view, the convention (along with plots in which female characters for a while disguised themselves as young men) allowed Shakespeare to say what some modern gender

critics say: Gender is a constructed role rather than a bio-
logical given, something we make, rather than a fixed binary
opposition of male and female (see Juliet Dusinberre, in
Shakespeare and the Nature of Women [1975]). On the other
hand, some scholars have maintained that the male disguise
assumed by some female characters serves only to reaffirm
traditional social distinctions since female characters who
don male garb (notably Portia in *The Merchant of Venice*
and Rosalind in *As You Like It*) return to their female garb
and at least implicitly (these critics say) reaffirm the status
quo. (For this last view, see Clara Claiborne Park, in an
essay in *The Woman's Part*, ed. Carolyn Ruth Swift Lenz et
al. [1980].) Perhaps no one answer is right for all plays; in
As You Like It cross-dressing empowers Rosalind, but in
Twelfth Night cross-dressing comically traps Viola.

Shakespeare's Dramatic Language: Costumes, Gestures and Silences; Prose and Poetry

Because Shakespeare was a dramatist, not merely a poet,
he worked not only with language but also with costume,
sound effects, gestures, and even silences. We have already
discussed some kinds of spectacle in the preceding section,
and now we will begin with other aspects of visual language;
a theater, after all, is literally a "place for seeing." Consider
the opening stage direction in *The Tempest*, the first play in
the first published collection of Shakespeare's plays: *"A
tempestuous noise of thunder and Lightning heard: Enter a
Ship-master, and a Boteswain."*

Costumes: What did that shipmaster and that boatswain
wear? Doubtless they wore something that identified them
as men of the sea. Not much is known about the costumes
that Elizabethan actors wore, but at least three points are
clear: (1) many of the costumes were splendid versions of
contemporary Elizabethan dress; (2) some attempts were
made to approximate the dress of certain occupations and of
antique or exotic characters such as Romans, Turks, and
Jews; (3) some costumes indicated that the wearer was

supernatural. Evidence for elaborate Elizabethan clothing can be found in the plays themselves and in contemporary comments about the "sumptuous" players who wore the discarded clothing of noblemen, as well as in account books that itemize such things as "a scarlet cloak with two broad gold laces, with gold buttons down the sides."

The attempts at approximation of the dress of certain occupations and nationalities also can be documented from the plays themselves, and it derives additional confirmation from a drawing of the first scene of Shakespeare's *Titus Andronicus*—the only extant Elizabethan picture of an identifiable episode in a play. (See pp. xxxviii–xxxix.) The drawing, probably done in 1594 or 1595, shows Queen Tamora pleading for mercy. She wears a somewhat medieval-looking robe and a crown; Titus wears a toga and a wreath, but two soldiers behind him wear costumes fairly close to Elizabethan dress. We do not know, however, if the drawing represents an actual stage production in the public theater, or perhaps a private production, or maybe only a reader's visualization of an episode. Further, there is some conflicting evidence: In *Julius Caesar* a reference is made to Caesar's doublet (a close-fitting jacket), which, if taken literally, suggests that even the protagonist did not wear Roman clothing; and certainly the lesser characters, who are said to wear hats, did not wear Roman garb.

It should be mentioned, too, that even ordinary clothing can be symbolic: Hamlet's "inky cloak," for example, sets him apart from the brightly dressed members of Claudius's court and symbolizes his mourning; the fresh clothes that are put on King Lear partly symbolize his return to sanity. Consider, too, the removal of disguises near the end of some plays. For instance, Rosalind in *As You Like It* and Portia and Nerissa in *The Merchant of Venice* remove their male attire, thus again becoming fully themselves.

Gestures and Silences: Gestures are an important part of a dramatist's language. King Lear kneels before his daughter Cordelia for a benediction (4.7.57–59), an act of humility that contrasts with his earlier speeches banishing her and that contrasts also with a comparable gesture, his ironic

kneeling before Regan (2.4.153–55). Northumberland's failure to kneel before King Richard II (3.3.71–72) speaks volumes. As for silences, consider a moment in *Coriolanus*: Before the protagonist yields to his mother's entreaties (5.3.182), there is this stage direction: *"Holds her by the hand, silent."* Another example of "speech in dumbness" occurs in *Macbeth*, when Macduff learns that his wife and children have been murdered. He is silent at first, as Malcolm's speech indicates: "What, man! Ne'er pull your hat upon your brows. Give sorrow words" (4.3.208–09). (For a discussion of such moments, see Philip C. McGuire's *Speechless Dialect: Shakespeare's Open Silences* [1985].)

Of course when we think of Shakespeare's work, we think primarily of his language, both the poetry and the prose.

Prose: Although two of his plays (*Richard II* and *King John*) have no prose at all, about half the others have at least one quarter of the dialogue in prose, and some have notably more: *1 Henry IV* and *2 Henry IV*, about half; *As You Like It*

and *Twelfth Night*, a little more than half; *Much Ado About Nothing*, more than three quarters; and *The Merry Wives of Windsor*, a little more than five sixths. We should remember that despite Molière's joke about M. Jourdain, who was amazed to learn that he spoke prose, most of us do not speak prose. Rather, we normally utter repetitive, shapeless, and often ungrammatical torrents; prose is something very different—a sort of literary imitation of speech at its most coherent.

Today we may think of prose as "natural" for drama; or even if we think that poetry is appropriate for high tragedy we may still think that prose is the right medium for comedy. Greek, Roman, and early English comedies, however, were written in verse. In fact, prose was not generally considered a literary medium in England until the late fifteenth century; Chaucer tells even his bawdy stories in verse. By the end of the 1580s, however, prose had established itself on the English comic stage. In tragedy, Marlowe made some use of prose, not simply in the speeches of clownish servants but even in the speech of a tragic hero, Doctor Faustus. Still, before Shakespeare, prose normally was used in the theater only for special circumstances: (1) letters and proclamations, to set them off from the poetic dialogue; (2) mad characters, to indicate that normal thinking has become disordered; and (3) low comedy, or speeches uttered by clowns even when they are not being comic. Shakespeare made use of these conventions, but he also went far beyond them. Sometimes he begins a scene in prose and then shifts into verse as the emotion is heightened; or conversely, he may shift from verse to prose when a speaker is lowering the emotional level, as when Brutus speaks in the Forum.

Shakespeare's prose usually is not prosaic. Hamlet's prose includes not only small talk with Rosencrantz and Guildenstern but also princely reflections on "What a piece of work is a man" (2.2.312). In conversation with Ophelia, he shifts from light talk in verse to a passionate prose denunciation of women (3.1.103), though the shift to prose here is perhaps also intended to suggest the possibility of madness. (Consult Brian Vickers, *The Artistry of Shakespeare's Prose* [1968].)

Poetry: Drama in rhyme in England goes back to the Middle Ages, but by Shakespeare's day rhyme no longer dominated poetic drama; a finer medium, blank verse (strictly speaking, unrhymed lines of ten syllables, with the stress on every second syllable) had been adopted. But before looking at unrhymed poetry, a few things should be said about the chief uses of rhyme in Shakespeare's plays. (1) A couplet (a pair of rhyming lines) is sometimes used to convey emotional heightening at the end of a blank verse speech; (2) characters sometimes speak a couplet as they leave the stage, suggesting closure; (3) except in the latest plays, scenes fairly often conclude with a couplet, and sometimes, as in *Richard II*, 2.1.145–46, the entrance of a new character within a scene is preceded by a couplet, which wraps up the earlier portion of that scene; (4) speeches of two characters occasionally are linked by rhyme, most notably in *Romeo and Juliet*, 1.5.95–108, where the lovers speak a sonnet between them; elsewhere a taunting reply occasionally rhymes with the previous speaker's last line; (5) speeches with sententious or gnomic remarks are sometimes in rhyme, as in the duke's speech in *Othello* (1.3.199–206); (6) speeches of sardonic mockery are sometimes in rhyme—for example, Iago's speech on women in *Othello* (2.1.146–58)—and they sometimes conclude with an emphatic couplet, as in Bolingbroke's speech on comforting words in *Richard II* (1.3.301–2); (7) some characters are associated with rhyme, such as the fairies in *A Midsummer Night's Dream*; (8) in the early plays, especially *The Comedy of Errors* and *The Taming of the Shrew*, comic scenes that in later plays would be in prose are in jingling rhymes; (9) prologues, choruses, plays-within-the-play, inscriptions, vows, epilogues, and so on are often in rhyme, and the songs in the plays are rhymed.

Neither prose nor rhyme immediately comes to mind when we first think of Shakespeare's medium: It is blank verse, unrhymed iambic pentameter. (In a mechanically exact line there are five iambic feet. An iambic foot consists of two syllables, the second accented, as in *away*; five feet make a pentameter line. Thus, a strict line of iambic pentameter contains ten syllables, the even syllables being stressed more heavily than the odd syllables. Fortunately, Shakespeare usually varies the line somewhat.) The first speech in *A Midsummer Night's Dream*, spoken by Duke Theseus to his betrothed, is an example of blank verse:

> Now, fair Hippolyta, our nuptial hour
> Draws on apace. Four happy days bring in
> Another moon; but, O, methinks, how slow
> This old moon wanes! She lingers my desires,
> Like to a stepdame, or a dowager,
> Long withering out a young man's revenue.   (1.1.1–6)

As this passage shows, Shakespeare's blank verse is not mechanically unvarying. Though the predominant foot is the iamb (as in *apace* or *desires*), there are numerous variations. In the first line the stress can be placed on "fair," as the regular metrical pattern suggests, but it is likely that "Now" gets almost as much emphasis; probably in the second line "Draws" is more heavily emphasized than "on," giving us a trochee (a stressed syllable followed by an unstressed one); and in the fourth line each word in the phrase "This old moon wanes" is probably stressed fairly heavily, conveying by two spondees (two feet, each of two stresses) the oppressive tedium that Theseus feels.

In Shakespeare's early plays much of the blank verse is end-stopped (that is, it has a heavy pause at the end of each line), but he later developed the ability to write iambic pentameter verse paragraphs (rather than lines) that give the illusion of speech. His chief techniques are (1) enjambing, i.e., running the thought beyond the single line, as in the first three lines of the speech just quoted; (2) occasionally replacing an iamb with another foot; (3) varying the position of the chief pause (the caesura) within a line; (4) adding an occasional unstressed syllable at the end of a line, traditionally called a feminine ending; (5) and beginning or ending a speech with a half line.

Shakespeare's mature blank verse has much of the rhythmic flexibility of his prose; both the language, though richly figurative and sometimes dense, and the syntax seem natural. It is also often highly appropriate to a particular character. Consider, for instance, this speech from *Hamlet*, in which Claudius, King of Denmark ("the Dane"), speaks to Laertes:

> And now, Laertes, what's the news with you?
> You told us of some suit. What is't, Laertes?
> You cannot speak of reason to the Dane
> And lose your voice. What wouldst thou beg, Laertes,
> That shall not be my offer, not thy asking? (1.2.42–46)

Notice the short sentences and the repetition of the name "Laertes," to whom the speech is addressed. Notice, too, the shift from the royal "us" in the second line to the more intimate "my" in the last line, and from "you" in the first three lines to the more intimate "thou" and "thy" in the last two lines. Claudius knows how to ingratiate himself with Laertes.

For a second example of the flexibility of Shakespeare's blank verse, consider a passage from *Macbeth*. Distressed by the doctor's inability to cure Lady Macbeth and by the imminent battle, Macbeth addresses some of his remarks to the doctor and others to the servant who is arming him. The entire speech, with its pauses, interruptions, and irresolution (in "Pull't off, I say," Macbeth orders the servant to remove the armor that the servant has been putting on him), catches Macbeth's disintegration. (In the first line, *physic* means "medicine," and in the fourth and fifth lines, *cast the water* means "analyze the urine.")

> Throw physic to the dogs, I'll none of it.
> Come, put mine armor on. Give me my staff.
> Seyton, send out.—Doctor, the thanes fly from me.—
> Come, sir, dispatch. If thou couldst, doctor, cast
> The water of my land, find her disease
> And purge it to a sound and pristine health,
> I would applaud thee to the very echo,
> That should applaud again.—Pull't off, I say.—
> What rhubarb, senna, or what purgative drug,
> Would scour these English hence? Hear'st thou of them?
>
> (5.3.47–56)

Blank verse, then, can be much more than unrhymed iambic pentameter, and even within a single play Shakespeare's blank verse often consists of several styles, depending on the speaker and on the speaker's emotion at the moment.

The Play Text as a Collaboration

Shakespeare's fellow dramatist Ben Jonson reported that the actors said of Shakespeare, "In his writing, whatsoever he penned, he never blotted out line," i.e., never crossed out material and revised his work while composing. None of Shakespeare's plays survives in manuscript (with the possible exception of a scene in *Sir Thomas More*), so we cannot fully evaluate the comment, but in a few instances the published work clearly shows that he revised his manuscript. Consider the following passage (shown here in facsimile) from the best early text of *Romeo and Juliet*, the Second Quarto (1599):

Ro. Would I were sleepe and peace so sweet to rest
The grey eyde morne smiles on the frowning night,
Checkring the Easterne Clouds with streaks of light,
And darknesse fleckted like a drunkard reeles,
From forth daies pathway, made by *Tytans* wheeles.
Hence will I to my ghostly Friers close cell,
His helpe to craue, and my deare hap to tell.

Exit.

Enter Frier alone with a basket.   (night,
Fri. The grey-eyed morne smiles on the frowning
Checking the Easterne clowdes with streaks of light:
And fleckeld darknesse like a drunkard reeles,
From forth daies path, and *Titans* burning wheeles:
Now ere the sun aduance his burning eie,

Romeo rather elaborately tells us that the sun at dawn is
dispelling the night (morning is smiling, the eastern clouds
are checked with light, and the sun's chariot—Titan's
wheels—advances), and he will seek out his spiritual father,
the Friar. He exits and, oddly, the Friar enters and says pretty
much the same thing about the sun. Both speakers say that
"the gray-eyed morn smiles on the frowning night," but there
are small differences, perhaps having more to do with the
business of printing the book than with the author's
composition: For Romeo's "checkring," "fleckted," and
"pathway," we get the Friar's "checking," "fleckeld," and
"path." (Notice, by the way, the inconsistency in Elizabethan
spelling: Romeo's "clouds" become the Friar's "clowdes.")

Both versions must have been in the printer's copy, and it
seems safe to assume that both were in Shakespeare's manuscript. He must have written one version—let's say he first
wrote Romeo's closing lines for this scene—and then he
decided, no, it's better to give this lyrical passage to the
Friar, as the opening of a new scene, but he neglected to
delete the first version. Editors must make a choice, and they
may feel that the reasonable thing to do is to print the text as
Shakespeare intended it. But how can we know what he
intended? Almost all modern editors delete the lines from

Romeo's speech, and retain the Friar's lines. They don't do this because they know Shakespeare's intention, however. They give the lines to the Friar because the first published version (1597) of *Romeo and Juliet* gives only the Friar's version, and this text (though in many ways inferior to the 1599 text) is thought to derive from the memory of some actors, that is, it is thought to represent a performance, not just a script. Maybe during the course of rehearsals Shakespeare—an actor as well as an author—unilaterally decided that the Friar should speak the lines; if so (remember that we don't know this to be a fact) his final intention was to give the speech to the Friar. Maybe, however, the actors talked it over and settled on the Friar, with or without Shakespeare's approval. On the other hand, despite the 1597 version, one might argue (if only weakly) on behalf of giving the lines to Romeo rather than to the Friar, thus: (1) Romeo's comment on the coming of the daylight emphasizes his separation from Juliet, and (2) the figurative language seems more appropriate to Romeo than to the Friar. Having said this, in the Signet edition we have decided in this instance to draw on the evidence provided by earlier text and to give the lines to the Friar, on the grounds that since Q1 reflects a production, in the theater (at least on one occasion) the lines were spoken by the Friar.

A playwright sold a script to a theatrical company. The script thus belonged to the company, not the author, and author and company alike must have regarded this script not as a literary work but as the basis for a play that the actors would create on the stage. We speak of Shakespeare as the author of the plays, but readers should bear in mind that the texts they read, even when derived from a single text, such as the First Folio (1623), are inevitably the collaborative work not simply of Shakespeare with his company—doubtless during rehearsals the actors would suggest alterations—but also with other forces of the age. One force was governmental censorship. In 1606 parliament passed "an Act to restrain abuses of players," prohibiting the utterance of oaths and the name of God. So where the earliest text of *Othello* gives us "By heaven" (3.3.106), the first Folio gives "Alas," presumably reflecting the compliance of stage practice with the law. Similarly, the 1623 version of *King Lear* omits the oath "Fut" (probably from "By God's foot") at 1.2.142, again presumably reflecting the line as it was spoken on the stage. Editors who seek to give the reader the play that Shakespeare initially conceived—the "authentic" play conceived by the solitary Shakespeare—probably will restore the missing oaths and references to God. Other editors, who see the play as a collaborative work, a construction made not only by Shakespeare but also by actors and compositors and even government censors, may claim that what counts is the play as it was actually performed. Such editors regard the censored text as legitimate, since it is the play that was (presumably) finally put on. A performed text, they argue, has more historical reality than a text produced by an editor who has sought to get at what Shakespeare initially wrote. In this view, the text of a play is rather like the script of a film; the script is not the film, and the play text is not the performed play. Even if we want to talk about the play that Shakespeare "intended," we will find ourselves talking about a script that he handed over to a company with the intention that it be implemented by actors. The "intended" play is the one that the actors—we might almost say "society"—would help to construct.

Further, it is now widely held that a play is also the work of readers and spectators, who do not simply receive meaning, but who create it when they respond to the play. This idea is fully in accord with contemporary post-structuralist critical thinking, notably Roland Barthes's "The Death of the Author," in *Image-Music-Text* (1977) and Michel Foucault's "What Is an Author?," in *The Foucault Reader* (1984). The gist of the idea is that an author is not an isolated genius; rather, authors are subject to the politics and other social structures of their age. A dramatist especially is a worker in a collaborative project, working most obviously with actors—parts may be written for particular actors—but working also with the audience. Consider the words of Samuel Johnson, written to be spoken by the actor David Garrick at the opening of a theater in 1747:

> The stage but echoes back the public voice;
> The drama's laws, the drama's patrons give,
> For we that live to please, must please to live.

The audience—the public taste as understood by the playwright—helps to determine what the play is. Moreover, even members of the public who are not part of the playwright's immediate audience may exert an influence through censorship. We have already glanced at governmental censorship, but there are also other kinds. Take one of Shakespeare's most beloved characters, Falstaff, who appears in three of Shakespeare's plays, the two parts of *Henry IV* and *The Merry Wives of Windsor*. He appears with this name in the earliest printed version of the first of these plays, *1 Henry IV*, but we know that Shakespeare originally called him (after an historical figure) Sir John Oldcastle. Oldcastle appears in Shakespeare's source (partly reprinted in the Signet edition of *1 Henry IV*), and a trace of the name survives in Shakespeare's play, 1.2.43–44, where Prince Hal punningly addresses Falstaff as "my old lad of the castle." But for some reason—perhaps because the family of the historical Oldcastle complained—Shakespeare had to change the name. In short, the play as we have it was (at least in this detail) subject to some sort of censorship. If we think that a text should present what we take to be the author's intention, we probably will want to replace *Falstaff* with *Oldcastle*. But if we recognize that a play is a collaboration, we may welcome the change, even if it was forced on Shakespeare. Somehow *Falstaff*, with its hint of *false-staff*, i.e., inadequate prop, seems just right for this fat knight who, to our delight, entertains the young prince with untruths. We can go as far as saying that, at least so far as a play is concerned, an insistence on the author's original intention (even if we could know it) can sometimes impoverish the text.

The tiny example of Falstaff's name illustrates the point that the text we read is inevitably only a version—something in effect produced by the collaboration of the playwright with his actors, audiences, compositors, and editors—of a fluid text that Shakespeare once wrote, just as the *Hamlet* that we see on the screen starring Kenneth Branagh is not the *Hamlet* that Shakespeare saw in an open-air playhouse starring Richard Burbage. *Hamlet* itself, as we shall note in a moment, also exists in several versions. It is not surprising that there is now much talk about the *instability* of Shakespeare's texts.

Because he was not only a playwright but was also an actor and a shareholder in a theatrical company, Shakespeare probably was much involved with the translation of the play from a manuscript to a stage production. He may or may not have done some rewriting during rehearsals, and he may or may not have been happy with cuts that were made. Some plays, notably *Hamlet* and *King Lear*, are so long that it is most unlikely that the texts we read were acted in their entirety. Further, for both of these plays we have more than one early text that demands consideration. In *Hamlet*, the Second Quarto (1604) includes some two hundred lines not found in the Folio (1623). Among the passages missing from the Folio are two of Hamlet's reflective speeches, the "dram of evil" speech (1.4.13–38) and "How all occasions do inform against me" (4.4.32–66). Since the Folio has more numerous and often fuller stage directions, it certainly looks as though in the Folio we get a theatrical version of the play, a text whose cuts were probably made—this is only a hunch, of course—not because Shakespeare was changing his conception of Hamlet but because the playhouse demanded a modified play. (The problem is complicated, since the Folio not only cuts some of the Quarto but adds some material. Various explanations have been offered.)

Or take an example from *King Lear*. In the First and Second Quarto (1608, 1619), the final speech of the play is given to Albany, Lear's surviving son-in-law, but in the First Folio version (1623), the speech is given to Edgar. The Quarto version is in accord with tradition—usually the highest-ranking character in a tragedy speaks the final words. Why does the Folio give the speech to Edgar? One possible answer is this: The Folio version omits some of Albany's speeches in earlier scenes, so perhaps it was decided (by Shakespeare? by the players?) not to give the final lines to so pale a character. In fact, the discrepancies are so many between the two texts, that some scholars argue we do not simply have texts showing different theatrical productions. Rather, these scholars say, Shakespeare substantially revised the play, and we really have two versions of *King Lear* (and of *Othello* also, say some)—two different plays—not simply two texts, each of which is in some ways imperfect.

In this view, the 1608 version of *Lear* may derive from Shakespeare's manuscript, and the 1623 version may derive from his later revision. The Quartos have almost three hundred lines not in the Folio, and the Folio has about a hundred lines not in the Quartos. It used to be held that all the texts were imperfect in various ways and from various causes—some passages in the Quartos were thought to have been set from a manuscript that was not entirely legible, other passages were thought to have been set by a compositor who was new to setting plays, and still other passages were thought to have been provided by an actor who misremembered some of the lines. This traditional view held that an editor must draw on the Quartos and the Folio in order to get Shakespeare's "real" play. The new argument holds (although not without considerable strain) that we have two authentic plays, Shakespeare's early version (in the Quarto) and Shakespeare's—or his theatrical company's—revised version (in the Folio). Not only theatrical demands but also Shakespeare's own artistic sense, it is argued, called for extensive revisions. Even the titles vary: Q1 is called *True Chronicle Historie of the life and death of King Lear and his three Daughters*, whereas the Folio text is called *The Tragedie of King Lear*. To combine the two texts in order to produce what the editor thinks is the play that Shakespeare intended to write is, according to this view, to produce a text that is false to the history of the play. If the new view is correct, and we do have texts of two distinct versions of *Lear* rather than two imperfect versions of one play, it supports in a textual way the post-structuralist view that we cannot possibly have an unmediated vision of (in this case) a play by Shakespeare; we can only recognize a plurality of visions.

Editing Texts

Though eighteen of his plays were published during his lifetime, Shakespeare seems never to have supervised their publication. There is nothing unusual here; when a playwright sold a play to a theatrical company he surrendered his ownership to it. Normally a company would not publish the play, because to publish it meant to allow competitors to acquire the piece. Some plays did get published: Apparently hard-up actors sometimes pieced together a play for a publisher; sometimes a company in need of money sold a play; and sometimes a company allowed publication of a play that no longer drew audiences. That Shakespeare did not concern himself with publication is not remarkable; of his contemporaries, only Ben Jonson carefully supervised the publication of his own plays.

In 1623, seven years after Shakespeare's death, John Heminges and Henry Condell (two senior members of Shakespeare's company, who had worked with him for about twenty years) collected his plays—published and unpublished—into a large volume, of a kind called a folio. (A folio is a volume consisting of large sheets that have been folded once, each sheet thus making two leaves, or four pages. The size of the page of course depends on the size of the sheet—a folio can range in height from twelve to sixteen inches, and in width from eight to eleven; the pages in the 1623 edition of Shakespeare, commonly called the First Folio, are approximately thirteen inches tall and eight inches wide.) The eighteen plays published during Shakespeare's lifetime had been issued one play per volume in small formats called quartos. (Each sheet in a quarto has been folded twice, making four leaves, or eight pages, each page being about nine inches tall and seven inches wide, roughly the size of a large paperback.)

Heminges and Condell suggest in an address "To the great variety of readers" that the republished plays are presented in better form than in the quartos:

> Before you were abused with diverse stolen and surreptitious copies, maimed and deformed by the frauds and stealths of injurious impostors that exposed them; even those, are now offered to your view cured and perfect of their limbs, and all the rest absolute in their numbers, as he [i.e., Shakespeare] conceived them.

There is a good deal of truth to this statement, but some of the quarto versions are better than others; some are in fact preferable to the Folio text.

Whoever was assigned to prepare the texts for publication

in the first Folio seems to have taken the job seriously and yet not to have performed it with uniform care. The sources of the texts seem to have been, in general, good unpublished copies or the best published copies. The first play in the collection, *The Tempest*, is divided into acts and scenes, has unusually full stage directions and descriptions of spectacle, and concludes with a list of the characters, but the editor was not able (or willing) to present all of the succeeding texts so fully dressed. Later texts occasionally show signs of carelessness: in one scene of *Much Ado About Nothing* the names of actors, instead of characters, appear as speech prefixes, as they had in the Quarto, which the Folio reprints; proofreading throughout the Folio is spotty and apparently was done without reference to the printer's copy; the pagination of *Hamlet* jumps from 156 to 257. Further, the proofreading was done while the presses continued to print, so that each play in each volume contains a mix of corrected and uncorrected pages.

Modern editors of Shakespeare must first select their copy; no problem if the play exists only in the Folio, but a considerable problem if the relationship between a Quarto and the Folio—or an early Quarto and a later one—is unclear. In the case of *Romeo and Juliet*, the First Quarto (Q1), published in 1597, is vastly inferior to the Second (Q2), published in 1599. The basis of Q1 apparently is a version put together from memory by some actors. Not surprisingly, it garbles many passages and is much shorter than Q2. On the other hand, occasionally Q1 makes better sense than Q2. For instance, near the end of the play, when the parents have assembled and learned of the deaths of Romeo and Juliet, in Q2 the Prince says (5.3.208–9),

Come, *Montague;* for thou art early vp
To see thy sonne and heire, now earling downe.

The last three words of this speech surely do not make sense, and many editors turn to Q1, which instead of "now earling downe" has "more early downe." Some modern editors take only "early" from Q1, and print "now early down"; others take "more early," and print "more early down." Further, Q1 (though, again, quite clearly a garbled and abbreviated text) includes some stage directions that are not found in Q2, and today many editors who base their text on Q2 are glad to add these stage directions, because the directions help to give us a sense of what the play looked like on Shakespeare's stage. Thus, in 4.3.58, after Juliet drinks the potion, Q1 gives us this stage direction, not in Q2: *"She falls upon her bed within the curtains."*

In short, an editor's decisions do not end with the choice of a single copy text. First of all, editors must reckon with Elizabethan spelling. If they are not producing a facsimile, they probably modernize the spelling, but ought they to preserve the old forms of words that apparently were pronounced quite unlike their modern forms—*lanthorn, alablaster*? If they preserve these forms are they really preserving Shakespeare's forms or perhaps those of a compositor in the printing house? What is one to do when one finds *lanthorn* and *lantern* in adjacent lines? (The editors of this series in general, but not invariably, assume that words should be spelled in their modern form, unless, for instance, a rhyme is involved.) Elizabethan punctuation, too, presents problems. For example, in the First Folio, the only text for the play, Macbeth rejects his wife's idea that he can wash the blood from his hand (2.2.60–62):

> No: this my Hand will rather
> The multitudinous Seas incarnardine,
> Making the Greene one, Red.

Obviously an editor will remove the superfluous capitals, and will probably alter the spelling to "incarnadine," but what about the comma before "Red"? If we retain the comma, Macbeth is calling the sea "the green one." If we drop the comma, Macbeth is saying that his bloody hand will make the sea ("the Green") *uniformly* red.

An editor will sometimes have to change more than spelling and punctuation. Macbeth says to his wife (1.7.46–47):

> I dare do all that may become a man,
> Who dares no more, is none.

For two centuries editors have agreed that the second line is unsatisfactory, and have emended "no" to "do": "Who dares do more is none." But when in the same play (4.2.21–22) Ross says that fearful persons

> Floate vpon a wilde and violent Sea
> Each way, and moue,

need we emend the passage? On the assumption that the compositor misread the manuscript, some editors emend "each way, and move" to "and move each way"; others emend "move" to "none" (i.e., "Each way and none"). Other editors, however, let the passage stand as in the original. The editors of the Signet Classic Shakespeare have restrained themselves from making abundant emendations. In their minds they hear Samuel Johnson on the dangers of emendation: "I have adopted the Roman sentiment, that it is more honorable to save a citizen than to kill an enemy." Some departures (in addition to spelling, punctuation, and lineation) from the copy text have of course been made, but the original readings are listed in a note following the play, so that readers can evaluate the changes for themselves.

Following tradition, the editors of the Signet Classic Shakespeare have prefaced each play with a list of characters, and throughout the play have regularized the names of the speakers. Thus, in our text of *Romeo and Juliet*, all speeches by Juliet's mother are prefixed "Lady Capulet," although the 1599 Quarto of the play, which provides our copy text, uses at various points seven speech tags for this one character: *Capu. Wi.* (i.e., Capulet's wife), *Ca. Wi., Wi., Wife, Old La.* (i.e., Old Lady), *La.,* and *Mo.* (i.e., Mother). Similarly, in *All's Well That Ends Well*, the character whom we regularly call "Countess" is in the Folio (the copy text) variously identified as *Mother, Countess, Old Countess, Lady,* and *Old Lady*. Admittedly there is some loss in regularizing, since the various prefixes may give us a hint of the way Shakespeare (or a scribe who copied Shakespeare's manuscript) was thinking of the character in a particular scene—for instance, as a mother, or as an old lady. But too much can be made of these differing prefixes, since the social relationships implied are *not* always relevant to the given scene.

We have also added line numbers and in many cases act and scene divisions as well as indications of locale at the beginning of scenes. The Folio divided most of the plays into acts and some into scenes. Early eighteenth-century editors increased the divisions. These divisions, which provide a convenient way of referring to passages in the plays, have been retained, but when not in the text chosen as the basis for the Signet Classic text they are enclosed within square brackets, [ ], to indicate that they are editorial additions. Similarly, though no play of Shakespeare's was equipped with indications of the locale at the heads of scene divisions, locales have here been added in square brackets for the convenience of readers, who lack the information that costumes, properties, gestures, and scenery afford to spectators. Spectators can tell at a glance they are in the throne room, but without an editorial indication the reader may be puzzled for a while. It should be mentioned, incidentally, that there are a few authentic stage directions—perhaps Shakespeare's, perhaps a prompter's—that suggest locales, such as *"Enter Brutus in his orchard,"* and *"They go up into the Senate house."* It is hoped that the bracketed additions in the Signet text will provide readers with the sort of help provided by these two authentic directions, but it is equally hoped that the reader will remember that the stage was not loaded with scenery.

Shakespeare on the Stage

Each volume in the Signet Classic Shakespeare includes a brief stage (and sometimes film) history of the play. When we read about earlier productions, we are likely to find them eccentric, obviously wrongheaded—for instance, Nahum Tate's version of *King Lear*, with a happy ending, which held the stage for about a century and a half, from the late seventeenth century until the end of the first quarter of the nineteenth. We see engravings of David Garrick, the greatest actor of the eighteenth century, in eighteenth-century garb

as King Lear, and we smile, thinking how absurd the production must have been. If we are more thoughtful, we say,
with the English novelist L. P. Hartley, "The past is a foreign
country: they do things differently there." But if the eighteenth-century staging is a foreign country, what of the plays
of the late sixteenth and seventeenth centuries? A foreign
language, a foreign theater, a foreign audience.

Probably all viewers of Shakespeare's plays, beginning
with Shakespeare himself, at times have been unhappy with
the plays on the stage. Consider three comments about production that we find in the plays themselves, which suggest
Shakespeare's concerns. The Chorus in *Henry V* complains
that the heroic story cannot possibly be adequately staged:

> But pardon, gentles all,
> The flat unraisèd spirits that hath dared
> On this unworthy scaffold to bring forth
> So great an object. Can this cockpit hold
> The vasty fields of France? Or may we cram
> Within this wooden *O* the very casques
> That did affright the air at Agincourt?
> . . . .
> Piece out our imperfections with your thoughts.
>
> (Prologue 1.8–14, 23)

Second, here are a few sentences (which may or may not
represent Shakespeare's own views) from Hamlet's longish
lecture to the players:

> Speak the speech, I pray you, as I pronounced it to you, trippingly
> on the tongue. But if you mouth it, as many of our players do, I had
> as lief the town crier spoke my lines. . . . O, it offends me to the
> soul to hear a robustious periwig-pated fellow tear a passion to tat-
> ters, to very rags, to split the ears of the groundlings. . . . And let
> those that play your clowns speak no more than is set down for
> them, for there be of them that will themselves laugh, to set on
> some quantity of barren spectators to laugh too, though in the
> meantime some necessary question of the play be then to be con-
> sidered. That's villainous and shows a most pitiful ambition in the
> fool that uses it. (3.2.1–47)

Finally, we can quote again from the passage cited earlier in this introduction, concerning the boy actors who played the female roles. Cleopatra imagines with horror a theatrical version of her activities with Antony:

> The quick comedians
> Extemporally will stage us, and present
> Our Alexandrian revels: Antony
> Shall be brought drunken forth, and I shall see
> Some squeaking Cleopatra boy my greatness
> I' th' posture of a whore.   (5.2.216–21)

It is impossible to know how much weight to put on such passages—perhaps Shakespeare was just being modest about his theater's abilities—but it is easy enough to think that he was unhappy with some aspects of Elizabethan production. Probably no production can fully satisfy a playwright, and for that matter, few productions can fully satisfy *us;* we regret this or that cut, this or that way of costuming the play, this or that bit of business.

One's first thought may be this: Why don't they just do "authentic" Shakespeare, "straight" Shakespeare, the play as Shakespeare wrote it? But as we read the plays—words written to be performed—it sometimes becomes clear that we do not know *how* to perform them. For instance, in *Antony and Cleopatra* Antony, the Roman general who has succumbed to Cleopatra and to Egyptian ways, says, "The nobleness of life / Is to do thus" (1.1.36–37). But what is "thus"? Does Antony at this point embrace Cleopatra? Does he embrace and kiss her? (There are, by the way, very few scenes of kissing on Shakespeare's stage, possibly because boys played the female roles.) Or does he make a sweeping gesture, indicating the Egyptian way of life?

This is not an isolated example; the plays are filled with lines that call for gestures, but we are not sure what the gestures should be. *Interpretation* is inevitable. Consider a passage in *Hamlet*. In 3.1, Polonius persuades his daughter, Ophelia, to talk to Hamlet while Polonius and Claudius eavesdrop. The two men conceal themselves, and Hamlet encounters Ophelia. At 3.1.131 Hamlet suddenly says to her, "Where's your father?" Why does Hamlet, apparently out of nowhere—they have not been talking about Polonius—ask this question? Is this an example of the "antic disposition" (fantastic behavior) that Hamlet earlier (1.5.172) had told Horatio and others—including us—he would display? That is, is the question about the whereabouts of her father a seemingly irrational one, like his earlier question (3.1.103) to Ophelia, "Ha, ha! Are you honest?" Or, on the other hand, has Hamlet (as in many productions) suddenly glimpsed Polonius's foot protruding from beneath a drapery at the rear? That is, does Hamlet ask the question because he has suddenly seen something suspicious and now is testing Ophelia? (By the way, in productions that do give Hamlet a physical cue, it is almost always Polonius rather than Claudius who provides the clue. This itself is an act of inter-pretation on the part of the director.) Or (a third possibility) does Hamlet get a clue from Ophelia, who inadvertently betrays the spies by nervously glancing at their place of hiding? This is the interpretation used in the BBC television version, where Ophelia glances in fear toward the hiding place just after Hamlet says "Why wouldst thou be a breeder of sinners?" (121–22). Hamlet, realizing that he is being ob-served, glances here and there *before* he asks "Where's your father?" The question thus is a climax to what he has been doing while speaking the preceding lines. Or (a fourth inter-pretation) does Hamlet suddenly, without the aid of any clue whatsoever, intuitively (insightfully, mysteriously, wonder-fully) sense that someone is spying? Directors must decide, of course—and so must readers.

Recall, too, the preceding discussion of the texts of the plays, which argued that the texts—though they seem to be before us in permanent black on white—are unstable. The Signet text of *Hamlet*, which draws on the Second Quarto (1604) and the First Folio (1623) is considerably longer than any version staged in Shakespeare's time. Our version, even if spoken very briskly and played without any intermission, would take close to four hours, far beyond "the two hours' traffic of our stage" mentioned in the Prologue to *Romeo and Juliet*. (There are a few contemporary references to the dura-tion of a play, but none mentions more than three hours.) Of Shakespeare's plays, only *The Comedy of Errors*, *Macbeth*, and *The Tempest* can be done in less than three hours without cutting. And even if we take a play that exists only in a short text, *Macbeth*, we cannot claim that we are experiencing the very play that Shakespeare conceived, partly because some of the Witches' songs almost surely are non-Shakespearean additions, and partly because we are not willing to watch the play performed without an intermission and with boys in the female roles.

Further, as the earlier discussion of costumes mentioned, the plays apparently were given chiefly in contemporary, that is, in Elizabethan dress. If today we give them in the costumes that Shakespeare probably saw, the plays seem not contemporary but curiously dated. Yet if we use our own dress, we find lines of dialogue that are at odds with what we see; we may feel that the language, so clearly not our own, is inappropriate coming out of people in today's dress. A common solution, incidentally, has been to set the plays in the nineteenth century, on the grounds that this attractively distances the plays (gives them a degree of foreignness, allowing for interesting costumes) and yet doesn't put them into a museum world of Elizabethan England.

Inevitably our productions are adaptations, *our* adaptations, and inevitably they will look dated, not in a century but in twenty years, or perhaps even in a decade. Still, we cannot escape from our own conceptions. As the director Peter Brook has said, in *The Empty Space* (1968):

> It is not only the hair-styles, costumes and make-ups that look dated. All the different elements of staging—the shorthands of behavior that stand for emotions; gestures, gesticulations and tones of voice—are all fluctuating on an invisible stock exchange all the time. . . . A living theatre that thinks it can stand aloof from anything as trivial as fashion will wilt. (p. 16)

As Brook indicates, it is through today's hairstyles, costumes, makeup, gestures, gesticulations, tones of voice—this includes our *conception* of earlier hairstyles, costumes, and so forth if we stage the play in a period other than our own—that we inevitably stage the plays.

It is a truism that every age invents its own Shakespeare, just as, for instance, every age has invented its own classical world. Our view of ancient Greece, a slave-holding society in which even free Athenian women were severely circumscribed, does not much resemble the Victorians' view of ancient Greece as a glorious democracy, just as, perhaps, our view of Victorianism itself does not much resemble theirs. We cannot claim that the Shakespeare on our stage is the true Shakespeare, but in our stage productions we find a Shakespeare that speaks to us, a Shakespeare that our ancestors doubtless did not know but one that seems to us to be the true Shakespeare—at least for a while.

Our age is remarkable for the wide variety of kinds of staging that it uses for Shakespeare, but one development deserves special mention. This is the now common practice of race-blind or color-blind or nontraditional casting, which allows persons who are not white to play in Shakespeare. Previously blacks performing in Shakespeare were limited to a mere three roles, Othello, Aaron (in *Titus Andronicus*), and the Prince of Morocco (in *The Merchant of Venice*), and there were no roles at all for Asians. Indeed, African-Americans rarely could play even one of these three roles, since they were not welcome in white companies. Ira Aldridge (c.1806–1867), a black actor of undoubted talent, was forced to make his living by performing Shakespeare in England and in Europe, where he could play not only Othello but also—in whiteface—other tragic roles such as King Lear. Paul Robeson (1898–1976) made theatrical history when he played Othello in London in 1930, and there was some talk about bringing the production to the United States, but there was more talk about whether American audiences would tolerate the sight of a black man—a real black man, not a white man in blackface—kissing and then killing a white woman. The idea was tried out in summer stock in 1942, the reviews were enthusiastic, and in the following year Robeson opened on Broadway in a production that ran an astounding 296 performances. An occasional all-black company sometimes performed Shakespeare's plays, but otherwise blacks (and other minority members) were in effect shut out from performing Shakespeare. Only since about 1970 has it been common for nonwhites to play major roles along with whites. Thus, in a 1996–97 production of *Antony and Cleopatra*, a white Cleopatra, Vanessa Redgrave, played opposite a black Antony, David Harewood.

Multiracial casting is now especially common at the New York Shakespeare Festival, founded in 1954 by Joseph Papp, and in England, where even siblings such as Claudio and Isabella in *Measure for Measure* or Lear's three daughters may be of different races. Probably most viewers today soon stop worrying about the lack of realism, and move beyond the color of the performers' skin to the quality of the performance.

Nontraditional casting is not only a matter of color or race; it includes sex. In the past, occasionally a distinguished woman of the theater has taken on a male role—Sarah Bernhardt (1844–1923) as Hamlet is perhaps the most famous example—but such performances were widely regarded as eccentric. Although today there have been some performances involving cross-dressing (a drag *As You Like It* staged by the National Theatre in England in 1966 and in the United States in 1974 has achieved considerable fame in the annals of stage history), what is more interesting is the casting of women in roles that traditionally are male but that need not be. Thus, a 1993–94 English production of *Henry V* used a woman—*not* cross-dressed—in the role of the governor of Harfleur. According to Peter Holland, who reviewed the production in *Shakespeare Survey* 48 (1995), "having a female Governor of Harfleur feminized the city and provided a direct response to the horrendous threat of rape and murder that Henry had offered, his language and her body in direct connection and opposition" (p. 210). Ten years from now the device may not play so effectively, but today it speaks to us. Shakespeare, born in the Elizabethan Age, has been dead nearly four hundred years, yet he is, as Ben Jonson said, "not of an age but for all time." We must understand, however, that he is "for all time" precisely because each age finds in his abundance something for itself and something of itself.

And here we come back to two issues discussed earlier in this introduction—the instability of the text and, curiously, the Bacon/Oxford heresy concerning the authorship of the plays. *Of course* Shakespeare wrote the plays, and we should daily fall on our knees to thank him for them—and yet there is something to the idea that he is not their only author. Every editor, every director and actor, and every reader to some degree shapes them, too, for when we edit, direct, act, or read, we inevitably become Shakespeare's collaborator and re-create the plays. The plays, one might say, are so cunningly contrived that they guide our responses, tell us how we ought to feel, and make a mark on us, but (for better or for worse) we also make a mark on them.

—SYLVAN BARNET
Tufts University

Introduction

The Comedy of Errors has come down to us solely through the First Folio, in a good text which seems not far removed from the author's manuscript, and which is particularly interesting for the explicitness of its stage directions. The play itself is the shortest, and may indeed be the earliest, of Shakespeare's dramatic works. As such, it is more explicitly linked to classical tradition than any of the others. In spite of a notorious gibe by Ben Jonson, it is quite evident that Shakespeare was acquainted with certain standard Latin authors. There is even an accredited rumor that, before entering the theater, he had taught in a country school, where the curriculum would have consisted of very little else. If he was to assay the range of the repertory, Seneca could not be "too heavy," in the phrase of Polonius, "nor Plautus too light." Titus Andronicus was Shakespeare's early experiment in the mode of Senecan tragedy; The Comedy of Errors marks, rather more happily, his assimilation and extension of Plautine comedy. In that case there was a specific model, the archetypal comedy of twins, the Menaechmi or Two Menaechmuses. A lively translation into Elizabethan prose by one W.W. (who is commonly identified as the minor poet William Warner) was published in 1595, some 1800 years after the appearance of Plautus' play on the Roman stage.

Whether Shakespeare could have seen an unpublished draft of this version, or whether W.W. was indebted to Shakespeare's free adaptation, has been argued back and forth by scholars. Certainly Shakespeare could have known the original at first hand, and the similar phrases used by both writers may be coincidences rather than echoes. At all events, the English Menaechmi offers a helpful basis of comparison whereby readers may observe for themselves how Shakespeare adapted and amplified Plautus. Such observations might well begin with W.W.'s title page: "A pleasant and fine Conceited Comedy taken out of the most excellent witty Poet Plautus, chosen purposely from out the rest as least harmful and yet delightful . . ." In other words, both the translator and the playwright chose to work from an untypical play—untypical in its all but complete reliance on chance and not on contrivance, not on malice or mischief but sheer luck. Not that fortune, often in the most commercial sense, was ever slow to intervene in the world of Greco-Roman comedy. But it was commonly sought through the profit motive on the part of the old, or sexual appetite on the part of the young, and the resultant conflicts were perennially exploited by parasites and abetted by slaves. Whereas tragedy took place in temples and palaces, the comic sphere was a round of urban shops and middle-class domiciles.

In the ancient theater the proscenium was not a picture frame but an architectural facade, whose practical doors and upper windows gave a stylized impression of a street scene in some Mediterranean seaport. By convention the side exits led to the marketplace in one direction (Shakespeare's Mart) and to the harbor in the other ("from the Bay"). Between them flowed the continual traffic of characters, pausing at one doorway or another to transact their business, and incidentally to inform the audience of the goings-on within. What Shakespeare calls "the stirring passage of the day" moved all the faster because it did not look beyond external appearances. Drama becomes more serious when it stresses characterization; farce, at the other extreme, tends to subordinate character to plot. Hence the *donnée* of Plautus was the very essence of the farcical: two characters sufficiently alike, so that each might fit interchangeably into the other's situation, could not afford to possess distinguishing characteristics. They are, by definition, altogether unexceptional. In general, the *dramatis personae* of New Comedy—the kind of comedy that was new with Menander, yet was by no means exhausted with Molière—are stock types rather than fully characterized individuals. With many changes of costume and scenery, they continue to present object lessons in

avarice, flattery, braggadocio, and other continuing devia-
tions from sound morality.

Comedy, as Sir Philip Sidney defined it for Shakespeare's
age, is "an imitation of the common errors of our life,"
which are represented "in the most ridiculous and scornful
sort that may be, so as it is impossible that any beholder can
be content to be such a one." Sidney, who was involved in
the defense of poetry, may bear down too heavily for our
taste upon the posture of dramatist as moralist; yet, in
emphasizing the correction of error, he shifts to the enlight-
enment of the spectator and to that civilized overview
which—through a process of confusion and clarification—
we finally attain: "There, but for the grace of God, go we!"
To err is proverbially human; and our tragic heroes go astray
grandly by committing some single and fatal mistake.
Comic figures, on the other hand, run through a whole train
of petty errors, and somehow manage to extricate themselves from the final consequences. Hence it is not surprising that Shakespeare's generic title had its lost
forerunners, notably a *History of Error* performed in 1577.
It is recorded, too, that a gala performance of the Shakespearean *Comedy of Errors* was played by the legal
gentlemen of Gray's Inn during the Christmas season of
1594 (probably two or three years after it was first publicly
produced), with such crowds and attendant confusions that
the festive occasion "was ever afterwards called *The Night
of Errors.*"

In his massive studies of Shakespeare's modest Latinity,
T. W. Baldwin has shown that the poet may well have
studied Plautus in the contemporaneous edition of Lam-
binus. There the text of the *Menaechmus* was flanked by a
commentary in which each successive twist or turn of the
plot is signalized by the Latin verb *errare* or the noun *error.*
Thus the key word utilized by Shakespeare would seem to
have had the force of a technical term. Along with it we may
consider another term, introduced by that versatile literary
innovator, George Gascoigne, through his English rendering
of Ariosto's prose comedy, *The Supposes.* Now a "suppose," as Gascoigne defined it and applied it through a series
of marginal comments on the action of the play, is "a mistaking or imagination of one thing for another," generally

one person supposed to be someone else because of deception, disguise, or impersonation. It requires no plotting or counterplotting in a Machiavellian sense; the only plotter is Shakespeare or Plautus himself; and what he hatches is fobbed off upon us as a trick of fate, a freak of nature, a practical joke conceived and executed by providence. The misapprehensions that gave rise to it are not poses nor supposes nor impostures; they are, plainly and simply, errors. We are at the roulette table, not the chessboard, here.

Where tragedy individualizes its protagonists, comedy underscores those broad resemblances which make it difficult to tell people apart. The closer the similarity between them, the easier it becomes for us to confound them. Blunders are most easily committed when two differing alternatives closely resemble one another, though the resemblance be no more than skin-deep. "Two faces that are alike," Pascal remarked, "though neither of them excites laughter in itself, make me laugh when together on account of the likeness." It was this sentence of Pascal's that Bergson developed into his theory of laughter as a protest of the natural and the humane against all attempts at mechanization and regimentation. Duplication, in particular, seems an affront to human dignity (one is almost tempted to call it a loss of face)—to be always mistaken for, to be almost indistinguishable from, somebody else. A set of identical twins, leading different lives, is a possibility but not a probability; and Coleridge would invoke that classic distinction to draw a line between comedy and farce. Upon his recommendation we entertain the initial hypothesis; we verily believe it because it is absurd; for, after all, absurdity is man's lot as the Existentialists have redefined it. Plautus offered Shakespeare a basic theme for the unforced interplay of cross-purposes. Shakespeare's variations, widely echoed in their turn, would be blithely syncopated by Rodgers and Hart in their appealing musical comedy *The Boys from Syracuse*.

The improbable assumption of Plautus was complicated to the very limits of the possible when Shakespeare dared to redouble the twins, and thereby to provide his pair of protagonists with a brace of retainers. Here he was acting on a hint from another Plautine source, a play so frequently imitated that Jean Giraudoux could number his treatment

Amphitryon 38. Its myth is that of Alcmena, wooed by Jupiter in the shape of her absent husband Amphitryon, while Jupiter's companion, Mercury, assumes the person of Sosia, the household slave. Two of Shakespeare's most effective scenes, where the homecoming master and man are turned away from their own threshold, are directly inspired by Plautus' *Amphitryon.* Consequently, since each of Shakespeare's masters has a bond-servant, he does not need to attach an officious parasite to the local Menaechmus as Plautus does. Messenio, the clever servant who accompanies the Syracusan Menaechmus, warns him with a pun against Epidamnum, where no one escapes "*sine damno* (without damage)"; but the Epidamnian pitfalls turn out to be unsolicited favors, which the visitor accepts with increasing insouciance. As for the citizen-twin, he is a solid man of affairs; but, having had a falling-out with his wife (and Plautus wastes no sympathy whatsoever upon the shrewish Uxor or Roman matron), he sets aside the day's business for a night's pleasure. In the true holiday spirit, both brothers are on the town.

Shakespeare, in amplifying the wife's role, reduced the part assigned to the Courtesan. The pivotal banquet is served not at her hangout, the Porpentine, but at the home of Antipholus above his shop, the Phoenix; while he, a normally faithful husband, seeks out her company only after he has reason to suspect his wife. The latter, Adriana, inherits the Uxor's misunderstanding with her husband; but Shakespeare sublimates it to a plane of genuine, if too possessive, conjugal love. Moreover, he endows her with a sister, to be courted by the bachelor Antipholus; and Luciana proves to be a *raisonneuse,* a mouthpiece of moderation, so that the twins occupy a place in the great Shakespearean debate on marriage, along with Kate and Petruchio or Rosaline and Berowne or Beatrice and Benedick. Shakespeare's characters live, as usual, in a Christian ethos. The perplexed traveler swears, "as I am a Christian," and—approached by the Courtesan—echoes Christ bidding Satan avaunt. The change in the ethical climate may be noted by the shift from Epidamnum, which is nonetheless mentioned along the way, to Ephesus. Plautus' Syracusans fear Epidamnum because it is an emporium of sharp practice, peopled by rogues and harlots and the usual comic types. Shakespeare's Syracusans are cautious too. "They say this town is full of cozenage," the traveling Antipholus warns himself.

Notwithstanding, the Ephesians he meets are not "disguised cheaters." They are, as the traveling Dromio puts it, "a gentle nation," who "speak us fair, give us gold." Shakespeare is more in his milieu where the setting is a room in the palace—or, better still, another part of the forest—than in the mercantile zones of New Comedy. It is not coney-catching but witchcraft and sorcery that envelop Ephesus in its mysterious aura. "Here we wander in illusions." This is a place of strangers and sojourners, given to curious arts, to echo the patron saint of travelers *in partibus infidelium,* the Apostle Paul. Not without pertinence, it has been suggested that Paul's Epistle to the Ephesians, with its injunctions for husbands and wives, and for servants and masters, may have been in the background of Shakespeare's mind. His far-flung romance of *Pericles,* based on the folk tale of Apollonius of Tyre as retold by John Gower, reaches its resolution in the famous Temple of Diana at Ephesus. Some of the elements of the late play are present in the early one, notably the vicissitudes of a family progressing through misadventure by sea to recognition under religious auspices. The pagan temple has its counterpart in the Priory, where—instead of a goddess in the machine—the flesh-and-blood Abbess is revealed to be the long-lost wife and mother.

The framing figure of Egeon contributes an emotional tension, at the very outset, to what would otherwise have remained a two-dimensional drama. His protracted expository narration is enlivened by the awareness that it is a plea, and probably a vain one, for his life. Rightly he blames his misfortunes on hap; for nowhere else in Shakespeare can a whole pattern of incidents be so directly traceable to sheer unmitigated contingency. Egeon is hopeless and helpless because he is hapless. But this is not to be a novel by Thomas Hardy; it is a knockabout farce, where bad fortune will change soon enough into good. The next scene not only offers a hint that the new arrival is one of Egeon's sons—through the mix-up of the Dromios—and that the other son is just around the corner, but virtually guarantees the ransom, since the sum mentioned in both scenes is exactly a thousand marks. Coincidence has already done its best, as well as its worst, and a happy ending has been implicit from the beginning. Meanwhile the sequence of farcical episodes has been framed by the tragicomic overplot; and Shakespeare, by enlisting our sympathies for the fate of Egeon, has charged the air with a suspense which cannot be resolved until the appointed hour of execution, five o'clock in the afternoon.

Both of the Antipholuses have appointments at that hour, one of them with the Merchant and the other with Angelo the Goldsmith; and since it is noon when the Syracusan arrives, and since the Ephesian Dromio gets into his troubles over the question of dinnertime, the time scheme is firmly fixed within the course of the afternoon. There are frequent reminders of time passing, to reinforce the structure of occurrences: when Komisarjevsky produced the play at Stratford-on-Avon, his setting was dominated by a gigantic clock. Adhering to the classical unities as Shakespeare does just once again in *The Tempest,* he takes the traditional city street as his horizon, moving his characters back and forth from port to Mart and in and out of the various doorways between. The play would seem to lend itself very conveniently to the simultaneous stage of a great hall, such as that of Gray's Inn, where three or four free-standing houses or so-called mansions would have corresponded to the labeled locations: the Phoenix, the Porpentine for the Courtesan, the Centaur inn, and the ultimate abbey near the place of execution. On the other hand, the recent production at Stratford, Ontario, demonstrated how well the play could adapt to the multilevel mobility of an Elizabethan playhouse.

The problem of staging ought not to be unduly strained by the presupposition that calls for identical twins. To be sure, the difficulty raised by the twins of two sexes in *Twelfth Night,* which would have been solved in Shakespeare's day when both parts were acted by young men, is virtually insoluble in the modern theater. But, granted an approximate equivalence of stature, plus the same costuming and make-up, the Antipholuses and Dromios ought to look enough alike to confuse the other characters without confusing the audience. Is it not our premise, in viewing a comedy, that we are brighter than those who are on the stage? In the theater, where the employment of masks eliminated the facial disparities, Plautus had to give a tassel to Mercury and a feather to Jupiter so that they would not be confused with Sosia and Amphitryon. At Stratford, Connecticut, in 1963, the same actor was cast as both twins, thereby combining histrionic virtuosity with artistic economy. This directorial tactic must create a bigger dilemma than the one it endeavors to solve, since the audience can never know the moment of catharsis, the visual illumination of seeing the two confusing elements discriminated from one another and exhibited side by side.

That way schizophrenia lies—which does not mean that it would be unproduceable in the Theater of the Absurd. It might turn out to be something in the vein of Pirandello, if not a dramatization of *Dr. Jekyll and Mr. Hyde*. But the actual predicament is that of two personalities forced into the same role, rather than that of one personality playing two roles, since the resident twin has the contacts and continuities, and the roving twin intercepts them, as it were. Tweedledum has got to match Tweedledee, more or less, in order to be taken for him; and yet, the less he feels like him, the more the dramatic irony. Plautus did not discriminate between his two very sharply; the discrepancies that emerged largely took the concrete form of objects which fell into the wrong hands; otherwise the interconnecting characters did not seem to notice much difference. The married Menaechmus was angry from the first, so that each new chagrin could be rationalized to his mood. The interloping Menaechmus, though considerably bewildered, had no cause for being dissatisfied with his reception. Neither of them was above the temptation to profit from the contretemps; and the interloper finally engaged in a stratagem of his own, when he joined the game and pretended to be a lunatic.

That sort of conduct is what we have agreed to label a suppose, a deception which is cultivated rather than casual. The most notable fact about Shakespeare's comedy is that it has no supposes, only errors: only mischances, and no contrivances by anybody except Shakespeare himself. There is no parallel scene of pretended madness; Shakespeare must have been saving the theme for *Hamlet*. Here the suspected madman, like Malvolio in *Twelfth Night,* protests his sanity. He does not act; he is acted upon; and Shakespeare, ever the psychologist, makes a good deal more out of the attempted diagnosis of demonic possession. He makes the exorcism so very painful, and goes so far out of his way to substitute the grim-visaged schoolmaster, Dr. Pinch, for the Plautine Medicus that we sense a virtual obsession, possibly connected with Holofernes, the pedant of *Love's Labor's Lost,* or with some other reminiscence from Shakespeare's own teaching days. It is as if the nightmare came so close that the misunderstood hero dare not pretend to be hallucinated. Again there is a precedent in Saint Paul's Epistle to the Ephesians, where the exorcist is exorcised. The customary rhetorical questions of comedy, in these mouths, become questions of existential bewilderment or expressions of cosmic vertigo: Do I dream or wake? Do we see double? Is he drunk or sober? Is she a liar or a fool? Who is crazy? Who is sane?

Contrasted with this constant inner questioning, the caricature of Dr. Pinch seems externalized. He is the one humorous personage of the play, in the Jonsonian usage, a man of obvious quirks and eccentric aspect, the crazy psychiatrist. If the others are funny, it is because of the plights they find themselves in. No, there is one other exception, though she is peripheral, and has a greater impact in her absence than in her presence onstage. This heroine, invoked indifferently as Luce or Nell, is generically a Dowsabel or, for that matter, a Dulcinea—a kitchen maid whose formidable proportions are vividly verbalized by the wrong Dromio, her brother-in-law, who is still quaking from the shock of having been claimed by her as a husband. This is the vulgar parallel to Adriana's claim upon her brother-in-law. Dromio's description of his brother's Nell, elicited by his master's queries as straight man, is a set-piece in the manner of Launce or Launcelot Gobbo, and may well have been assigned to the same comedian. With its geographical conceits, comparing the parts of her person to foreign countries (and containing, incidentally, the sole direct allusion that Shakespeare makes to America), it might almost be a ribald reversal of Othello's traveler's tales when wooing Desdemona.

But it is by no means a far-fetched gag, since it embodies—on a more than miniature scale—the principal contrast of the play: on the one hand, extensive voyaging; on the other, intensive domesticity. In using an underplot which burlesques the main plot, Shakespeare employs a device as old as Medwall's pioneer interlude of *Fulgens and Lucres,* where the rival suitors have servants who court the mistress' maid under the diagrammatic designations of A and B. With Nell, as with the demanding Adriana, the normal approaches of courtship are reversed. The closest we come to romantic love is the sketchy relationship between her brother-in-law and her husband's sister-in-law. Yet that is a good deal closer than Plautus brings us; and though both masters are suitably mated in the end, the concluding dialogue of the servants emphasizes the pairing of twins, not spouses. Parents and children are reunited, family ties are reasserted; but Dromio of Syracuse remains a free agent. His greatest moment has been the midpoint of the play, when he acted as doorkeeper and kept out his fellow Dromio, as well as that Dromio's master, the master of the house. This is the one point before the denouement when Shakespeare permits his twins to meet and talk, and the door between them seems to keep the mutual visibility fairly obscure.

It is worth noting that their brief colloquy reverts to the doggerel style of *Ralph Roister Doister,* the oldest English imitation of Plautus, in its stichomythic interchanges of rhyming fourteeners. This is the main scene (the first of Act 3) that Shakespeare borrowed from the *Amphitryon* (the first of Act 1), eking out the comedy of the *Menaechmi* with the underplot of the two Sosias to complete—with a vengeance—the Elizabethan requirements for a double plot. He develops it to the very pitch of the dramatic subversion that he has been exploiting, with the outsider inside and the insider excluded, the stranger in possession of the house and the householder cast into outer darkness. Both parties are translated, as Quince will affirm of Bottom; and they could not have been so completely translated, had they not been facsimiles to begin with. The most fundamental alteration that Shakespeare made in his Plautine material was to shift the focus from the homekeeping twin to his errant brother, whose sobriquet, Antipholus Erotes, may be a variation on

Erratus or Errans. The *Menaechmi* starts out with the other twin, and with the reassurance of familiar surroundings, into which the disturbing factor will be injected. *The Comedy of Errors* starts with the newcomer, and his impressions of strangeness: the witchery of Ephesus, not the bustle of Epidamnum.

Having a head start, and having to alternate scenes with Antipholus of Ephesus who does not appear until the third act, Antipholus of Syracuse has a much larger part: roughly 272 lines to the other's 207. The disproportion is even clearer between the parts of the two Dromios: there the score is Syracuse 233, Ephesus 162. The *Menaechmi,* though it is the shorter play, has fewer characters and longer speeches; accordingly, its Syracusan twin has 251 lines, whereas the Epidamnian twin has 300. We therefore tend to visualize what goes on in the Latin play from the denizen's standpoint, and what goes on in the English play from the alien's. Epidamnum could be any old town, where everything should be in its place, *in situ:* where everyone expects his fellow citizen, Menaechmus, to go through the round of his habitual day. No one could suspect that there was another Menaechmus, whose chance encounters would lead to incongruities and discontinuities, except for his one follower, who shares and compounds his perplexities. Ephesus is another story, however. We are put off at once by the hostile reception of Egeon; and when the two other foreigners enter, Antipholus and Dromio, they are the first of those names whom we have met.

We share their misgivings all the more readily because they too have been risking their lives, and because the object of their travels has so far eluded them. When this Antipholus gets caught up in his brother's existence, it is as new to us as it is to him. We participate in an adventure; what might be matter-of-fact to an Ephesian is, for him and ourselves, a fantasy out of the *Arabian Nights.* "What error drives our eyes and ears amiss?" he wonders, after Adriana accosts him, reprimands him, and invites him to dinner. And tentatively he resolves,

> Until I know this sure uncertainty,
> I'll entertain the offered fallacy.   (2.2.186–87)

Then, after dinner, smitten with Luciana, he asks her to unfold the mystery:

> Teach me, dear creature, how to think and speak:
> Lay open to my earthy-gross conceit,
> Smoth'red in errors, feeble, shallow, weak,
> The folded meaning of your words' deceit.   (3.2.33–36)

But the undeception does not come about until all the participants in this "sympathizèd one day's error"—for so the Abbess sums it up—have sought the illumination of sanctuary within her abbey. In that cloistered serenity, far from urban corruption, the deferred recognition scenes can coincide at long last. The confessions and counteraccusations piece together a step-by-step recapitulation of how "these errors are arose." The maternal figure of the Abbess is something of a surprise, as Bertrand Evans points out in his recent study, *Shakespeare's Comedies.* Running through all of them, Mr. Evans finds their common structural principle in what he calls a "discrepant awareness." Characteristically, the humor springs from "the exploitable gulf spread between the participants' understanding and ours."

In Shakespeare's development of this resource, *The Comedy of Errors* is primordial, since it is his single comedy where the audience knows all and all the characters are in the dark. Mr. Evans' suggestive analysis can be perfectly fitted to the *Menaechmi.* Plautus, in effect, is always saying, "I told you so." But Shakespeare is always asking, "Can such things be?" The exceptional position of the Abbess not only rounds out the recognitions; it lays the spell of wonderment again upon the concluding scene; and it reminds us, as other touches do, of Shakespeare's romances. Even within the venal and angular precincts of Latinate Comedy, he can make us aware of unpathed waters, undreamed shores, and things in heaven and earth that philosophy has not fathomed. Yet philosophers can tell us much, particularly about the processes of learning; and Bergson tells us much about *The Comedy of Errors* when, in his essay on laughter, he borrows a concept from optics and writes of "the reciprocal interference of series." At length we can put our supposes or errors down in scientific terminology. "A situation is invari-

ably comic," Bergson explains, "when it belongs simultaneously to two independent series of events, and is capable of
being interpreted in two entirely different meanings at the
same time."

It would be hard to conceive of a better illustration than
the two different series of events in the respective days of
the two Antipholuses, and the ways in which they are im-
perceptibly crisscrossed. Antipholus of Syracuse has no
particular expectations or plans. He derives a gratuitous
enjoyment from the inexplicable services rendered and
favors due his brother. This interference or substitution
induces a certain amnesia on the brother's part, when the
bills come in and the witnesses testify; naturally, he cannot remember the items attested. As one error engenders
another, suspicion is bound to mount and disgruntlement
spread, rising to their climax in hot pursuit toward the mad-
house or the jail, and ending at the Priory. Now the brunt of
these displacements is borne by Antipholus of Ephesus. Of
all those discomfited, he comes nearest to being a victim
of the situation, since it is his situation, in the last analysis.
It is his routine which is broken up, his standing in the com-
munity undermined; his normal expectations are interfered
with, and—to add insult to injury—he is expected to pay
for what he has been deprived of. In short, the rug has
been pulled out from under the very preconditions of his
existence.

Other people's bafflement can be fun, and Plautus makes
the most of it. From the heights of our spectatorial vantage
point, we need not worry too much about what befalls
whom. We are not playing blind man's buff, we are
watching the game. But Shakespeare makes us feel what it
is like to be this or that Antipholus—all the difference in the
world, if we happened to start by being the other one—and
the interaction of opposite numbers ends by demonstrating *a
fortiori* the uniqueness of the individual. When Adriana and
her husband appeal to the Duke, the stories they tell of their
day's experience are mutually contradictory; but the discrepancies would disappear if the shadow of the interfering
Antipholus were retraced through their reciprocal patterns.
(Latter-day readers or viewers may be reminded of the
Japanese story or film *Rashomon.*) It has been a lesson for

Adriana, brought home by the gentle rebuke of the Abbess, and penitently acknowledged. For Antipholus of Ephesus, it has been an eye-opening misadventure. Apparently, he has never felt the impetus that has incited his brother and his father to sally forth in search of him. Unconcerned with his foundling origin, he rejoices in the good graces of the Duke and takes for granted the stable comforts of his Ephesian citizenship.

What greater shock for him, then, than to bring a party of fellow citizens home to his well-established household for lunch and to discover that household preempted by roistering strangers, to be shut out in the street, to have one's own door slammed in one's own face? Or is it one's own? The sense of alienation, that *Verfremdungseffekt* so characteristic of Brecht and of the twentieth-century theater, is all the greater when our image of ourselves depends for its corroboration upon a settled context, and when we come to realize—what tragedy teaches us—that it is our destiny to be displaced. When Messenio saw the two Menaechmuses together, he declared that water was not more like water. After Shakespeare has adapted the metaphor, it stands not for an easy correspondence but for an unending quest.

> I to the world am like a drop of water
> That in the ocean seeks another drop, (1.2.35–36)

Antipholus of Syracuse confesses sadly, realizing that he is less likely to find a mother and a brother than to be irretrievably lost himself. Later, Adriana, addressing him as if he were Antipholus of Ephesus, likens their imperiled love to a drop of water into the sea; and he has a similar exchange with Luciana. The Syracusan twin is conscious that he must lose his identity in order to find it; the Ephesian twin is not; but he must, and he does. And Dromio too—both Dromios, whichever is which—must undergo their crises of identity: "Am I Dromio? Am I your man? Am I myself?" (3.2.73–74)

Modern psychological fiction is haunted by doubles, sometimes as overtly as in the tales of Hoffmann, Poe, and Dostoevsky, or in "The Jolly Corner" of Henry James, where the Black Stranger is recognized as the self that might have been. The other self—best friend, worst enemy—stares back at the poets from Heine's pallid ghost *("Du! Doppelgänger, du bleicher Geselle!")* or Baudelaire's hypocritical reader *("mon semblable! mon frère!")*. That alter ego may be demon or devil, good angel or evil genius. It may be the retribution of conscience—Philip Drunk reprehended by Philip Sober—or, at the other extreme, the vicarious pleasure the artist enjoys through the playboy, the envy of Shem for Shaun. All this may well be a far cry from Plautine or even Shakespearean farce, to which we should be glad that we can escape from our more introspective dilemmas. There all aberrations come home to roost, and are sorted out by the happy ending; we acknowledge the error of our ways, and false suppositions are replaced by truths. No one really gets damaged in Epidamnum, and everyone enjoys a new lease of life when Egeon is ransomed and reprieved. Everything will be explained at a feast, after the conventional manner of comedy. Debts will be paid, relationships renewed, and daily routine taken up where it broke off. Having been restored once more to our familiar world, we laugh away the shudder of estrangement.

—HARRY LEVIN
Harvard University

The Comedy of Errors

The Comedy of Errors

ACT 1

Scene 1. [*A public place.*]

Enter the Duke of Ephesus, with [Egeon] the Mer-
chant of Syracusa,°1 *Jailer, and other Attendants.*

Egeon. Proceed, Solinus, to procure my fall,
    And by the doom° of death end woes and all.

Duke. Merchant of Syracusa, plead no more;
    I am not partial° to infringe our laws.
    The enmity and discord which of late   5
    Sprung from the rancorous outrage of your Duke
    To merchants, our well-dealing countrymen,
    Who, wanting guilders° to redeem their lives,
    Have sealed his rigorous statutes with their bloods,
    Excludes all pity from our threat'ning looks.   10
    For, since the mortal and intestine jars°
    'Twixt thy seditious countrymen and us,

¹ The degree sign (°) indicates a footnote, which is keyed to the
text by line number. Text references are printed in **boldface** type; the
annotation follows in roman type.
1.1. s.d. **Syracusa** Syracuse, ancient capital of Sicily   2 **doom** sentence   4 **partial** predisposed   8 **guilders** Dutch coins worth about forty
cents   11 **intestine jars** internal conflicts

It hath in solemn synods been decreed,
Both by the Syracusians and ourselves,
15   To admit no traffic to our adverse° towns.
Nay more; if any born at Ephesus°
Be seen at Syracusian marts and fairs;
Again, if any Syracusian born
Come to the bay of Ephesus, he dies,
20   His goods confiscate to the Duke's dispose,°
Unless a thousand marks° be levièd
To quit° the penalty and to ransom him.
Thy substance, valued at the highest rate,
Cannot amount unto a hundred marks;
25   Therefore by law thou art condemned to die.

Egeon. Yet this my comfort: when your words are
        done,
My woes end likewise with the evening sun.

Duke. Well, Syracusian, say, in brief, the cause
Why thou departed'st from thy native home,
30   And for what cause thou cam'st to Ephesus.

Egeon. A heavier task could not have been imposed
Than I to speak my griefs unspeakable;
Yet, that the world may witness that my end
Was wrought by nature, not by vile offense,
35   I'll utter what my sorrow gives me leave.
In Syracusa was I born, and wed
Unto a woman happy but for me,
And by me, had not our hap been bad.
With her I lived in joy, our wealth increased
40   By prosperous voyages I often made
To Epidamnum,° till my factor's° death
And the great care of goods at random left
Drew me from kind embracements of my spouse;
From whom my absence was not six months old,
45   Before herself—almost at fainting under
The pleasing punishment that women bear—

15 **adverse** hostile   16 **Ephesus** (rich city on the coast of Asia Minor)
20 **dispose** disposal   21 **marks** (valued at somewhat more than three
dollars)   22 **quit** acquit   41 **Epidamnum** (Adriatic seaport)   41 **factor's** agent's

Had made provision for her following me,
And soon and safe arrivèd where I was.
There had she not been long, but she became
A joyful mother of two goodly sons;   50
And, which was strange, the one so like the other,
As could not be distinguished but by names.
That very hour, and in the self-same inn,
A mean° woman was deliverèd
Of such a burden male, twins both alike.   55
Those, for° their parents were exceeding poor,
I bought, and brought up to attend my sons.
My wife, not meanly° proud of two such boys,
Made daily motions° for our home return.
Unwilling I agreed; alas, too soon   60
We came aboard.
A league from Epidamnum had we sailed
Before the always wind-obeying deep
Gave any tragic instance° of our harm.
But longer did we not retain much hope;   65
For what obscurèd light the heavens did grant
Did but convey unto our fearful minds
A doubtful warrant° of immediate death,
Which, though myself would gladly have embraced,
Yet the incessant weepings of my wife,   70
Weeping before for what she saw must come,
And piteous plainings° of the pretty babes,
That mourned for fashion,° ignorant what to fear,
Forced me to seek delays for them and me.
And this it was—for other means was none: 75
The sailors sought for safety by our boat,
And left the ship, then sinking-ripe,° to us.
My wife, more careful for the latter-born,°
Had fast'ned him unto a small spare mast,
Such as seafaring men provide for storms;   80
To him one of the other twins was bound,
Whilst I had been like heedful of the other.

---

54 **mean** poor   56 **for** because   58 **not meanly** more than a little
59 **motions** proposals   64 **instance** token   68 **doubtful warrant** om-
inous sign   72 **plainings** wails   73 **fashion** custom   77 **sinking-ripe**
ready to sink   78 **latter-born** (but see line 124)

The children thus disposed, my wife and I,
Fixing our eyes on whom our care was fixed,
85 Fast'ned ourselves at either end the mast;
And floating straight, obedient to the stream,
Was carried towards Corinth,° as we thought.
At length the sun, gazing upon the earth,
Dispersed those vapors that offended us,
90 And, by the benefit of his wishèd° light,
The seas waxed calm, and we discoverèd
Two ships from far, making amain° to us:
Of Corinth that, of Epidaurus° this.
But ere they came—O, let me say no more!
95 Gather the sequel by that went before.

Duke. Nay, forward, old man; do not break off so,
For we may pity, though not pardon thee.

Egeon. O, had the gods done so, I had not now
Worthily° termed them merciless to us.
100 For, ere the ships could meet by twice five leagues,
We were encount'red by a mighty rock,
Which being violently borne upon,
Our helpful ship° was splitted in the midst;
So that, in this unjust divorce of us,
105 Fortune had left to both of us alike
What to delight in, what to sorrow for.
Her part, poor soul, seeming as burdenèd
With lesser weight, but not with lesser woe,
Was carried with more speed before the wind;
110 And in our sight they three were taken up
By fishermen of Corinth, as we thought.
At length another ship had seized on us,
And, knowing whom it was their hap to save,
Gave healthful welcome to their shipwracked guests,
115 And would have reft° the fishers of their prey,
Had not their bark been very slow of sail;
And therefore homeward did they bend their course.

87 **Corinth** (major Greek seaport) 90 **his wishèd** its wished-for
92 **amain** with full speed 93 **Epidaurus** (ancient name for both a
Greek and an Adriatic town) 99 **Worthily** deservedly 103 **ship**
i.e., the mast 115 **reft** robbed

Thus have you heard me severed from my bliss,
That by misfortunes was my life prolonged
To tell sad stories of my own mishaps.   *120*

Duke. And, for the sake of them thou sorrowest for,
Do me the favor to dilate° at full
What have befall'n of them and thee till now.

Egeon. My youngest boy, and yet my eldest care,
At eighteen years became inquisitive   *125*
After his brother, and importuned me
That his attendant—so his case was like,
Reft of his brother, but retained his name—
Might bear him company in the quest of him;
Whom whilst I labored of a love° to see,   *130*
I hazarded the loss of whom I loved.
Five summers have I spent in farthest Greece,
Roaming clean through the bounds of Asia,
And coasting homeward, came to Ephesus,
Hopeless to find,° yet loath to leave unsought   *135*
Or° that or any place that harbors men.
But here must end the story of my life;
And happy were I in my timely death,
Could all my travels° warrant me they live.

Duke. Hapless Egeon, whom the fates have marked   *140*
To bear the extremity of dire mishap!
Now trust me, were it not against our laws,
Against my crown, my oath, my dignity,°
Which princes, would they, may not disannul,°
My soul should sue as advocate for thee.   *145*
But though thou art adjudgèd° to the death,
And passèd sentence may not be recalled
But to our honor's great disparagement,°
Yet will I favor thee in what I can;
Therefore, merchant, I'll limit thee this day   *150*
To seek thy health by beneficial help.
Try all the friends thou hast in Ephesus—

---

122 **dilate** relate   130 **of a love** out of love   135 **Hopeless to find**
without hope of finding   136 **Or** either   139 **travels** (with the further implication of "travails")   143 **dignity** office   144 **disannul**
cancel   146 **adjudgèd** sentenced   148 **disparagement** injury

Beg thou, or borrow, to make up the sum,
And live; if no, then thou art doomed to die.
155   Jailer, take him to thy custody.

Jailer. I will, my lord.

Egeon. Hopeless and helpless doth Egeon wend,
But to procrastinate° his lifeless end.   *Exeunt.*

Scene 2. [*The Mart.*°]

*Enter Antipholus [of Syracuse], a Merchant,
and Dromio [of Syracuse].*

Merchant. Therefore, give out you are of Epidamnum,
Lest that your goods too soon be confiscate.
This very day a Syracusian merchant
Is apprehended for arrival here,
5   And not being able to buy out° his life,
According to the statute of the town,
Dies ere the weary sun set in the west.
There is your money that I had to keep.

S. Antipholus. Go bear it to the Centaur,° where we
host,°
10   And stay there, Dromio, till I come to thee;
Within this hour it will be dinnertime;
Till that, I'll view the manners of the town,
Peruse the traders, gaze upon the buildings,
And then return and sleep within mine inn;
15   For with long travel I am stiff and weary.
Get thee away.

S. Dromio. Many a man would take you at your word,
And go indeed, having so good a mean.°

Exit Dromio.

158 **procrastinate** postpone   1.2. s.d. **Mart** marketplace   5 **buy out**
redeem   9 **Centaur** (name and sign of an inn)   9 **host** lodge   18
mean means

S. Antipholus. A trusty villain,° sir, that very oft,
　　When I am dull with care and melancholy,   20
　　Lightens my humor° with his merry jests.
　　What, will you walk with me about the town,
　　And then go to my inn and dine with me?

Merchant. I am invited, sir, to certain merchants,
　　Of whom I hope to make much benefit.   25
　　I crave your pardon; soon at five o'clock,
　　Please you, I'll meet with you upon the Mart,
　　And afterward consort° you till bedtime.
　　My present business calls me from you now.

S. Antipholus. Farewell till then. I will go lose myself,   30
　　And wander up and down to view the city.

Merchant. Sir, I commend you to your own content.
　　　　　　　　　　　　　　　　　　　Exit.

S. Antipholus. He that commends me to mine own
　　　content
　　Commends me to the thing I cannot get.
　　I to the world am like a drop of water   35
　　That in the ocean seeks another drop,
　　Who, falling there to find his fellow forth,°
　　Unseen, inquisitive, confounds° himself.
　　So I, to find a mother and a brother,
　　In quest of them, unhappy,° lose myself.   40

　　　　　　　Enter Dromio of Ephesus.

　　Here comes the almanac° of my true date.
　　What now? How chance thou art returned so soon?

E. Dromio. Returned so soon! Rather approached too
　　　late.
　　The capon burns, the pig falls from the spit;
　　The clock hath strucken twelve° upon the bell;   45
　　My mistress made it one upon my cheek.
　　She is so hot because the meat is cold;

19 **villain** (in the original sense of "bondman") 21 **humor** mood
28 **consort** accompany 37 **find his fellow forth** seek his fellow out
38 **confounds** loses 40 **unhappy** unlucky 41 **almanac** (Dromio
reminds Antipholus of his own age) 45 **twelve** (dinnertime or later)

The meat is cold because you come not home;
You come not home because you have no stomach;°
50   You have no stomach, having broke your fast.
But we, that know what 'tis to fast and pray,
Are penitent for your default° today.

S. Antipholus. Stop in your wind,° sir; tell me this,
    I pray:
Where have you left the money that I gave you?

55 *E. Dromio.* O, sixpence, that I had o' Wednesday last,
To pay the saddler for my mistress' crupper?°
The saddler had it, sir, I kept it not.

S. Antipholus. I am not in a sportive humor now.
Tell me, and dally not, where is the money?
60   We being strangers here, how dar'st thou trust
So great a charge from thine own custody?

E. Dromio. I pray you, jest, sir, as you sit at dinner.
I from my mistress come to you in post;°
If I return, I shall be post° indeed,
65   For she will score° your fault upon my pate.
Methinks your maw,° like mine, should be your
    clock,
And strike you home without a messenger.

S. Antipholus. Come, Dromio, come, these jests are
    out of season;
Reserve them till a merrier hour than this.
70   Where is the gold I gave in charge to thee?

E. Dromio. To me, sir? Why, you gave no gold to me.

S. Antipholus. Come on, sir knave, have done your
    foolishness,
And tell me how thou hast disposed thy charge.

---

49 **stomach** appetite 52 **default** (1) sin (2) failure to appear 53
wind breath 56 **crupper** strap from saddle to horse's tail 63 **post**
haste 64 **post** posted (to pay account, with pun meaning "beaten")
65 **score** (with pun on "scour," beat) 66 **maw** stomach (ordinarily
used of animals)

E. Dromio. My charge was but to fetch you from the
　　Mart
　　Home to your house, the Phoenix,° sir, to dinner.　75
　　My mistress and her sister stays for you.

S. Antipholus. Now, as I am a Christian, answer me,
　　In what safe place you have bestowed° my money;
　　Or I shall break that merry sconce° of yours
　　That stands on° tricks when I am undisposed.　80
　　Where is the thousand marks thou hadst of me?

E. Dromio. I have some marks of yours upon my pate,
　　Some of my mistress' marks upon my shoulders,
　　But not a thousand marks between you both.
　　If I should pay° your worship those again,　85
　　Perchance you will not bear them patiently.

S. Antipholus. Thy mistress' marks? What mistress,
　　slave, hast thou?

E. Dromio. Your worship's wife, my mistress at the
　　Phoenix;
　　She that doth fast till you come home to dinner,
　　And prays that you will hie you home to dinner.　90

S. Antipholus. What, wilt thou flout me thus unto my
　　face,
　　Being forbid? There, take you that, sir knave.
　　　　　　　　　　　　　　　　　　[*Beats him.*]

E. Dromio. What mean you, sir? For God's sake, hold
　　your hands!
　　Nay, and° you will not, sir, I'll take my heels.
　　　　　　　　　　　　　　　　　Exit Dromio E.

S. Antipholus. Upon my life, by some device or other,　95
　　The villain is o'er-raught° of all my money.
　　They say this town is full of cozenage:°
　　As° nimble jugglers that deceive the eye,

---

75 **Phoenix** i.e., house of Antipholus, denoted by the sign of his shop
78 **bestowed** deposited　79 **sconce** head　80 **stands on** insists upon
85 **pay** (also meaning "beat")　94 **and** if　96 **o'er-raught** over-
reached　97 **cozenage** cheating　98 **As** such as

Dark-working sorcerers that change the mind,
100   Soul-killing witches that deform the body,
Disguisèd cheaters, prating mountebanks,°
And many suchlike liberties° of sin.
If it prove so, I will be gone the sooner.
I'll to the Centaur, to go seek this slave.
105   I greatly fear my money is not safe.   *Exit.*

101 **mountebanks** quacks   102 **liberties** uninhibited acts

ACT 2

Scene 1. [*The Phoenix.*]

Enter Adriana, wife to Antipholus [of Ephesus], with Luciana, her sister.

Adriana. Neither my husband nor the slave returned,
That in such haste I sent to seek his master.
Sure, Luciana, it is two o'clock.

Luciana. Perhaps some merchant hath invited him,
And from the Mart he's somewhere gone to dinner.   5
Good sister, let us dine, and never fret;
A man is master of his liberty.
Time is their master, and when they see time,
They'll go or come; if so, be patient, sister.

Adriana. Why should their liberty than ours be more?   10

Luciana. Because their business still° lies out o' door.

Adriana. Look when° I serve him so, he takes it ill.

Luciana. O, know he is the bridle of your will.

Adriana. There's none but asses will be bridled so.

Luciana. Why, headstrong liberty is lashed° with woe.   15
There's nothing situate under heaven's eye
But hath his bound, in earth, in sea, in sky.
The beasts, the fishes, and the wingèd fowls
Are their males' subjects, and at their controls;°

2.1.11 **still** always   12 **Look when** whenever   15 **lashed** whipped
19 **controls** commands

13

20 Man, more divine, the master of all these,
Lord of the wide world and wild wat'ry seas,
Indued with intellectual sense° and souls,
Of more preeminence than fish and fowls,
Are masters to their females, and their lords;
25 Then let your will attend on their accords.

Adriana. This servitude makes you to keep unwed.

Luciana. Not this, but troubles of the marriage bed.

Adriana. But, were you wedded, you would bear some
sway.°

Luciana. Ere I learn love, I'll practice to obey.

Adriana. How if your husband start some other
30 where?°

Luciana. Till he come home again, I would forbear.

Adriana. Patience unmoved! no marvel though she
pause;°
They can be meek that have no other cause.°
A wretched soul, bruised with adversity,
35 We bid be quiet when we hear it cry;
But were we burd'ned with like weight of pain,
As much or more we should ourselves complain:
So thou, that hast no unkind mate to grieve thee,
With urging helpless° patience would relieve me;
40 But, if thou live to see like right bereft,°
This fool-begged° patience in thee will be left.

Luciana. Well, I will marry one day, but to try.
Here comes your man, now is your husband nigh.

Enter Dromio of Ephesus.

Adriana. Say, is your tardy master now at hand?

_____

22 **intellectual sense** reason   28 **sway** authority   30 **start some other
where** pursue another woman   32 **pause** delay in getting married
33 **cause** motive   39 **helpless** unavailing   40 **like right bereft** your
own rights denied   41 **fool-begged** i.e., assumed as one would assume
responsibility for a fool

E. Dromio. Nay, he's at two hands with me, and that   45
  my two ears can witness.

Adriana. Say, didst thou speak with him? Know'st thou
  his mind?

E. Dromio. Ay, ay, he told° his mind upon mine ear.
  Beshrew his hand, I scarce could understand it.

Luciana. Spake he so doubtfully,° thou couldst not   50
  feel his meaning?

E. Dromio. Nay, he struck so plainly, I could too well
  feel his blows; and withal so doubtfully, that I could
  scarce understand° them.

Adriana. But say, I prithee, is he coming home?   55
  It seems he hath great care to please his wife.

E. Dromio. Why, mistress, sure my master is horn-mad.

Adriana. Horn-mad,° thou villain!

E. Dromio.   I mean not cuckold-mad,
  But sure he is stark mad.
  When I desired him to come home to dinner,   60
  He asked me for a thousand marks in gold.
  " 'Tis dinnertime," quoth I. "My gold!" quoth he.
  "Your meat doth burn," quoth I. "My gold!" quoth
    he.
  "Will you come?" quoth I. "My gold!" quoth he.
  "Where is the thousand marks I gave thee, villain?"   65
  "The pig," quoth I, "is burned." "My gold!" quoth
    he.
  "My mistress, sir—" quoth I. "Hang up° thy mis-
    tress!
  I know not thy mistress, out on° thy mistress!"

Luciana. Quoth who?

E. Dromio. Quoth my master.   70
  "I know," quoth he, "no house, no wife, no mistress."

48 **told** (with a pun on "tolled") 50 **doubtfully** uncertainly 54 **understand** (pun on "stand under") 58 **Horn-mad** (1) like a mad bull
(2) a cuckold 67 **Hang up** be hanged 68 **out on** (angry interjection)

So that my errand due unto° my tongue,
I thank him, I bare° home upon my shoulders;
For, in conclusion, he did beat me there.

Adriana. Go back again, thou slave, and fetch him
75   home.

E. Dromio. Go back again, and be new beaten home?
For God's sake, send some other messenger.

Adriana. Back, slave, or I will break thy pate across.°

E. Dromio. And he will bless that cross with other
beating;
80   Between you, I shall have a holy° head.

Adriana. Hence, prating peasant! Fetch thy master
home.

E. Dromio. Am I so round° with you, as you with me,
That like a football you do spurn me thus?
You spurn me hence, and he will spurn me hither;
85   If I last in this service, you must case me in leather.
                                            [*Exit.*]

Luciana. Fie, how impatience lowereth° in your face!

Adriana. His company must do his minions° grace,
Whilst I at home starve° for a merry look:
Hath homely age th' alluring beauty took
90   From my poor cheek? Then he hath wasted it.
Are my discourses° dull? Barren my wit?
If voluble and sharp discourse be marred,
Unkindness blunts it more than marble hard.
Do their gay vestments his affections bait?°
95   That's not my fault; he's master of my state.
What ruins are in me that can be found,
By him not ruined? Then is he the ground
Of my defeatures.° My decayèd fair°

72 **due unto** appropriate to   73 **bare** bore   78 **across** (taken by
Dromio as "a cross")   80 **holy** (quibbling on "full of holes")   82
round (1) plain-spoken (2) spherical   86 **lowereth** frowns   87 **min-
ions** paramours   88 **starve** pine away   91 **discourses** conversations
94 **bait** entice   98 **defeatures** disfigurements   98 **decayèd fair** im-
paired beauty

A sunny look of his would soon repair.
But, too unruly deer,° he breaks the pale,°   *100*
And feeds from° home; poor I am but his stale.°

Luciana. Self-harming jealousy! fie, beat it hence.

Adriana. Unfeeling fools can with such wrongs dis-
    pense.°
I know his eye doth homage otherwhere,°
Or else what lets° it but he would be here?   *105*
Sister, you know he promised me a chain.
Would that alone, alone he would detain,°
So he would keep fair quarter° with his bed!
I see the jewel best enamelèd
Will lose his° beauty; yet the gold bides still   *110*
That others touch, and often touching will
Wear gold, and no man that hath a name
But falsehood and corruption doth it shame.°
Since that my beauty cannot please his eye,
I'll weep what's left away, and weeping die.   *115*

Luciana. How many fond° fools serve mad jealousy!
                   Exit [with Adriana].

Scene 2. [*The Mart.*]

Enter Antipholus [of Syracuse].

S. Antipholus. The gold I gave to Dromio is laid up
Safe at the Centaur, and the heedful slave
Is wand'red forth, in care to seek me out,
By computation° and mine host's report.

---

100 **deer** (pun on "dear")   100 **pale** enclosure   101 **from** away from
101 **stale** dupe   103 **dispense** offer a dispensation   104 **otherwhere**
elsewhere   105 **lets** prevents   107 **detain** keep back   108 **keep fair**
quarter keep the peace   110 **his** its   109–113 **I see ... it shame**
(through these ambiguous metaphors Adriana seems to imply that
she still values her husband, though he is made less attractive by
promiscuity)   116 **fond** foolish   2.2.4 **computation** calculation

5   I could not speak with Dromio since at first
I sent him from the Mart! See, here he comes.

Enter Dromio of Syracuse.

How now, sir, is your merry humor altered?
As you love strokes, so jest with me again.
You know no Centaur? You received no gold?
10   Your mistress sent to have me home to dinner?
My house was at the Phoenix? Wast thou mad,
That thus so madly thou didst answer me?

S. Dromio. What answer, sir? When spake I such a
word?

S. Antipholus. Even now, even here, not half an hour
since.

15 *S. Dromio.* I did not see you since you sent me hence,
Home to the Centaur, with the gold you gave me.

S. Antipholus. Villain, thou didst deny the gold's
receipt,
And told'st me of a mistress, and a dinner;
For which, I hope, thou felt'st I was displeased.

20 *S. Dromio.* I am glad to see you in this merry vein.
What means this jest? I pray you, master, tell me.

S. Antipholus. Yea, dost thou jeer, and flout me in the
teeth?°
Think'st thou, I jest? Hold, take thou that! And that!
Beats Dromio.

S. Dromio. Hold, sir, for God's sake! Now your jest is
earnest.°
25   Upon what bargain do you give it me?

S. Antipholus. Because that I familiarly sometimes
Do use you for my fool and chat with you,
Your sauciness will jest upon my love,
And make a common° of my serious hours.
30   When the sun shines, let foolish gnats make sport;

22 **in the teeth** to my face   24 **earnest** (1) serious (2) a deposit
29 **common** public property

But creep in crannies, when he hides his beams.
If you will jest with me, know my aspect,°
And fashion your demeanor to my looks,
Or I will beat this method in your sconce.°

S. Dromio. Sconce, call you it? So you would leave   35
battering, I had rather have it a head. And you use
these blows long, I must get a sconce for my head,
and ensconce° it too, or else I shall seek my wit° in
my shoulders. But, I pray, sir, why am I beaten?

S. Antipholus. Dost thou not know?   40

S. Dromio. Nothing, sir, but that I am beaten.

S. Antipholus. Shall I tell you why?

S. Dromio. Ay, sir, and wherefore; for they say every
why hath a wherefore.

S. Antipholus. Why, first for flouting me, and then
wherefore,   45
For urging it the second time to me.

S. Dromio. Was there ever any man thus beaten out of
season,
When in the why and the wherefore is neither rhyme
nor reason?
Well, sir, I thank you.

S. Antipholus.   Thank me, sir, for what?

S. Dromio. Marry,° sir, for this something that you   50
gave me for nothing.

S. Antipholus. I'll make you amends next, to give you
nothing for something. But say, sir, is it dinnertime?

S. Dromio. No, sir. I think the meat wants that° I
have.   55

S. Antipholus. In good time,° sir. What's that?

---

32 **aspect** attitude (astrological term for planetary influence)   34
sconce (1) head (2) fortification   38 **ensconce** screen   38 **wit** brains
50 **Marry** (mild exclamation, originally an oath by the Virgin Mary)
54 **wants that** lacks what   56 **In good time** indeed

S. Dromio. Basting.°

S. Antipholus. Well, sir, then 'twill be dry.

S. Dromio. If it be, sir, I pray you eat none of it.

60 *S. Antipholus.* Your reason?

S. Dromio. Lest it make you choleric° and purchase me another dry° basting.

S. Antipholus. Well, sir, learn to jest in good time; there's a time for all things.

65 *S. Dromio.* I durst have denied that, before you were so choleric.

S. Antipholus. By what rule, sir?

S. Dromio. Marry, sir, by a rule as plain as the plain bald pate of Father Time himself.

70 *S. Antipholus.* Let's hear it.

S. Dromio. There's no time for a man to recover his hair that grows bald by nature.

S. Antipholus. May he not do it by fine and recovery?°

75 *S. Dromio.* Yes, to pay a fine for a periwig and recover the lost hair of another man.

S. Antipholus. Why is Time such a niggard of hair, being, as it is, so plentiful an excrement?°

S. Dromio. Because it is a blessing that he bestows on
80 beasts: and what he hath scanted men in hair, he hath given them in wit.

S. Antipholus. Why, but there's many a man hath more hair than wit.

---

57 **Basting** (1) moistening meat (2) thrashing   61 **choleric** irascible (from a surplus of choler, the humor of dryness)   62 **dry** bloodless   73–74 **fine and recovery** (legal form of conveyance, with a pun on "foin," the fur of a polecat)   78 **excrement** outgrowth

S. Dromio. Not a man of those but he hath the wit to
lose his hair.   85

S. Antipholus. Why, thou didst conclude hairy men
plain dealers without wit.

S. Dromio. The plainer dealer, the sooner lost; yet he
loseth it in a kind of jollity.°

S. Antipholus. For what reason?   90

S. Dromio. For two; and sound° ones too.

S. Antipholus. Nay, not sound, I pray you.

S. Dromio. Sure ones, then.

S. Antipholus. Nay, not sure, in a thing falsing.°

S. Dromio. Certain ones, then.   95

S. Antipholus. Name them.

S. Dromio. The one, to save the money that he spends
in tiring;° the other, that at dinner they should not
drop in his porridge.

S. Antipholus. You would all this time have proved   100
there is no time for all things.

S. Dromio. Marry, and did, sir: namely, e'en no time
to recover hair lost by nature.

S. Antipholus. But your reason was not substantial why
there is no time to recover.   105

S. Dromio. Thus I mend it: Time himself is bald, and
therefore, to the world's end, will have bald fol-
lowers.

S. Antipholus. I knew 'twould be a bald° conclusion.

Enter Adriana and Luciana.

But soft, who wafts° us yonder?   110

89 **loseth it in a kind of jollity** (as a consequence of venereal disease)
91 **sound** (1) cogent (2) healthy   94 **falsing** deceptive   98 **tiring**
hairdressing   109 **bald** (with a quibble on "trivial")   110 **wafts**
beckons

Adriana. Ay, ay, Antipholus, look strange° and frown;
    Some other mistress hath thy sweet aspects.
    I am not Adriana, nor thy wife.
    The time was once when thou unurged wouldst vow
115   That never words were music to thine ear,
    That never object pleasing in thine eye,
    That never touch well welcome to thy hand,
    That never meat sweet-savored in thy taste,
    Unless I spake or looked or touched or carved° to
        thee.
120   How comes it now, my husband, O how comes it,
    That thou art then estrangèd from thyself?
    Thyself I call it, being strange to me,
    That, undividable, incorporate,
    Am better than thy dear self's better part.°
125   Ah, do not tear away thyself from me;
    For know, my love, as easy mayst thou fall°
    A drop of water in the breaking gulf,
    And take unmingled thence that drop again
    Without addition or diminishing
130   As take from me thyself, and not me too.
    How dearly° would it touch thee to the quick,
    Shouldst thou but hear I were licentious,
    And that this body, consecrate to thee,
    By ruffian lust should be contaminate!
135   Wouldst thou not spit at me, and spurn at me,
    And hurl the name of husband in my face,
    And tear the stained skin off my harlot brow,
    And from my false hand cut the wedding ring,
    And break it with a deep-divorcing vow?
140   I know thou canst, and therefore see thou do it.
    I am possessed with an adulterate blot.
    My blood is mingled with the crime° of lust;
    For, if we two be one, and thou play false,
    I do digest the poison of thy flesh,
145   Being strumpeted by thy contagion.

---

111 **strange** distant   119 **carved** (a way of flirting at the dinner table)
124 **better part** soul   126 **fall** let fall   131 **dearly** grievously   142
crime sin

Keep then fair league and truce with thy true bed,°
I live distained,° thou undishonorèd.

S. Antipholus. Plead you to me, fair dame? I know
    you not.
In Ephesus I am but two hours old,
As strange unto your town as to your talk;   150
Who,° every word by all my wit being scanned,
Wants wit in all one word to understand.

Luciana. Fie, brother, how the world is changed with
    you.
When were you wont to use my sister thus?
She sent for you by Dromio home to dinner.   155

S. Antipholus. By Dromio?

S. Dromio. By me?

Adriana. By thee, and this thou didst return from
    him:
That he did buffet thee, and in his blows
Denied my house for his, me for his wife.   160

S. Antipholus. Did you converse, sir, with this gentle-
    woman?
What is the course and drift° of your compact?°

S. Dromio. I, sir? I never saw her till this time.

S. Antipholus. Villain, thou liest; for even her very
    words
Didst thou deliver to me on the Mart.   165

S. Dromio. I never spake with her in all my life.

S. Antipholus. How can she thus then call us by our
    names,
Unless it be by inspiration?

Adriana. How ill agrees it with your gravity
To counterfeit thus grossly° with your slave,   170

146 **Keep then ... true bed** i.e., if you are faithful to your marriage
147 **distained** unstained   151 **Who** (refers to "I")   162 **course and
drift** general meaning   162 **compact** confederacy   170 **grossly** obviously

Abetting him to thwart me in my mood!
Be it my wrong you are from me exempt,°
But wrong not that wrong with a more contempt.°
Come, I will fasten on° this sleeve of thine:
175 Thou art an elm, my husband, I a vine,
Whose weakness, married to thy stronger state,
Makes me with thy strength to communicate.°
If aught possess thee° from me, it is dross,
Usurping ivy, briar, or idle° moss,
180 Who, all for want of pruning, with intrusion
Infect thy sap and live on thy confusion.°

S. Antipholus. [*Aside*] To me she speaks, she moves
    me for her theme;°
What, was I married to her in my dream?
Or sleep I now, and think I hear all this?
185 What error drives our eyes and ears amiss?
Until I know this sure uncertainty,
I'll entertain the offered fallacy.°

Luciana. Dromio, go bid the servants spread for
    dinner.

S. Dromio. O, for my beads!° I cross me for a sinner.
190 This is the fairy land. O spite of spites!
We talk with goblins, owls, and sprites;
If we obey them not, this will ensue:
They'll suck our breath, or pinch us black and blue.

Luciana. Why prat'st thou to thyself and answer'st
    not?
Dromio, thou drone, thou snail, thou slug, thou
195 sot.°

S. Dromio. I am transformèd, master, am not I?

S. Antipholus. I think thou art in mind, and so am I.

---

172 **exempt** cut off   173 **But wrong ... more contempt** i.e., do not
compound it by adding insult to injury   174 **fasten on** cling to
177 **communicate** share   178 **possess thee** take you away   179 **idle**
worthless   181 **confusion** ruin   182 **moves me for her theme** appeals to me as her subject   187 **fallacy** delusion   189 **beads** rosary
195 **sot** dolt

S. Dromio. Nay, master, both in mind and in my
    shape.

S. Antipholus. Thou hast thine own form.

S. Dromio.   No, I am an ape.°

Luciana. If thou art changed to aught, 'tis to an ass.   *200*

S. Dromio. 'Tis true, she rides° me and I long for
    grass.
  'Tis so, I am an ass; else it could never be
  But I should know her as well as she knows me.

Adriana. Come, come, no longer will I be a fool,
  To put the finger in the eye and weep,   *205*
  Whilst man and master laughs my woes to scorn.
  Come, sir, to dinner. Dromio, keep the gate.
  Husband, I'll dine above° with you today,
  And shrive° you of a thousand idle pranks.
  Sirrah,° if any ask you for your master,   *210*
  Say he dines forth,° and let no creature enter.
  Come, sister. Dromio, play the porter well.

S. Antipholus. [*Aside*] Am I in earth, in heaven, or in
    hell?
  Sleeping or waking, mad or well-advised?°
  Known unto these, and to myself disguised?   *215*
  I'll say as they say, and persever so,
  And in this mist at all adventures° go.

S. Dromio. Master, shall I be porter at the gate?

Adriana. Ay, and let none enter, lest I break your
    pate.

Luciana. Come, come, Antipholus, we dine too late. *220*
                           [*Exeunt.*]

---

199 **ape** imitation (or fool) 201 **rides** teases 208 **above** upstairs
(represented by the upper stage) 209 **shrive** hear confession and
absolve 210 **Sirrah** (term used in addressing inferiors) 211 **forth**
out 214 **well-advised** of sound mind 217 **adventures** hazards

ACT 3

Scene 1. [*Before the Phoenix.*]

*Enter Antipholus of Ephesus, his man Dromio,
Angelo the Goldsmith, and Balthasar the Merchant.*

E. Antipholus. Good Signor° Angelo, you must ex-
    cuse us all;
My wife is shrewish when I keep not hours.
Say that I lingered with you at your shop
To see the making of her carcanet,°
5   And that tomorrow you will bring it home.
But here's a villain that would face me down°
He met me on the Mart, and that I beat him,
And charged him with a thousand marks in gold,
And that I did deny° my wife and house.
10   Thou drunkard, thou, what didst thou mean by this?

E. Dromio. Say what you will, sir, but I know what
    I know—
That you beat me at the Mart, I have your hand° to
    show;
If the skin were parchment and the blows you gave
    were ink,
Your own handwriting would tell you what I think.

E. Antipholus. I think thou art an ass.

3.1.1 **Signor** (the Italian title of respect is applied rather broadly by
Shakespeare) 4 **carcanet** jeweled necklace 6 **face me down** con-
tradict me by declaring 9 **deny** disown 12 **hand** (1) handwriting
(2) blows

E. Dromio.   Marry, so it doth appear   *15*
By the wrongs I suffer and the blows I bear.
I should kick, being kicked, and being at that pass,°
You would keep from my heels and beware of an
    ass.

E. Antipholus. You're sad,° Signor Balthasar; pray
    God, our cheer°
May answer° my good will and your good welcome
    here.   *20*

Balthasar. I hold your dainties cheap, sir, and your
    welcome dear.

E. Antipholus. O, Signor Balthasar, either at flesh or
    fish,
A tableful of welcome makes scarce one dainty
    dish.

Balthasar. Good meat, sir, is common; that every
    churl° affords.

E. Antipholus. And welcome more common, for that's
    nothing but words.   *25*

Balthasar. Small cheer and great welcome makes a
    merry feast.

E. Antipholus. Ay, to a niggardly host and more spar-
    ing guest.
But though my cates° be mean, take them in good
    part;
Better cheer may you have, but not with better
    heart.
But soft, my door is locked; go, bid them let us in.   *30*

E. Dromio. Maud, Bridget, Marian, Cicely, Gillian,
    Ginn!

S. Dromio. [*Within*] Mome, malt-horse, capon, cox-
    comb, idiot, patch!°

17 **at that pass** in that predicament 19 **sad** serious 19 **cheer** entertainment 20 **answer** accord with 24 **churl** peasant 28 **cates**
dainties 32 **Mome ... patch** blockhead, drudge, cuckold, fool, idiot,
jester

Either get thee from the door or sit down at the
hatch.°
Dost thou conjure for wenches, that thou call'st for
such store,°
When one is one too many? Go, get thee from the
35 door.

E. Dromio. What patch is made our porter? My
master stays in the street.

S. Dromio. Let him walk from whence he came, lest
he catch cold on's° feet.

E. Antipholus. Who talks within there? Ho, open the
door!

S. Dromio. Right sir, I'll tell you when, and you'll tell
me wherefore.

E. Antipholus. Wherefore? For my dinner; I have not
40 dined today.

S. Dromio. Nor today here you must not; come again
when you may.

E. Antipholus. What art thou that keep'st me out
from the house I owe?°

S. Dromio. The porter for this time, sir, and my name
is Dromio.

E. Dromio. O villain, thou hast stol'n both mine office
and my name.
The one ne'er got me credit, the other mickle°
45 blame.
If thou hadst been Dromio today in my place,
Thou wouldst have changed thy face for a name,
or thy name for an ass.°

Enter Luce [above].

---

33 **hatch** lower part of a divided door   34 **store** abundance   37 **on's**
in his   42 **owe** own   45 **mickle** much   47 **Thou wouldst . . . an ass**
you would have been confused with someone else, or been made a
fool of (?)

Luce. What a coil° is there, Dromio? Who are those
    at the gate?

E. Dromio. Let my master in, Luce.

Luce.   Faith, no, he comes too late.
    And so tell your master.

E. Dromio.   O Lord, I must laugh!   50
    Have at you with a proverb:° "Shall I set in my
    staff?"°

Luce. Have at you with another: that's "When? Can
    you tell?"°

S. Dromio. If thy name be called Luce—Luce, thou
    hast answered him well.

E. Antipholus. Do you hear, you minion?° You'll let
    us in, I trow?

Luce. I thought to have asked you.

S. Dromio.   And you said no.   55

E. Dromio. So, come help! Well struck! There was
    blow for blow.

E. Antipholus. Thou baggage, let me in.

Luce.   Can you tell for whose sake?

E. Dromio. Master, knock the door hard.

Luce.   Let him knock till it ache.

E. Antipholus. You'll cry for this, minion, if I beat the
    door down.

Luce. What needs all that, and a pair of stocks° in
    the town?   60

                Enter Adriana [above].

_____

48 **coil** turmoil   51 **proverb** (they bandy proverbial phrases)   51 **set
in my staff** move in   52 **When? Can you tell?** (a contemptuous re-
tort)   54 **minion** hussy   60 **stocks** device for the public confinement
of offenders

Adriana. Who is that at the door that keeps all this
      noise?

S. Dromio. By my troth, your town is troubled with
      unruly boys.°

E. Antipholus. Are you there, wife? You might have
      come before.

Adriana. Your wife, sir knave! Go, get you from the
      door.   [*Exit with Luce.*]

   E. Dromio. If you went in pain, master, this knave
65   would go sore.

Angelo. Here is neither cheer, sir, nor welcome; we
      would fain have either.

Balthasar. In debating which was best, we shall part°
      with neither.

E. Dromio. They stand at the door, master. Bid them
      welcome hither.

E. Antipholus. There is something in the wind, that
      we cannot get in.

   E. Dromio. You would say so, master, if your gar-
70   ments were thin.
      Your cake here is warm within; you stand here in
         the cold.
      It would make a man mad as a buck° to be so
         bought and sold.°

E. Antipholus. Go, fetch me something. I'll break ope
      the gate.

S. Dromio. Break any breaking here, and I'll break
      your knave's pate.

75 *E. Dromio.* A man may break° a word with you, sir,
      and words are but wind;°

---

62 **boys** fellows   67 **part** depart   72 **buck** male deer (with an im-
.plication of "horn-mad")   72 **bought and sold** cheated   75 **break**
exchange   75 **words are but wind** (a proverb, which Dromio vul-
garly quibbles upon)

Ay, and break it in your face, so he break it not
  behind.

S. Dromio. It seems thou want'st breaking.° Out upon
  thee,° hind!°

E. Dromio. Here's too much "out upon thee." I pray
  thee, let me in.

S. Dromio. Ay, when fowls have no feathers, and fish
  have no fin.

E. Antipholus. Well, I'll break in. Go borrow me a
  crow.°   80

E. Dromio. A crow without feather? Master, mean
  you so?
  For a fish without a fin, there's a fowl without a
  feather.
  If a crow help us in, sirrah, we'll pluck a crow°
  together.

E. Antipholus. Go, get thee gone, fetch me an iron
  crow.

Balthasar. Have patience, sir, O, let it not be so!   85
  Herein you war against your reputation,
  And draw within the compass of suspect°
  Th' unviolated honor of your wife.
  Once this°—your long experience of her wisdom,
  Her sober virtue, years, and modesty,   90
  Plead on her part some cause to you unknown;
  And doubt not, sir, but she will well excuse°
  Why at this time the doors are made° against you.
  Be ruled by me, depart in patience,
  And let us to the Tiger° all to dinner.   95
  And, about evening, come yourself alone,
  To know the reason of this strange restraint.
  If by strong hand you offer° to break in,

77 **breaking** beating 77 **Out upon thee** (a mild curse) 77 **hind**
menial 80 **crow** crowbar 83 **pluck a crow** pick a bone 87 **suspect** suspicion 89 **Once this** in summary 92 **excuse** explain 93
made shut 95 **Tiger** (name and sign of an inn) 98 **offer** attempt

Now in the stirring passage° of the day,
100   A vulgar° comment will be made of it;
And that supposèd by the common rout°
Against your yet ungallèd estimation,°
That may with foul intrusion enter in
And dwell upon your grave when you are dead;
105   For slander lives upon succession,°
For ever housed where it gets possession.

E. Antipholus. You have prevailed. I will depart in
        quiet,
And, in despite of mirth,° mean to be merry.
I know a wench of excellent discourse,
110   Pretty and witty; wild and yet, too, gentle;
There will we dine: this woman that I mean,
My wife—but, I protest, without desert—
Hath oftentimes upbraided me withal.
To her will we to dinner. [*To Angelo*] Get you home,
115   And fetch the chain; by this,° I know, 'tis made;
Bring it, I pray you, to the Porpentine,°
For there's the house. That chain will I bestow—
Be it for nothing but to spite my wife—
Upon mine hostess there. Good sir, make haste.
120   Since mine own doors refuse to entertain me,
I'll knock elsewhere, to see if they'll disdain me.

Angelo. I'll meet you at that place some hour hence.

E. Antipholus. Do so. This jest shall cost me some
        expense.   *Exeunt.*

99 **stirring passage** busy traffic   100 **vulgar** public   101 **rout** multi-
tude   102 **ungallèd estimation** unblemished repute   105 **succession**
its consequences   108 **in despite of mirth** though disinclined to mer-
riment   115 **by this** by this time   116 **Porpentine** porcupine (name
of the Courtesan's house)

Scene 2. [*Above.*]

Enter Luciana, with Antipholus of Syracuse.

Luciana. And may it be that you have quite forgot
   A husband's office? Shall, Antipholus, hate
   Even in the spring of love thy love-springs° rot?
   Shall love, in building, grow so ruinate?°
   If you did wed my sister for her wealth,   *5*
   Then for her wealth's sake use her with more kind-
      ness;
   Or, if you like elsewhere,° do it by stealth,
   Muffle your false love with some show of blindness.
   Let not my sister read it in your eye;
   Be not thy tongue thy own shame's orator;   *10*
   Look sweet, speak fair, become disloyalty;°
   Apparel vice like virtue's harbinger.
   Bear a fair presence, though your heart be tainted,
   Teach sin the carriage° of a holy saint,
   Be secret-false: what need she be acquainted?   *15*
   What simple thief brags of his own attaint?°
   'Tis double wrong to truant° with your bed
   And let her read it in thy looks at board.°
   Shame hath a bastard fame,° well managèd;
   Ill deeds is doubled with an evil word.   *20*
   Alas, poor women! Make us but believe,
   Being compact of credit,° that you love us;
   Though others have the arm, show us the sleeve:
   We in your motion° turn, and you may move us.
   Then, gentle brother, get you in again;   *25*

3.2.3 **love-springs** young plants of love 4 **ruinate** ruinous 7 **like elsewhere** have some other love 11 **become disloyalty** make infidelity seem becoming 14 **carriage** bearing 16 **attaint** disgrace 17 **truant** play truant 18 **board** table 19 **bastard fame** illegitimate honor 22 **compact of credit** disposed to trust 24 **in your motion** by your moves

      Comfort my sister, cheer her, call her wife;
      'Tis holy sport, to be a little vain,°
      When the sweet breath of flattery conquers strife.

S. *Antipholus.* Sweet mistress, what your name is else,
      I know not;
30   Nor by what wonder you do hit of° mine;
      Less in your knowledge and your grace you show°
         not
      Than our earth's wonder,° more than earth divine.
      Teach me, dear creature, how to think and speak:
      Lay open to my earthy-gross conceit,°
35   Smoth'red in errors, feeble, shallow, weak,
      The folded° meaning of your words' deceit.
      Against my soul's pure truth why labor you
      To make it wander in an unknown field?
      Are you a god? Would you create me new?
40   Transform me, then, and to your pow'r I'll yield.
      But if that I am I, then well I know
      Your weeping sister is no wife of mine,
      Nor to her bed no homage do I owe;
      Far more, far more, to you do I decline.°
45   O, train° me not, sweet mermaid, with thy note,
      To drown me in thy sister's flood of tears.
      Sing, siren, for thyself, and I will dote;
      Spread o'er the silver waves thy golden hairs;
      And as a bed I'll take them, and there lie,
50   And, in that glorious supposition, think
      He gains by death that hath such means to die.°
      Let Love, being light,° be drownèd if she sink!

Luciana. What, are you mad, that you do reason so?

S. *Antipholus.* Not mad, but mated°—how, I do not
      know.

55 *Luciana.* It is a fault that springeth from your eye.

27 **be a little vain** use a little flattery 30 **hit of** hit on 31 **show**
appear 32 **earth's wonder** (these lines are sometimes taken as a
compliment to Queen Elizabeth) 34 **conceit** apprehension 36
folded hidden 44 **decline** incline 45 **train** lure 51 **die** (with an
implication of sexual fulfillment) 52 **light** (1) not heavy (2) wanton
54 **mated** (1) confounded (2) wedded

S. Antipholus. For gazing on your beams, fair sun,
   being by.

Luciana. Gaze where you should, and that will clear
   your sight.

S. Antipholus. As good to wink,° sweet love, as look
   on night.

Luciana. Why call you me love? Call my sister so.

S. Antipholus. Thy sister's sister.

Luciana.   That's my sister.

S. Antipholus.   No,   *60*
   It is thyself, mine own self's better part,
   Mine eye's clear eye, my dear heart's dearer heart;
   My food, my fortune, and my sweet hope's aim;
   My sole earth's heaven, and my heaven's claim.°

Luciana. All this my sister is, or else should be.   *65*

S. Antipholus. Call thyself sister, sweet, for I am thee;
   Thee will I love, and with thee lead my life;
   Thou hast no husband yet, nor I no wife.
   Give me thy hand.

Luciana.   O, soft, sir, hold you still
   I'll fetch my sister, to get her good will.   *Exit.*   *70*

Enter Dromio of Syracuse.

S. Antipholus. Why, how now, Dromio! Where run'st
   thou so fast?

S. Dromio. Do you know me, sir? Am I Dromio? Am
   I your man? Am I myself?

S. Antipholus. Thou art Dromio, thou art my man,   *75*
   thou art thyself.

S. Dromio. I am an ass; I am a woman's man, and
   besides myself.

---

58 **wink** shut one's eyes   64 **heaven's claim** claim on heaven

S. Antipholus. What woman's man? And how besides
80   thyself?

S. Dromio. Marry, sir, besides myself,° I am due° to
a woman: one that claims me, one that haunts me,
one that will have me.

S. Antipholus. What claim lays she to thee?

85   *S. Dromio.* Marry, sir, such claim as you would lay
to your horse; and she would have me as a beast°—
not that, I being a beast, she would have me, but
that she, being a very beastly creature, lays claim
to me.

90   *S. Antipholus.* What is she?

S. Dromio. A very reverend body; ay, such a one as
a man may not speak of without he say "sir-
reverence."° I have but lean luck in the match, and
yet is she a wondrous fat marriage.

95   *S. Antipholus.* How dost thou mean a fat marriage?

S. Dromio. Marry, sir, she's the kitchen-wench,
and all grease;° and I know not what use to put her
to, but to make a lamp of her, and run from her
by her own light. I warrant her rags and the tallow in
100   in them will burn a Poland winter. If she lives
till doomsday, she'll burn a week° longer than
the whole world.

S. Antipholus. What complexion is she of?

S. Dromio. Swart,° like my shoe, but her face noth-
105   ing like so clean kept; for why? She sweats; a man
may go over-shoes° in the grime of it.

S. Antipholus. That's a fault that water will mend.

---

81 **besides myself** (1) out of my mind (2) in addition to me   81 **due**
belonging   86 **a beast** (Elizabethan pronunciation made possible a
pun on "abased")   92–93 **sir-reverence** save your reverence (meaning "pardon the expression")   97 **grease** (with a pun on "grace")
101 **week** (with a pun on "wick")   104 **Swart** swarthy   106 **over-
shoes** shoe-deep

S. Dromio. No, sir, 'tis in grain;° Noah's flood could not do it.

S. Antipholus. What's her name?   *110*

S. Dromio. Nell,° sir; but her name and three quarters—that's an ell° and three quarters—will not measure her from hip to hip.

S. Antipholus. Then she bears some breadth?

S. Dromio. No longer from head to foot than from hip to hip. She is spherical, like a globe. I could find out countries in her.   *115*

S. Antipholus. In what part of her body stands Ireland?

S. Dromio. Marry, sir, in her buttocks; I found it out by the bogs.   *120*

S. Antipholus. Where Scotland?

S. Dromio. I found it by the barrenness, hard in the palm of the hand.

S. Antipholus. Where France?   *125*

S. Dromio. In her forehead, armed and reverted,° making war against her heir.°

S. Antipholus. Where England?

S. Dromio. I looked for the chalky cliffs,° but I could find no whiteness in them. But I guess, it stood in her chin, by the salt rheum° that ran between France and it.   *130*

S. Antipholus. Where Spain?

S. Dromio. Faith, I saw it not; but I felt it hot in her breath.   *135*

S. Antipholus. Where America, the Indies?

---

108 **in grain** inherent   111 **Nell** (called Luce, 3.1.49)   112 **ell** forty-five inches   126 **reverted** revolted   127 **heir** (interpreted as a contemporary allusion to the struggle of the Catholic League against Henry of Navarre, who succeeded to the throne of France in 1593)   129 **chalky cliffs** teeth   131 **rheum** moisture from the nose

S. Dromio. O, sir, upon her nose, all o'er embellished
with rubies, carbuncles, sapphires, declining° their
rich aspect to the hot breath of Spain, who sent
140   whole armadoes of carracks° to be ballast° at her
nose.

S. Antipholus. Where stood Belgia, the Netherlands?°

S. Dromio. O, sir, I did not look so low. To conclude, this drudge, or diviner,° laid claim to me,
145   called me Dromio, swore I was assured° to her,
told me what privy marks I had about me, as the
mark of my shoulder, the mole in my neck, the
great wart on my left arm, that I, amazed, ran from
her as a witch.
And, I think, if my breast had not been made of
150   faith, and my heart of steel,
She had transformed me to a curtal dog,° and made
me turn i' th' wheel.°

S. Antipholus. Go, hie thee presently,° post to the
road,°
And if° the wind blow any way from shore,
I will not harbor° in this town tonight.
155   If any bark put forth, come to the Mart,
Where I will walk till thou return to me.
If everyone knows us, and we know none,
'Tis time, I think, to trudge, pack, and begone.°

S. Dromio. As from a bear a man would run for life,
160   So fly I from her that would be my wife.   *Exit.*

S. Antipholus. There's none but witches do inhabit
here,
And therefore 'tis high time that I were hence.
She that doth call me husband, even my soul
Doth for a wife abhor. But her fair sister,

138 **declining** inclining   140 **armadoes of carracks** fleets of galleons
(with possible reference to the Spanish Armada of 1588)   140 **ballast**
loaded   142 **Belgia, the Netherlands** the Low Countries   144 **diviner** witch   145 **assured** betrothed   151 **curtal dog** dog with
docked tail   151 **wheel** spit   152 **presently** immediately   152 **road**
harbor   153 **And if** if   154 **harbor** lodge   158 **trudge, pack, and
begone** (synonyms)

Possessed with such a gentle sovereign grace,   165
Of such enchanting presence and discourse,
Hath almost made me traitor to myself.
But, lest myself be guilty to° self-wrong,
I'll stop mine ears against the mermaid's song.

Enter Angelo with the chain.

Angelo. Master Antipholus—

S. Antipholus.   Ay, that's my name.   170

Angelo. I know it well, sir. Lo, here is the chain.
   I thought to have ta'en you at the Porpentine.
   The chain unfinished made me stay thus long.

S. Antipholus. What is your will that I shall do with
   this?

Angelo. What please yourself, sir; I have made it for
   you.   175

S. Antipholus. Made it for me, sir? I bespoke° it not.

Angelo. Not once, nor twice, but twenty times you
   have.
   Go home with it and please your wife withal,
   And soon at suppertime I'll visit you,
   And then receive my money for the chain.   180

S. Antipholus. I pray you, sir, receive the money now,
   For fear you ne'er see chain nor money more.

Angelo. You are a merry man, sir. Fare you well.
                                                    Exit.

S. Antipholus. What I should think of this, I cannot
   tell:
   But this I think, there's no man is so vain°   185
   That would refuse so fair an offered chain.
   I see a man here needs not live by shifts,°
   When in the streets he meets such golden gifts.
   I'll to the Mart, and there for Dromio stay;
   If any ship put out, then straight° away.   *Exit.* 190

168 **to** of   176 **bespoke** ordered   185 **vain** silly   187 **shifts** tricks
190 **straight** without delay

ACT 4

Scene 1. [*The Mart.*]

Enter a Merchant, [Angelo the] Goldsmith,
and an Officer.

Merchant. You know since Pentecost° the sum is due,
    And since I have not much importuned you,
    Nor now I had not, but that I am bound
    To Persia, and want guilders for my voyage;
5   Therefore make present° satisfaction,
    Or I'll attach° you by this officer.

Angelo. Even just the sum that I do owe to you
    Is growing° to me by Antipholus,
    And in the instant that I met with you
10   He had of me a chain. At five o'clock
    I shall receive the money for the same.
    Pleaseth° you, walk with me down to his house;
    I will discharge my bond, and thank you too.

Enter Antipholus of Ephesus, [and] Dromio
[of Ephesus] from the Courtesan's.

Officer. That labor may you save. See where he
    comes.

15 **E. Antipholus.** While I go to the goldsmith's house,
    go thou

4.1.1 **Pentecost** the fiftieth day after Easter 5 **present** immediate
6 **attach** arrest 8 **growing** accruing 12 **Pleaseth** may it please

And buy a rope's end;° that will I bestow
Among my wife and her confederates,
For locking me out of my doors by day.
But soft, I see the goldsmith; get thee gone,
Buy thou a rope, and bring it home to me.   20

E. Dromio. I buy a thousand pound a year! I buy a
   rope!°   *Exit Dromio.*

E. Antipholus. A man is well holp° up that trusts to
   you!
I promisèd your presence and the chain,
But neither chain nor goldsmith came to me.
Belike you thought our love would last too long,   25
If it were chained together, and therefore came not.

Angelo. Saving your merry humor, here's the note
How much your chain weighs to the utmost carat,
The fineness of the gold and chargeful° fashion—
Which doth amount to three odd ducats° more   30
Than I stand debted to this gentleman.
I pray you, see him presently° discharged,
For he is bound to sea, and stays but for it.

E. Antipholus. I am not furnished with the present
   money.
Besides, I have some business in the town.   35
Good signor, take the stranger to my house,
And with you take the chain, and bid my wife
Disburse the sum on the receipt thereof.
Perchance I will be there as soon as you.

Angelo. Then you will bring the chain to her yourself?   40

E. Antipholus. No, bear it with you, lest I come not
   time enough.°

---

16 **rope's end** (for flogging)   21 **I buy ... a rope!** (Dromio's obscure irony seems motivated by his awareness that the rope's end
could be used on him)   22 **holp** helped   29 **chargeful** costly   30
ducats gold coins of varying origin and value   32 **presently** instantly
41 **time enough** in time

Angelo. Well, sir, I will. Have you the chain about
  you?

E. Antipholus. And if I have not, sir, I hope you
  have,
  Or else you may return without your money.

45 *Angelo.* Nay, come, I pray you, sir, give me the chain:
  Both wind and tide stays for this gentleman,
  And I, to blame,° have held him here too long.

E. Antipholus. Good Lord, you use this dalliance°
  to excuse
  Your breach of promise to the Porpentine.
50 I should have chid you for not bringing it,
  But, like a shrew,° you first begin to brawl.

Merchant. The hour steals on; I pray you, sir, dispatch.

Angelo. You hear how he importunes me—the chain!

E. Antipholus. Why, give it to my wife, and fetch
  your money.

Angelo. Come, come, you know, I gave it you even
55 now;
  Either send the chain or send me by some token.

E. Antipholus. Fie, now you run this humor out of
  breath.
  Come, where's the chain? I pray you, let me see it.

Merchant. My business cannot brook this dalliance.
60 Good sir, say whe'er° you'll answer° me or no:
  If not, I'll leave him to the officer.

E. Antipholus. I answer you! What should I answer
  you?

Angelo. The money that you owe me for the chain.

E. Antipholus. I owe you none till I receive the chain.

65 *Angelo.* You know I gave it you half an hour since.

---

47 **to blame** blameworthy 48 **dalliance** tarrying 51 **shrew** scold
(male or female) 60 **whe'er** whether 60 **answer** pay

E. Antipholus. You gave me none; you wrong me
    much to say so.

Angelo. You wrong me more, sir, in denying it.
    Consider how it stands upon° my credit.

Merchant. Well, officer, arrest him at my suit.

Officer. I do,   70
    And charge you in the Duke's name to obey me.

Angelo. This touches me in reputation.
    Either consent to pay this sum for me,
    Or I attach you by this officer.

E. Antipholus. Consent to pay thee that I never had! 75
    Arrest me, foolish fellow, if thou dar'st.

Angelo. Here is thy fee; arrest him, officer.
    I would not spare my brother in this case,
    If he should scorn me so apparently.°

Officer. I do arrest you, sir; you hear the suit.   80

E. Antipholus. I do obey thee, till I give thee bail.
    But, sirrah, you shall buy this sport as dear
    As all the metal in your shop will answer.

Angelo. Sir, sir, I shall have law in Ephesus,
    To your notorious shame, I doubt it not.   85

      Enter Dromio of Syracuse from the Bay.

S. Dromio. Master, there's a bark of Epidamnum,
    That stays but till her owner comes aboard,
    And then she bears away. Our fraughtage,° sir,
    I have conveyed aboard, and I have bought
    The oil, the balsamum,° and aqua-vitae.°   90
    The ship is in her trim,° the merry wind
    Blows fair from land; they stay for nought at all
    But for their owner, master,° and yourself.

---

68 **stands upon** concerns 79 **apparently** openly 88 **fraughtage**
cargo 90 **balsamum** balm 90 **aqua-vitae** brandy 91 **in her trim**
ready to sail 93 **master** captain (?)

   E. Antipholus. How now! a madman? Why, thou
      peevish° sheep,°
95 What ship of Epidamnum stays for me?

   S. Dromio. A ship you sent me to, to hire waftage.°

   E. Antipholus. Thou drunken slave, I sent thee for a
      rope,
    And told thee to what purpose and what end.

   S. Dromio. You sent me for a rope's end° as soon.
100   You sent me to the bay, sir, for a bark.

   E. Antipholus. I will debate this matter at more leisure,
    And teach your ears to list° me with more heed.
    To Adriana, villain, hie thee straight;
    Give her this key, and tell her, in the desk
105   That's covered o'er with Turkish tapestry
    There is a purse of ducats; let her send it.
    Tell her I am arrested in the street,
    And that shall bail me. Hie thee, slave, begone.
    On, officer, to prison till it come.
                Exeunt [all but Dromio].

110 *S. Dromio.* To Adriana—that is where we dined,
    Where Dowsabel° did claim me for her husband.
    She is too big, I hope, for me to compass.°
    Thither I must, although against my will;
    For servants must their masters' minds fulfill.
                          Exit.

---

94 **peevish** silly   94 **sheep** (with a pun on "ship")   96 **waftage** passage by sea   99 **rope's end** (in the sense of "halter" here)   102 **list**
listen to   111 **Dowsabel** (from *douce et belle,* sweet and pretty, an
elaborate name for a heroine, ironically applied to Nell)   112 **compass** (1) obtain (2) embrace

Scene 2. [*Before the Phoenix.*]

Enter Adriana and Luciana.

Adriana. Ah, Luciana, did he tempt thee so?
  Mightst thou perceive austerely° in his eye,
  That he did plead in earnest, yea or no?
  Looked he or red or pale, or sad or merrily?
  What observation mad'st thou in this case   5
  Of his heart's meteors tilting° in his face?

Luciana. First, he denied you had in him no right.°

Adriana. He meant he did me none; the more my
    spite.°

Luciana. Then swore he that he was a stranger here.

Adriana. And true he swore, though yet forsworn he
    were.   10

Luciana. Then pleaded I for you.

Adriana.   And what said he?

Luciana. That love I begged for you he begged of me.

Adriana. With what persuasion did he tempt thy love?

Luciana. With words that in an honest° suit might
    move.
  First he did praise my beauty, then my speech.   15

Adriana. Didst speak him fair?°

Luciana.   Have patience, I beseech.

4.2.2 **austerely** by the austerity   6 **heart's meteors tilting** emotions
tossing   7 **denied ... no right** (double negative)   8 **spite** vexation
14 **honest** honorable   16 **speak him fair** speak to him kindly

Adriana. I cannot, nor I will not, hold me still.
   My tongue, though not my heart, shall have his°
      will.
   He is deformèd, crookèd, old and sere,
20   Ill-faced, worse bodied, shapeless° everywhere:
   Vicious, ungentle, foolish, blunt, unkind,
   Stigmatical in making,° worse in mind.

Luciana. Who would be jealous then of such a one?
   No evil lost is wailed when it is gone.

25 *Adriana.* Ah, but I think him better than I say;
   And yet would herein others' eyes were worse.
   Far from her nest the lapwing° cries away;
   My heart prays for him, though my tongue do
      curse.

Enter Dromio of Syracuse.

S. Dromio. Here, go—the desk, the purse! Sweet,
   now, make haste.

Luciana. How hast thou lost thy breath?

30 *S. Dromio.*   By running fast.

Adriana. Where is thy master, Dromio? Is he well?

S. Dromio. No, he's in Tartar limbo,° worse than
   hell:
   A devil in an everlasting garment° hath him;
   One whose hard heart is buttoned up with steel:
35   A fiend, a fairy,° pitiless and rough:
   A wolf, nay worse, a fellow all in buff:°
   A back-friend,° a shoulder-clapper,° one that coun-
      termands°
   The passages of alleys, creeks,° and narrow lands;

---

18 **his** its   20 **shapeless** unshapely   22 **Stigmatical in making** deformed in appearance   27 **lapwing** peewit (who draws intruders away from its nest in the manner described)   32 **Tartar limbo** prison, as well as the outskirts of hell (the pagan Tartarus)   33 **everlasting garment** leather coat, the police uniform   35 **fairy** malignant spirit   36 **buff** ox-hide   37 **back-friend** false friend (with a quibble on the mode of arrest)   37 **shoulder-clapper** bailiff   37 **countermands** prohibits   38 **creeks** winding alleys

   A hound that runs counter,° and yet draws dry-
     foot° well;
   One that, before the judgment, carries poor souls
     to hell.   40

Adriana. Why, man, what is the matter?

S. Dromio. I do not know the matter, he is 'rested°
   on the case.°

Adriana. What, is he arrested? Tell me, at whose suit.

S. Dromio. I know not at whose suit he is arrested
   well;
   But is in a suit of buff which 'rested him, that can
    I tell.   45
   Will you send him, Mistress Redemption, the
    money in his desk?

Adriana. Go fetch it, sister. This I wonder at,
                         Exit Luciana.
   Thus he, unknown to me, should be in debt.
   Tell me, was he arrested on a band?°

S. Dromio. Not on a band, but on a stronger thing: 50
   A chain, a chain! Do you not hear it ring?

Adriana. What, the chain?

S. Dromio.   No, no, the bell; 'tis time
   that I were gone.
   It was two ere I left him, and now the clock strikes
    one.°

Adriana. The hours come back! That did I never
   hear.

S. Dromio. O yes. If any hour° meet a sergeant, 'a°
   turns back for very fear.   55

---

39 **counter** (1) contrary   (2) **Counter,** a debtors' prison   39 **draws
dry-foot** hunts by scent   42 **'rested** arrested   42 **case** (1) special
case at law (2) suit of clothes   49 **band** bond   53 **one** (with a pun
on "on")   55 **hour** (pun on "whore")   55 **'a** (colloquial form of
"he," "she," or "it")

Adriana. As if time were in debt! How fondly° dost
　　thou reason!

S. Dromio. Time is a very bankrupt, and owes more
　　than he's worth to season.°
　　Nay, he's a thief too: have you not heard men say,
　　That time comes stealing on by night and day?
60　If 'a be in debt and theft, and a sergeant in the way,
　　Hath he not reason to turn back an hour in a day?

Enter Luciana.

Adriana. Go, Dromio. There's the money, bear it
　　straight,
　　And bring thy master home immediately.
　　Come, sister. I am pressed down with conceit:°
65　Conceit, my comfort and my injury.
　　　　　　　　Exit [with Luciana and Dromio].

Scene 3. [*The Mart.*]

Enter Antipholus of Syracuse.

S. Antipholus. There's not a man I meet but doth
　　salute me
　　As if I were their well-acquainted friend;
　　And everyone doth call me by my name.
　　Some tender money to me, some invite me;
5　Some other° give me thanks for kindnesses;
　　Some offer me commodities to buy.
　　Even now a tailor called me in his shop
　　And showed me silks that he had bought for me,
　　And therewithal took measure of my body.
10　Sure, these are but imaginary wiles,°
　　And Lapland° sorcerers inhabit here.

---

56 **fondly** foolishly　57 **season** occasion (?), ripen (?)　64 **conceit**
imagination　4.3.5 **other** others　10 **imaginary wiles** tricks of the
imagination　11 **Lapland** (notorious for sorcery)

Enter Dromio of Syracuse.

S. Dromio. Master, here's the gold you sent me for.
What, have you got the picture of old Adam° new-
appareled?

S. Antipholus. What gold is this? What Adam dost   15
thou mean?

S. Dromio. Not that Adam that kept the paradise, but
that Adam that keeps the prison; he that goes in the
calf's skin° that was killed for the Prodigal; he that
came behind you, sir, like an evil angel, and bid   20
you forsake your liberty.

S. Antipholus. I understand thee not.

S. Dromio. No? Why, 'tis a plain case:° he that went,
like a bass-viol, in a case of leather; the man, sir,
that, when gentlemen are tired gives them a sob°   25
and 'rests them; he, sir, that takes pity on decayed
men, and gives them suits of durance;° he that sets
up his rest° to do more exploits with his mace°
than a morris-pike.°

S. Antipholus. What, thou mean'st an officer?   30

S. Dromio. Ay, sir, the sergeant of the band: he that
brings any man to answer it that breaks his band;°
one that thinks a man always going to bed, and
says, "God give you good rest!"°

S. Antipholus. Well, sir, there rest in your foolery.   35
Is there any ships puts forth tonight? May we be
gone?

S. Dromio. Why, sir, I brought you word an hour

13 **old Adam** the sergeant in his buff coat (?)   18–19 **goes in the
calf's skin** wears the leather garb (with a quibble on the fatted
calf in the parable)   23 **case** (1) situation (2) box (3) suit   25 **sob**
rest given a horse to recover its wind (with quibbles)   27 **suits
of durance** durable clothing (with puns on "lawsuits" and "imprison-
ment")   27–28 **sets up his rest** stakes all   28 **mace** staff of authority   29 **morris-pike** Moorish lance   32 **band** (with pun on "bond")
34 **rest** (with the usual pun)

since that the bark° *Expedition* put forth tonight,
40 and then were you hind'red by the sergeant to tarry
for the hoy° *Delay.* Here are the angels° that you
sent for to deliver you.

S. Antipholus. The fellow is distract, and so am I,
And here we wander in illusions.
45 Some blessèd power deliver us from hence!

Enter a Courtesan.

Courtesan. Well met, well met, Master Antipholus.
I see, sir, you have found the goldsmith now.
Is that the chain you promised me today?

S. Antipholus. Satan, avoid!° I charge thee, tempt me
not!

50 *S. Dromio.* Master, is this Mistress Satan?

S. Antipholus. It is the devil.

S. Dromio. Nay, she is worse, she is the devil's dam;°
and here she comes in the habit° of a light° wench,
and thereof comes that the wenches say, "God
55 damn me." That's as much to say, "God make me
a light wench." It is written, they appear to men
like angels of light. Light is an effect of fire, and
fire will burn: ergo,° light wenches will burn.°
Come not near her.

Courtesan. Your man and you are marvelous merry,
60   sir.
Will you go with me? We'll mend° our dinner here.

S. Dromio. Master, if you do, expect spoon-meat,° or
bespeak a long spoon.

S. Antipholus. Why, Dromio?

39 **bark** ship (allegorically named by Dromio)   41 **hoy** coasting ves-
sel   41 **angels** coins worth ten shillings (with pun)   49 **avoid** begone
(Matthew 4:10)   52 **dam** mother   53 **habit** dress   53 **light** (with
implication of loose morals)   58 **ergo** it follows logically   58 **burn**
infect with disease   61 **mend** complete   62 **spoon-meat** soft food
(introducing an allusion to the proverb about the devil)

S. Dromio. Marry, he must have a long spoon that   65
    must eat with the devil.

S. Antipholus. Avoid, then, fiend! What tell'st thou
    me of supping?
    Thou art, as you are all, a sorceress.
    I conjure° thee to leave me and be gone.

Courtesan. Give me the ring of mine you had at
    dinner,   70
    Or, for my diamond, the chain you promised,
    And I'll be gone, sir, and not trouble you.

S. Dromio. Some devils ask but the parings° of one's
    nail,
    A rush, a hair, a drop of blood, a pin,
    A nut, a cherry-stone;   75
    But she, more covetous, would have a chain.
    Master, be wise; and if you give it her,
    The devil will shake her chain, and fright us with it.

Courtesan. I pray you, sir, my ring, or else the chain.°
    I hope you do not mean to cheat me so!   80

S. Antipholus. Avaunt,° thou witch! Come, Dromio,
    let us go.

S. Dromio. Fly pride, says the peacock.° Mistress,
    that you know.   *Exit [with Antipholus].*

Courtesan. Now, out of doubt, Antipholus is mad,
    Else would he never so demean° himself.
    A ring he hath of mine worth forty ducats,   85
    And for the same he promised me a chain;
    Both one and other he denies me now.
    The reason that I gather he is mad,
    Besides this present instance of his rage,°
    Is a mad tale he told today at dinner,   90
    Of his own doors being shut against his entrance.
    Belike his wife, acquainted with his fits,

69 **conjure** solemnly call on   73 **parings** (witchcraft requires such ap-
purtenances in order to cast a spell)   79 **chain** (cf. Revelation, 20:1–2)
81 **Avaunt** away   82 **peacock** (emblem of pride, which was also
personified by a harlot)   84 **demean** behave   89 **rage** madness

On purpose shut the doors against his way.
My way is now to hie home to his house,
95   And tell his wife that, being lunatic,
He rushed into my house and took perforce°
My ring away. This course I fittest choose,
For forty ducats is too much to lose.   [*Exit.*]

Scene 4. [*The same.*]

Enter Antipholus of Ephesus with a Jailer.

E. Antipholus. Fear me not, man, I will not break
   away.
I'll give thee, ere I leave thee, so much money,
To warrant° thee, as I am 'rested for.
My wife is in a wayward mood today,
5   And will not lightly trust the messenger
That I should be attached° in Ephesus;
I tell you, 'twill sound harshly in her ears.

Enter Dromio of Ephesus, with a rope's end.

Here comes my man, I think he brings the money.
How now, sir! Have you that I sent you for?

E. Dromio. Here's that, I warrant you, will pay° them
10   all.

E. Antipholus. But where's the money?

E. Dromio. Why, sir, I gave the money for the rope.

E. Antipholus. Five hundred ducats, villain, for a
   rope?

E. Dromio. I'll serve you,° sir, five hundred at the
   rate.

96 **perforce** by force   4.4.3 **warrant** secure   6 **attached** arrested
10 **pay** (with a beating)   14 **serve you** supply you with

E. Antipholus. To what end° did I bid thee hie thee
    home? 15

E. Dromio. To a rope's end, sir, and to that end am
    I returned.

E. Antipholus. And to that end, sir, I will welcome
    you. [*Beats Dromio.*]

Officer. Good sir, be patient.

E. Dromio. Nay, 'tis for me to be patient; I am in
    adversity. 20

Officer. Good° now, hold thy tongue.

E. Dromio. Nay, rather persuade him to hold his
    hands.

E. Antipholus. Thou whoreson,° senseless villain!

E. Dromio. I would I were senseless, sir, that I might 25
    not feel your blows.

E. Antipholus. Thou art sensible° in nothing but
    blows, and so is an ass.

E. Dromio. I am an ass, indeed; you may prove it by
    my long ears.° I have served him from the hour of 30
    my nativity to this instant, and have nothing at his
    hands for my service but blows. When I am cold,
    he heats me with beating; when I am warm, he
    cools me with beating. I am waked with it when I
    sleep, raised with it when I sit, driven out of 35
    doors with it when I go from home, welcomed
    home with it when I return; nay, I bear it on my
    shoulders, as a beggar wont° her brat; and, I think,
    when he hath lamed me, I shall beg with it from
    door to door. 40

    Enter Adriana, Luciana, Courtesan, and a
    Schoolmaster called Pinch.

---

15 **end** purpose (on which Dromio quibbles) 21 **Good** (used voca-
tively) 24 **whoreson** bastard 27 **sensible** (1) reasonable (2) sensitive
30 **ears** (pun on "years") 38 **wont** habitually does

E. Antipholus. Come, go along; my wife is coming
yonder.

E. Dromio. Mistress, *"respice finem,"*° respect your
end; or rather, the prophecy like the parrot,° "beware the rope's end."

45 *E. Antipholus.* Wilt thou still talk?   [*Beats Dromio.*]

Courtesan. How say you now? Is not your husband
mad?

Adriana. His incivility confirms no less.
Good Doctor Pinch, you are a conjurer;°
Establish him in his true sense again,
50   And I will please° you what you will demand.

Luciana. Alas, how fiery and how sharp he looks!

Courtesan. Mark how he trembles in his ecstasy!°

Pinch. Give me your hand, and let me feel your pulse.
                         [*Antipholus strikes him.*]

E. Antipholus. There is my hand, and let it feel your
ear!

55 *Pinch.* I charge thee, Satan, housed within this man,
To yield possession to my holy prayers,
And to thy state of darkness hie thee straight;
I conjure thee by all the saints in heaven.

E. Antipholus. Peace, doting wizard, peace; I am not
mad.

60 *Adriana.* O, that thou wert not, poor distressèd soul!

E. Antipholus. You minion,° you, are these your cus-
tomers?
Did this companion° with the saffron° face
Revel and feast it at my house today,

42 **respice finem** (this proverbial phrase, which Dromio translates,
was sometimes punningly altered to *"respice funem,"* remember the
rope)   43 **parrot** (parrots were taught to cry "rope")   48 **conjurer**
(who can exorcise evil spirits, also called "Doctor" because of his
learning)   50 **please** satisfy   52 **ecstasy** frenzy   61 **minion** harlot
62 **companion** low fellow   62 **saffron** yellow

Whilst upon me the guilty doors were shut,
And I denied° to enter in my house?   65

Adriana. O, husband, God doth know you dined at
     home,
Where would you had remained until this time,
Free from these slanders and this open shame!

E. Antipholus. Dined at home! Thou villain, what
     sayest thou?

E. Dromio. Sir, sooth to say, you did not dine at
     home.   70

E. Antipholus. Were not my doors locked up, and I
     shut out?

E. Dromio. Perdie,° your doors were locked, and you
     shut out.

E. Antipholus. And did not she herself revile me
     there?

E. Dromio. Sans fable,° she herself reviled you there.

E. Antipholus. Did not her kitchen maid rail, taunt,
     and scorn me?   75

E. Dromio. Certes,° she did; the kitchen vestal°
     scorned you.

E. Antipholus. And did not I in rage depart from
     thence?

E. Dromio. In verity, you did; my bones bears wit-
     ness,
That since have felt the vigor of his rage.

Adriana. Is't good to soothe° him in these contraries?   80

Pinch. It is no shame; the fellow finds his vein,
And yielding to him humors well his frenzy.

---

65 **denied** not allowed   72 **Perdie** by God (*"par Dieu"*)   74 **Sans
fable** without lying (French)   76 **Certes** certainly   76 **kitchen vestal**
(so called, as Dr. Johnson pointed out, because she kept the fire
burning, like the vestal virgins of Rome)   80 **soothe** humor

E. Antipholus. Thou hast suborned° the goldsmith to
    arrest me.

Adriana. Alas, I sent you money to redeem you,
85   By Dromio here, who came in haste for it.

E. Dromio. Money by me? Heart and goodwill you
    might,
    But, surely, master, not a rag° of money.

E. Antipholus. Went'st not thou to her for a purse
    of ducats?

Adriana. He came to me, and I delivered it.

90 *Luciana.* And I am witness with her that she did.

E. Dromio. God and the rope-maker bear me witness
    That I was sent for nothing but a rope.

Pinch. Mistress, both man and master is possessed;
    I know it by their pale and deadly looks.
95   They must be bound, and laid in some dark room.

E. Antipholus. Say, wherefore didst thou lock me
    forth° today,
    And why dost thou deny the bag of gold?

Adriana. I did not, gentle husband, lock thee forth.

E. Dromio. And, gentle master, I received no gold;
100   But I confess, sir, that we were locked out.

Adriana. Dissembling villain, thou speak'st false in
    both.

E. Antipholus. Dissembling harlot, thou art false in
    all,
    And art confederate° with a damnèd pack°
    To make a loathsome abject scorn of me;
105   But with these nails I'll pluck out these false eyes
    That would behold in me this shameful sport.

Enter three or four, and offer to bind him.
He strives.

---

83 **suborned** colluded with 87 **rag** (slang for farthing) 96 **forth**
out 103 **confederate** in conspiracy 103 **pack** gang of rogues

Adriana. O, bind him, bind him, let him not come
     near me!

Pinch. More company! The fiend is strong within him.

Luciana. Ay me,° poor man, how pale and wan he
     looks.

E. Antipholus. What, will you murder me? Thou
     jailer, thou,   *110*
   I am thy prisoner; wilt thou suffer them
   To make a rescue?°

Officer.   Masters, let him go.
   He is my prisoner, and you shall not have him.

Pinch. Go, bind this man, for he is frantic too.

Adriana. What wilt thou do, thou peevish° officer?   *115*
   Hast thou delight to see a wretched man
   Do outrage and displeasure° to himself?

Officer. He is my prisoner; if I let him go,
   The debt he owes will be required of me.

Adriana. I will discharge° thee ere I go from thee.   *120*
   Bear me forthwith unto his creditor,
   And, knowing how the debt grows, I will pay it.
   Good master doctor, see him safe conveyed
   Home to my house. O most unhappy° day!

E. Antipholus. O most unhappy strumpet!   *125*

E. Dromio. Master, I am here ent'red in bond for you.

E. Antipholus. Out on thee, villain! Wherefore dost
     thou mad° me?

E. Dromio. Will you be bound for nothing? Be mad,
     good master;
   Cry, "The devil!"

Luciana. God help, poor souls, how idly° do they
     talk!   *130*

109 **Ay me** (expression of sympathy)   112 **rescue** deliverance by force
115 **peevish** stupid   117 **displeasure** offense   120 **discharge** pay
124 **unhappy** unfortunate   127 **mad** madden   130 **idly** foolishly

Adriana. Go bear him hence. Sister, go you with me.

*Exeunt [Pinch and others with Antipholus of
Ephesus and Dromio of Ephesus]. Manet° Officer,
Adriana, Luciana, Courtesan.*

Say now, whose suit is he arrested at?

Officer. One Angelo, a goldsmith, do you know him?

Adriana. I know the man. What is the sum he owes?

Officer. Two hundred ducats.

135 *Adriana.*   Say, how grows° it due?

Officer. Due for a chain your husband had of him.

Adriana. He did bespeak a chain for me, but had it
    not.

Courtesan. Whenas your husband, all in rage, today
    Came to my house, and took away my ring—
140 The ring I saw upon his finger now—
    Straight after did I meet him with a chain.

Adriana. It may be so, but I did never see it.
    Come, jailer, bring me where the goldsmith is;
    I long to know the truth hereof at large.

*Enter Antipholus of Syracuse, with his rapier
drawn, and Dromio of Syracuse.*

145 *Luciana.* God for thy mercy, they are loose again.

Adriana. And come with naked° swords. Let's call
    more help
    To have them bound again.

Officer.   Away, they'll kill us!

*Run all out. Exeunt omnes as fast as may be,
frighted.*

S. Antipholus. I see these witches are afraid of swords.

131s.d. **Manet** remains (Latin; third person singular, but common
with a plural subject)   135 **grows** comes   146 **naked** drawn

S. Dromio. She that would be your wife now ran from
   you.

S. Antipholus. Come to the Centaur; fetch our stuff°
   from thence.   *150*
   I long that we were safe and sound aboard.

S. Dromio. Faith, stay here this night; they will surely
   do us no harm. You saw they speak us fair, give
   us gold. Methinks they are such a gentle nation
   that, but for the mountain of mad flesh that claims   *155*
   marriage of me, I could find in my heart to stay here
   still,° and turn witch.

S. Antipholus. I will not stay tonight for all the town;
   Therefore away, to get our stuff aboard.   *Exeunt.*

150 **stuff** baggage   157 **still** always

ACT 5

Scene 1. [*Before the Phoenix.*]

*Enter [Another] Merchant and
[Angelo] the Goldsmith.*

Angelo. I am sorry, sir, that I have hind'red you;
But I protest he had the chain of me.
Though most dishonestly he doth deny it.

Merchant. How is the man esteemed here in the city?

5 **Angelo.** Of very reverend reputation, sir,
Of credit infinite, highly beloved,
Second to none that lives here in the city.
His word might bear° my wealth at any time.

Merchant. Speak softly; yonder, as I think, he walks.

Enter Antipholus and Dromio of Syracuse again.

10 **Angelo.** 'Tis so; and that self° chain about his neck,
Which he forswore° most monstrously to have.
Good sir, draw near to me; I'll speak to him.
Signor Antipholus, I wonder much
That you would put me to this shame and trouble,
15 And not without some scandal to yourself,
With circumstance° and oaths so to deny
This chain which now you wear so openly.

5.1.8 **bear** command the support of   10 **self** same   11 **forswore** denied on oath   16 **circumstance** detailed argument

    Beside the charge,° the shame, imprisonment,
    You have done wrong to this my honest friend,
    Who, but for staying on our controversy,   *20*
    Had hoisted sail and put to sea today.
    This chain you had of me, can you deny it?

S. Antipholus. I think I had; I never did deny it.

Merchant. Yes, that you did, sir, and forswore it too.

S. Antipholus. Who heard me to deny it or forswear
    it?   *25*

Merchant. These ears of mine, thou know'st, did hear
    thee.
    Fie on thee, wretch! 'Tis pity that thou liv'st
    To walk where any honest men resort.

S. Antipholus. Thou art a villain to impeach° me thus.
    I'll prove mine honor and mine honesty   *30*
    Against thee presently,° if thou dar'st stand.°

Merchant. I dare, and do defy thee for a villain!

        They draw. Enter Adriana, Luciana,
            Courtesan, and others.

Adriana. Hold, hurt him not, for God's sake! He is
    mad.
    Some get within him,° take his sword away.
    Bind Dromio too, and bear them to my house.   *35*

S. Dromio. Run, master, run; for God's sake, take a
    house!°
    This is some priory. In, or we are spoiled.
                Exeunt to the Priory.

        Enter Lady Abbess.

Abbess. Be quiet, people. Wherefore throng you
    hither?

Adriana. To fetch my poor distracted husband hence.

---

18 **charge** expense 29 **impeach** accuse 31 **presently** at once 31
stand prepare to fight 34 **within him** inside his guard 36 **take a
house** get inside

40   Let us come in, that we may bind him fast,
      And bear him home for his recovery.

Angelo. I knew he was not in his perfect wits.

Merchant. I am sorry now that I did draw on him.

Abbess. How long hath this possession° held the man?

45 *Adriana.* This week he hath been heavy, sour, sad,
      And much different from the man he was;
      But till this afternoon his passion
      Ne'er brake into extremity of rage.

Abbess. Hath he not lost much wealth by wrack of
      sea?°
50   Buried some dear friend? Hath not else his eye
      Strayed° his affection in unlawful love—
      A sin prevailing much in youthful men,
      Who give their eyes the liberty of gazing?
      Which of these sorrows is he subject to?

55 *Adriana.* To none of these, except it be the last,
      Namely, some love that drew him oft from home.

Abbess. You should for that have reprehended him.

Adriana. Why, so I did.

Abbess. Ay, but not rough enough.

Adriana. As roughly as my modesty would let me.

Abbess. Haply, in private.

60 *Adriana.* And in assemblies too.

Abbess. Ay, but not enough.

Adriana. It was the copy° of our conference.
      In bed he slept not for° my urging it;
      At board he fed not for my urging it;
65   Alone, it was the subject of my theme:
      In company I often glancèd° it;
      Still° did I tell him it was vile and bad.

---

44 **possession** (by evil spirits)   49 **wrack of sea** shipwreck   51
Strayed led astray   62 **copy** topic   63 **for** because of   66 **glancèd**
touched on   67 **Still** continually

Abbess. And thereof came it that the man was mad.
   The venom° clamors of a jealous woman
   Poisons more deadly than a mad dog's tooth.   70
   It seems his sleeps were hind'red by thy railing,
   And thereof comes it that his head is light.
   Thou say'st his meat was sauced with thy upbraid-
     ings;
   Unquiet meals make ill digestions;
   Thereof the raging fire of fever bred—   75
   And what's a fever but a fit of madness?
   Thou sayest his sports were hind'red by thy brawls;
   Sweet recreation barred, what doth ensue
   But moody and dull melancholy,
   Kinsman to grim and comfortless despair,   80
   And at her heels a huge infectious troop
   Of pale distemperatures° and foes to life?
   In food, in sport, and life-preserving rest
   To be disturbed, would mad° or man or beast.
   The consequence is, then, thy jealous fits   85
   Hath scared thy husband from the use of wits.

Luciana. She never reprehended him but mildly,
   When he demeaned° himself rough, rude, and wildly.
   Why bear you these rebukes and answer not?

Adriana. She did betray me to my own reproof.°   90
   Good people, enter and lay hold on him.

Abbess. No, not a creature enters in my house.

Adriana. Then, let your servants bring my husband
   forth.

Abbess. Neither. He took this place for sanctuary,°
   And it shall privilege him° from your hands   95
   Till I have brought him to his wits again,
   Or lose my labor in assaying° it.

---

69 **venom** venomous   82 **distemperatures** disorders   84 **mad** madden   88 **demeaned** conducted   90 **my own reproof** self-accusation
94 **sanctuary** right of asylum   95 **privilege him** grant him immunity
97 **assaying** attempting

Adriana. I will attend my husband, be his nurse,
    Diet his sickness, for it is my office,
100   And will have no attorney° but myself;
    And therefore let me have him home with me.

Abbess. Be patient, for I will not let him stir
    Till I have used the approvèd° means I have,
    With wholesome syrups, drugs, and holy prayers,
105   To make of him a formal° man again.
    It is a branch and parcel° of mine oath,
    A charitable duty of my order;
    Therefore depart, and leave him here with me.

Adriana. I will not hence, and leave my husband here;
110   And ill it doth beseem your holiness
    To separate the husband and the wife.

Abbess. Be quiet and depart, thou shalt not have him.
                              [Exit.]

Luciana. Complain unto the Duke of this indignity.

Adriana. Come, go. I will fall prostrate at his feet,
115   And never rise until my tears and prayers
    Have won his Grace to come in person hither,
    And take perforce my husband from the Abbess.

Merchant. By this, I think, the dial points at five:
    Anon, I'm sure, the Duke himself in person
120   Comes this way to the melancholy vale,
    The place of death and sorry° execution,
    Behind the ditches of the abbey here.

Angelo. Upon what cause?

Merchant. To see a reverend Syracusian merchant,
125   Who put unluckily into this bay
    Against the laws and statutes of this town,
    Beheaded publicly for his offense.

Angelo. See, where they come. We will behold his
    death.

---

100 **attorney** agent   103 **approvèd** tested   105 **formal** normal   106
branch and parcel part and parcel   121 **sorry** sorrowful

Luciana. Kneel to the Duke before he pass the abbey.

> *Enter the Duke of Ephesus and [Egeon] the Merchant of Syracuse, barehead, with the Headsman and other Officers.*

Duke. Yet once again proclaim it publicly,   *130*
  If any friend will pay the sum for him,
  He shall not die; so much we tender° him.

Adriana. Justice, most sacred Duke, against the Abbess!

Duke. She is a virtuous and a reverend lady.
  It cannot be that she hath done thee wrong.   *135*

Adriana. May it please your Grace, Antipholus, my husband,
  Who I made lord of me and all I had
  At your important° letters, this ill day
  A most outrageous fit of madness took him:
  That° desp'rately he hurried through the street,   *140*
  With him his bondman° all as mad as he,
  Doing displeasure° to the citizens
  By rushing in their houses, bearing thence
  Rings, jewels, anything his rage did like.
  Once did I get him bound, and sent him home,   *145*
  Whilst to take order° for the wrongs I went,
  That here and there his fury had committed.
  Anon, I wot° not by what strong° escape,
  He broke from those that had the guard of him,
  And with his mad attendant and himself,   *150*
  Each one with ireful passion, with drawn swords,
  Met us again and, madly bent on us,
  Chased us away, till, raising of more aid,
  We came again to bind them. Then they fled
  Into this abbey, whither we pursued them;   *155*
  And here the Abbess shuts the gates on us,
  And will not suffer us to fetch him out,
  Nor send him forth that we may bear him hence.

132 **tender** regard   138 **important** pressing   140 **That** so that
141 **bondman** slave   142 **displeasure** harm   146 **take order** settle
148 **wot** know   148 **strong** violent

Therefore, most gracious Duke, with thy command,
160   Let him be brought forth and borne hence for help.

Duke. Long since thy husband served me in my wars;
    And I to thee engaged a prince's word,
    When thou didst make him master of thy bed,
    To do him all the grace and good I could.
165   Go, some of you, knock at the abbey gate,
    And bid the Lady Abbess come to me.
    I will determine this before I stir.

Enter a Messenger.

Messenger. O mistress, mistress, shift and save your-
        self.
    My master and his man are both broke loose,
170   Beaten the maids a-row,° and bound the doctor,
    Whose beard they have singed off with brands of
        fire,
    And ever as it blazed, they threw on him
    Great pails of puddled° mire to quench the hair.
    My master preaches patience to him, and the while
175   His man with scissors nicks him like a fool;°
    And, sure, unless you send some present help,
    Between them they will kill the conjurer.

Adriana. Peace, fool, thy master and his man are here,
    And that is false thou dost report to us.

180   *Messenger.* Mistress, upon my life, I tell you true;
    I have not breathed almost° since I did see it.
    He cries for you and vows, if he can take you,
    To scorch your face and to disfigure you.

Cry within.

Hark, hark! I hear him, mistress. Fly, begone.

185   *Duke.* Come, stand by me; fear nothing. Guard with
        halberds!°

---

170 **a-row** one after another   173 **puddled** muddied   175 **fool** (Elizabethan fools had their hair cut off)   181 **not breathed almost** hardly
breathed   185 **halberds** (poles with heads like battle-axes)

Adriana. Ay me, it is my husband! Witness you,
   That he is borne about invisible.
   Even now we housed him° in the abbey here,
   And now he's there, past thought of human rea-
      son.

> *Enter Antipholus and Dromio of Ephesus.*

E. Antipholus. Justice, most gracious Duke! O, grant
      me justice,   *190*
   Even for the service that long since I did thee,
   When I bestrid° thee in the wars, and took
   Deep scars to save thy life; even for the blood
   That then I lost for thee, now grant me justice.

Egeon. Unless the fear of death doth make me dote, *195*
   I see my son Antipholus and Dromio.

E. Antipholus. Justice, sweet Prince, against that woman
      there!
   She whom thou gav'st to me to be my wife;
   That hath abusèd and dishonored me,
   Even in the strength and height° of injury: *200*
   Beyond imagination is the wrong
   That she this day hath shameless thrown on me.

Duke. Discover° how, and thou shalt find me just.

E. Antipholus. This day, great Duke, she shut the
      doors upon me,
   While she with harlots° feasted in my house.   *205*

Duke. A grievous fault. Say, woman, didst thou so?

Adriana. No, my good lord. Myself, he, and my sister
   Today did dine together; so befall my soul
   As this is false he burdens me withal.°

Luciana. Ne'er may I look on day, nor sleep on night,° *210*
   But she tells to your Highness simple truth.

---

188 **housed him** pursued him to shelter   192 **bestrid** defended by
standing over   200 **in the strength and height** to the strongest degree   203 **Discover** reveal   205 **harlots** rascals   208–09 **so befall . . .
me withal** i.e., I stake my soul that what he charges me with is
false   210 **on night** at night

Angelo. O perjured woman! They are both forsworn.
In this the madman justly chargeth them.

E. Antipholus. My liege, I am advisèd° what I say,
215 Neither disturbed with the effect of wine,
Nor heady-rash, provoked with raging ire,
Albeit my wrongs might make one wiser mad.
This woman locked me out this day from dinner.
That goldsmith there, were he not packed° with her,
220 Could witness it; for he was with me then,
Who parted with me to go fetch a chain,
Promising to bring it to the Porpentine,
Where Balthasar and I did dine together.
Our dinner done, and he not coming thither,
225 I went to seek him. In the street I met him,
And in his company that gentleman.
There did this perjured goldsmith swear me down
That I this day of him received the chain,
Which, God he knows, I saw not; for the which,
230 He did arrest me with an officer.
I did obey, and sent my peasant° home
For certain ducats; he with none returned.
Then fairly I bespoke° the officer
To go in person with me to my house.
235 By th' way we met
My wife, her sister, and a rabble more
Of vile confederates. Along with them
They brought one Pinch, a hungry lean-faced villain;
A mere anatomy,° a mountebank,
240 A threadbare juggler° and a fortune-teller,
A needy-hollow-eyed-sharp-looking wretch;
A living dead man. This pernicious slave,
Forsooth, took on him as° a conjurer;
And, gazing in mine eyes, feeling my pulse,

---

214 **advisèd** well aware of 219 **packed** conspiring 231 **peasant** bondman 233 **fairly I bespoke** politely I addressed 239 **mere anatomy** sheer skeleton 240 **juggler** sorcerer 243 **took on him as** assumed the part of

And with no face, as 'twere, out-facing me,   245
Cries out, I was possessed. Then all together
They fell upon me, bound me, bore me thence,
And in a dark and dankish vault at home
There left me and my man, both bound together,
Till gnawing with my teeth my bonds in sunder,°   250
I gained my freedom; and immediately
Ran hither to your Grace, whom I beseech
To give me ample satisfaction
For these deep shames and great indignities.

Angelo. My lord, in truth, thus far I witness with him: 255
That he dined not at home, but was locked out.

Duke. But had he such a chain of thee, or no?

Angelo. He had, my lord, and when he ran in here
These people saw the chain about his neck.

Merchant. Besides, I will be sworn these ears of mine   260
Heard you confess you had the chain of him,
After you first forswore it on the Mart;
And, thereupon, I drew my sword on you;
And then you fled into this abbey here,
From whence, I think, you are come by miracle.   265

E. Antipholus. I never came within these abbey walls,
Nor ever didst thou draw thy sword on me.
I never saw the chain, so help me Heaven!
And this is false you burden me withal.

Duke. Why, what an intricate impeach° is this!   270
I think you all have drunk of Circe's cup.°
If here you housed him, here he would have been;
If he were mad, he would not plead so coldly.°
You say he dined at home, the goldsmith here
Denies that saying. Sirrah, what say you?   275

E. Dromio. Sir, he dined with her there at the Porpentine.

250 **in sunder** asunder   270 **impeach** accusation   271 **Circe's cup**
(potion which, in Greek mythology, turns men into beasts)   273
coldly rationally

Courtesan. He did, and from my finger snatched that
    ring.

E. Antipholus. 'Tis true, my liege, this ring I had of
    her.

Duke. Saw'st thou him enter at the abbey here?

280 *Courtesan.* As sure, my liege, as I do see your Grace.

Duke. Why, this is strange. Go call the Abbess hither.
    I think you are all mated,° or stark mad.
                         Exit One to the Abbey.

Egeon. Most mighty Duke, vouchsafe me° speak a
    word.
    Haply° I see a friend will save my life,
285   And pay the sum that may deliver me.

Duke. Speak freely, Syracusian, what thou wilt.

Egeon. Is not your name, sir, called Antipholus?
    And is not that your bondman Dromio?

E. Dromio. Within this hour I was his bondman, sir,
290   But he, I thank him, gnawed in two my cords.
    Now am I Dromio, and his man, unbound.

Egeon. I am sure you both of you remember me.

E. Dromio. Ourselves we do remember, sir, by you;
    For lately we were bound,° as you are now.
295   You are not Pinch's patient, are you, sir?

Egeon. Why look you strange on me? You know me
    well.

E. Antipholus. I never saw you in my life till now.

Egeon. O, grief hath changed me since you saw me
    last,
    And careful° hours with time's deformèd hand
300   Have written strange defeatures° in my face.

282 **mated** confounded   283 **vouchsafe me** allow me to   284 **Haply**
perchance   294 **bound** (pun on being a bondservant and being literally bound as a madman)   299 **careful** full of care   300 **defeatures**
disfigurements

But tell me yet, dost thou not know my voice?

E. Antipholus. Neither.

Egeon. Dromio, nor thou?

E. Dromio.   No, trust me, sir, nor I.

Egeon. I am sure thou dost!

E. Dromio. Ay, sir, but I am sure I do not; and what-   *305*
soever a man denies, you are now bound° to believe
him.

Egeon. Not know my voice! O, time's extremity,
Hast thou so cracked and splitted my poor tongue
In seven short years, that here my only son   *310*
Knows not my feeble key of untuned cares?°
Though now this grainèd° face of mine be hid
In sap-consuming winter's drizzled snow,
And all the conduits of my blood froze up,
Yet hath my night of life some memory;   *315*
My wasting lamps° some fading glimmer left;
My dull deaf ears a little use to hear.
All these old witnesses—I cannot err—
Tell me thou art my son Antipholus.

E. Antipholus. I never saw my father in my life.   *320*

Egeon. But seven years since, in Syracusa, boy,
Thou know'st we parted; but perhaps, my son,
Thou sham'st to acknowledge me in misery.

E. Antipholus. The Duke and all that know me in the
   city
Can witness with me that it is not so.   *325*
I ne'er saw Syracusa in my life.

Duke. I tell thee, Syracusian, twenty years
Have I been patron to Antipholus,
During which time he ne'er saw Syracusa.   *330*
I see thy age and dangers make thee dote.

306 **bound** (a further quibble) 311 **feeble key of untuned cares**
voice enfeebled by discordant cares 312 **grainèd** furrowed 316
wasting lamps dimming eyes

*Enter the Abbess with Antipholus of Syracuse
and Dromio of Syracuse.*

Abbess. Most mighty Duke, behold a man much wronged.
                        All gather to see them.

Adriana. I see two husbands, or mine eyes deceive me.

Duke. One of these men is genius° to the other;
    And so of these, which is the natural man,
335   And which the spirit? Who deciphers them?

S. Dromio. I, sir, am Dromio; command him away.

E. Dromio. I, sir, am Dromio; pray let me stay.

S. Antipholus. Egeon art thou not, or else his ghost?

S. Dromio. O, my old master! Who hath bound him
    here?

340 *Abbess.* Whoever bound him, I will loose his bonds,
    And gain a husband by his liberty.
    Speak, old Egeon, if thou beest the man
    That hadst a wife once called Emilia,
    That bore thee at a burden° two fair sons!
345   O, if thou beest the same Egeon, speak;
    And speak unto the same Emilia.

Duke. [*Aside*] Why, here begins his morning story right:
    These two Antipholus', these two so like,
    And these two Dromios, one in semblance,°
350   Besides her urging° of her wrack at sea;
    These are the parents to these children,
    Which accidentally are met together.

Egeon. If I dream not, thou art Emilia.
    If thou art she, tell me where is that son
355   That floated with thee on the fatal raft?

Abbess. By men of Epidamnum, he and I
    And the twin Dromio, all were taken up;

---

333 **genius** attendant spirit   344 **burden** birth   349 **semblance** appearance   350 **urging** account

But by and by rude fishermen of Corinth
By force took Dromio and my son from them,
And me they left with those of Epidamnum.   *360*
What then became of them, I cannot tell;
I to° this fortune that you see me in.

Duke. Antipholus, thou cam'st from Corinth first.

S. Antipholus. No, sir, not I; I came from Syracuse.

Duke. Stay, stand apart; I know not which is which.   *365*

E. Antipholus. I came from Corinth, my most gracious lord.

E. Dromio. And I with him.

E. Antipholus. Brought to this town by that most
famous warrior,
Duke Menaphon, your most renownèd uncle.

Adriana. Which of you two did dine with me today?   *370*

S. Antipholus. I, gentle mistress.

Adriana.   And are not you my husband?

E. Antipholus. No, I say nay to that.

S. Antipholus. And so do I, yet did she call me so;
And this fair gentlewoman, her sister here,
Did call me brother. What I told you then   *375*
I hope I shall have leisure to make good,
If this be not a dream I see and hear.

Angelo. That is the chain, sir, which you had of me.

S. Antipholus. I think it be, sir; I deny it not.

E. Antipholus. And you, sir, for this chain arrested
me.   *380*

Angelo. I think I did, sir. I deny it not.

Adriana. I sent you money, sir, to be your bail,
By Dromio; but I think he brought it not.

E. Dromio. No, none by me.

362 **I to** I came to

S. Antipholus. This purse of ducats I received from
385 you,
  And Dromio, my man, did bring them me.
  I see we still° did meet each other's man,
  And I was ta'en for him, and he for me,
  And thereupon these errors are arose.

E. Antipholus. These ducats pawn I for my father
390 here.

Duke. It shall not need; thy father hath his life.

Courtesan. Sir, I must have that diamond from you.

E. Antipholus. There, take it, and much thanks for
  my good cheer.

Abbess. Renownèd Duke, vouchsafe to take the pains
395 To go with us into the abbey here,
  And hear at large discoursèd all our fortunes;
  And all that are assembled in this place,
  That by this sympathizèd° one day's error
  Have suffered wrong, go, keep us company,
400 And we shall make full satisfaction.
  Thirty-three years have I but gone in travail°
  Of you, my sons, and till this present hour
  My heavy burden ne'er delivered.
  The Duke, my husband, and my children both,
405 And you the calendars° of their nativity,
  Go to a gossips'° feast, and joy with me
  After so long grief such nativity.°

Duke. With all my heart I'll gossip° at this feast.
       Exeunt [all except] the two Dromios
          and two Brothers.

S. Dromio. Master, shall I fetch your stuff from ship-
  board?

387 **still** repeatedly 398 **sympathizèd** shared 401 **travail** child-
birth (with a pun on "travel") 405 **calendars** (the Dromios mark
the age of the Antipholuses) 406 **gossips** godparents 407 **nativity**
a christening party (suggested emendations are "festivity" and
"felicity") 408 **gossip** make merry

E. Antipholus. Dromio, what stuff of mine hast thou
    embarked?   410

S. Dromio. Your goods that lay at host,° sir, in the
    Centaur.

S. Antipholus. He speaks to me. I am your master,
    Dromio.
    Come, go with us; we'll look to that anon.
    Embrace thy brother there; rejoice with him.
           Exit [with Antipholus of Ephesus].

S. Dromio. There is a fat friend at your master's
    house,   415
    That kitchened° me for you today at dinner;
    She now shall be my sister, not my wife.

E. Dromio. Methinks you are my glass, and not my
    brother;
    I see by you I am a sweet-faced° youth.
    Will you walk in to see their gossiping?   420

S. Dromio. Not I, sir, you are my elder.

E. Dromio. That's a question; how shall we try it?

S. Dromio. We'll draw cuts for the senior; till then,
    lead thou first.

E. Dromio. Nay, then, thus: 425
    We came into the world like brother and brother:
    And now let's go hand in hand, not one before
    another.   *Exeunt.*

FINIS

411 **at host** in the care of the host   416 **kitchened** entertained in the
kitchen   419 **sweet-faced** good-looking

Textual Note

The Comedy of Errors was first published in the Folio of 1623, which provides the only authoritative text. It is possible that the copy for the Folio was Shakespeare's manuscript; the ambiguity of some names in stage directions and in speech prefixes would have been confusing in a promptbook. For example, Egeon is *Mer(chant)* in 1.1., but other merchants appear in other scenes without distinctive titles. More important, *E. Dro(mio)* is, as might be expected, *Dromio of Ephesus;* but *E. Ant.* is Antipholus of Syracuse, an abbreviation of his earlier designation, *Ant. Errotis*—which is perhaps an approximation of *erraticus,* wandering. A promptbook doubtless would have clarified the nomenclature.

The Folio's text is a good one, presenting the editor with relatively few problems. In the present edition the speech prefixes and names in stage directions have been regularized, spelling and punctuation have been modernized, and obvious typographical errors have been corrected. A few passages that the Folio prints as prose are given in verse, and the positions of a few stage directions have been slightly altered. Act division (translated from the Latin) is that of the Folio; scene division is that of the Globe text. Other departures from the Folio are listed below, with the adopted reading first, in italics, and the original reading next, in roman.

1.1.17 *at* at any   42 *the* he   102 *upon* vp   116 *bark* backe   123 *thee* they   151 *health* helpe

1.2.s.d. *Antipholus of Syracuse* Antipholis Erotes   4 *arrival* a riuall   30 *lose* loose   32s.d. *Exit* Exeunt   40 *unhappy* vnhappie a   65 *score* scoure   66 *clock* cooke   93 *God's* God   94s.d. *Exit* Exeunt

2.1.s.d. *Antipholus of Ephesus* Antipholis Sereptus   11 *o' door* adore   12 *ill* thus   45 *two* too   61 *thousand* hundred   72 *errand* arrant   107 *alone, alone* alone, a loue   112 *Wear* Where   113 *But* By

2.2.s.d. *Antipholus of Syracuse* Antipholis Errotis   12 *didst* did didst   80 *men* them   98 *tiring* trying   102 *e'en* in   176 *stronger* stranger   187 *offered* free'd   195 *drone* Dromio   196 *am not I* am I not

3.1.54 *trow* hope   75 *you* your   89 *her* your   91 *her* your

3.2.s.d. *Luciana* Iuliana   1 *Luciana* Iulia   2 *Antipholus, hate* Antipholus 4 *building* buildings   16 *attaint* attaine   21 *but* not   26 *wife* wise   46 *sister's* sister   49 *bed* bud   49 *them* thee   57 *where* when   111 *and* is 129 *chalky* chalkle   171 *here is* here's

4.1.17 *her* their   28 *carat* charect   47 *to blame* too blame   88 *then she* then sir she

4.2.6 *Of* Oh   60 *'a* I

4.3.1 *S. Antipholus* [F omits]   62 *if you do* if do

5.1.s.d. *Another Merchant* the Merchant   33 *God's* God   121 *death* depth   168 *Messenger* [F omits]   246 *all together* altogether   282s.d. *Abbey* Abbesse   403 *ne'er* are   406 *joy with* go with   408s.d. *Exeunt* Exeunt omnes. Manet   423 *senior* Signior

The Source of
The Comedy of Errors

Titus Maccius Plautus, who was born during the third century B.C. and died during the second, was the most popular of the Roman playwrights. Freely adapted into the Latin vernacular from the New Comedy of the Greeks, his plays were distinguished by their broad humor, fast movement, vivid language, and nimble versification. Among the twenty-one Plautine comedies that have come down to us, the *Menaechmi* is one of the best known and the most influential, doubtless because it reduces the dilemmas of mistaken identity to an archetypal pattern. The Elizabethan translation, which Shakespeare may or may not have known in some form, was published in 1595, presumably a few years after the first production of *The Comedy of Errors*. The initials of the translator, W.W., are generally thought to stand for William Warner, a man of letters who is sometimes remembered for his historical poem, *Albion's England*. His prose version of Plautus' comedy is rough, lively, and actable. Occasionally it substitutes a colloquial turn of phrase for a literal expression that would sound pedantic. Though it does not translate the prologue, which sets the scene and recapitulates the plot, it does begin with the synopsis in verse (added to Plautus by a later hand), which originally took the form of an acrostic spelling the title of the play. For the underplot of the twin servants, Shakespeare is indebted to the *Amphitruo* of Plautus, particularly the opening scene and the fourth act.

A Pleasant and Fine Conceited Comedy

Called *Menaechmus,*

Taken Out of the Most Excellent Poet

Plautus.

THE ARGUMENT

Two twin-born sons a Sicil merchant had:
Menaechmus one, and Sosicles the other.
The first his father lost, a little lad;
The grandsire named the latter like his brother.
This, grown a man, long travel took to seek
His brother, and to Epidamnum came,
Where th'other dwelt enriched, and him so like
That citizens there take him for the same.
Father, wife, neighbors, each mistaking either,
Much pleasant error, ere they meet together.

Act 1. Scene 1.

Enter Peniculus, a Parasite.

[*Peniculus.*] Peniculus was given me for my name when I
was young, because like a broom I swept all clean away,
wheresoe'er I be come: namely all the victuals which are
set before me. Now, in my judgment, men that clap iron
bolts on such captives as they would keep safe, and tie

those servants in chains who they think will run away, they commit an exceeding great folly. My reason is: these poor wretches, enduring one misery upon another, never cease devising how, by wrenching asunder their gyves or by some subtlety or other, they may escape such cursed bonds. If, then, ye would keep a man without all suspicion of running away from ye, the surest way is to tie him with meat, drink, and ease. Let him ever be idle, eat his belly-ful, and carouse while his skin will hold, and he shall never, I warrant ye, stir a foot. These strings to tie one by the teeth pass all the bands of iron, steel, or what metal soever; for, the more slack and easy ye make them, the faster shall they tie the party which is in them. I speak this upon experience of myself, who am now going for Menaechmus, there willingly to be tied to his good cheer. He is commonly so exceeding bountiful and liberal in his fare, as no marvel though such guests as myself be drawn to his table and tied there in his dishes. Now because I have lately been a stranger there, I mean to visit him at dinner; for my stomach, methinks, even thrusts me into the fetters of his dainty fare. But yonder I [see] his door open, and himself ready to come forth.

Scene 2.

*Enter Menaechmus, talking back
to his Wife within.*

[*Menaechmus.*] If ye were not such a brabbling fool and mad-brain scold as ye are, ye would never thus cross your husband in all actions. 'Tis no matter; let her serve me thus once more, I'll send her home to her dad with a vengeance. I can never go forth a-doors but she asketh me whither I go, what I do, what business, what I fetch, what I carry, as though she were a constable or a toll-gatherer. I have pampered her too much; she hath servants about her, wool, flax, and all things necessary to busy her withal; yet she watcheth and wondreth whither I go. Well, sith it is so, she shall now have some cause; I mean to dine this day abroad with a sweet friend of mine.

Peniculus. Yea, marry, now comes he to the point that pricks me: this last speech galls me as much as it would do his wife. If he dine not at home, I am dressed.

Menaechmus. We that have loves abroad and wives at home are miserably hampered; yet would every man could tame his shrew as well as I do mine! I have now filched away a fine riding cloak of my wife's, which I mean to bestow upon one that I love better. Nay, if she be so wary and watchful over me, I count it an alms-deed to deceive her.

Peniculus. Come, what share have I in that same?

Menaechmus. Out alas! I am taken.

Peniculus. True, but by your friend.

Menaechmus. What, mine own Peniculus?

Peniculus. Yours, i' faith, body and goods—if I had any.

Menaechmus. Why, thou hast a body.

Peniculus. Yea, but neither goods nor good body.

Menaechmus. Thou couldst never come fitter in all thy life.

Peniculus. Tush, I ever do so to my friends; I know how to come always in the nick. Where dine ye today?

Menaechmus. I'll tell thee of a notable prank.

Peniculus. What, did the cook mar your meat in the dressing? Would I might see the reversion.

Menaechmus. Tell me didst thou see a picture how Jupiter's eagle snatched away Ganymede, or how Venus stole away Adonis?

Peniculus. Often; but what care I for shadows? I want substance.

Menaechmus. Look thee here, look not I like such a picture?

Peniculus. O ho! What cloak have ye got here?

Menaechmus. Prithee say I am now a brave fellow.

Peniculus. But hark ye, where shall we dine?

Menaechmus. Tush, say as I bid thee, man.

Peniculus. Out of doubt, ye are a fine man.

Menaechmus. What, canst add nothing of thine own?

Peniculus. Ye are a most pleasant gentleman.

Menaechmus. On yet.

Peniculus. Nay, not a word more, unless ye tell me how you and your wife be fallen out.

Menaechmus. Nay I have a greater secret than that to impart to thee.

Peniculus. Say your mind.

Menaechmus. Come farther this way from my house.

Peniculus. So, let me hear.

Menaechmus. Nay, farther yet.

Peniculus. I warrant ye, man.

Menaechmus. Nay, yet farther.

Peniculus. 'Tis pity ye were not made a water-man to row in a wherry.

Menaechmus. Why?

Peniculus. Because ye go one way and look another still, lest your wife should follow ye. But what's the matter? Is't not almost dinnertime?

Menaechmus. Seest thou this cloak?

Peniculus. Not yet. Well, what of it?

Menaechmus. This same I mean to give to Erotium.

Peniculus. That's well, but what of all this?

Menaechmus. There I mean to have a delicious dinner prepared for her and me.

Peniculus. And me?

Menaechmus. And thee.

Peniculus. O sweet word! What, shall I knock presently at her door?

Menaechmus. Aye, knock. But stay too, Peniculus, let's not be too rash. Oh see, she is in good time coming forth.

Peniculus. Ah, he now looks against the sun; how her beams dazzle his eyes!

Enter Erotium.

Erotium. What, mine own Menaechmus! Welcome, sweetheart.

Peniculus. And what am I? Welcome too?

Erotium. You, sir? Ye are out of the number of my welcome guests.

Peniculus. I am like a voluntary soldier, out of pay.

Menaechmus. Erotium, I have determined that here shall be pitched a field this day; we mean to drink for the heavens; and which of us performs the bravest service at his weapon, the wine bowl, yourself as captain shall pay him his wages according to his deserts.

Erotium. Agreed.

Peniculus. I would we had the weapons, for my valor pricks me to the battle.

Menaechmus. Shall I tell thee, sweet mouse? I never look upon thee, but I am quite out of love with my wife.

Erotium. Yet ye cannot choose but ye must still wear something of hers. What's this same?

Menaechmus. This? Such a spoil, sweetheart, as I took from her to put on thee.

Erotium. Mine own Menaechmus, well worthy to be my dear of all dearest!

Peniculus. Now she shows herself in her likeness; when she finds him in the giving vein, she draws close to him.

Menaechmus. I think Hercules got not the garter from Hippolyta so hardly as I got this from my wife. Take this, and with the same take my heart.

Peniculus. Thus they must do that are right lovers—especially if they mean to [be] beggars with any speed.

Menaechmus. I bought this same of late for my wife; it stood me, I think, in some ten pound.

Peniculus. There's ten pound bestowed very thriftily.

Menaechmus. But know ye what I would have ye do?

Erotium. It shall be done: your dinner shall be ready.

Menaechmus. Let a good dinner be made for us three. Hark ye, some oysters, a marrowbone pie or two, some artichokes, and potato roots; let our other dishes be as you please.

Erotium. You shall, sir.

Menaechmus. I have a little business in this city; by that time dinner will be prepared. Farewell till then, sweet Erotium. Come, Peniculus.

Peniculus. Nay, I mean to follow ye. I will sooner lose my life than sight of you till this dinner be done.

Exeunt.

Erotium. Who's there? Call me Cylindrus, the cook, hither.

Enter Cylindrus.

Cylindrus, take the handbasket; and here, there's ten shillings, is there not?

Cylindrus. 'Tis so, mistress.

Erotium. Buy me of all the daintiest meals ye can get, ye know what I mean, so as three may dine passing well, and yet no more than enough.

Cylindrus. What guests have ye today, mistress?

Erotium. Here will be Menaechmus and his parasite and myself.

Cylindrus. That's ten persons in all.

Erotium. How many?

Cylindrus. Ten; for I warrant you, that parasite may stand for eight at his victuals.

Erotium. Go, dispatch as I bid you, and look ye return with all speed.

Cylindrus. I will have all ready with a trice.

Exeunt.

Act 2. Scene 1.

*Enter Menaechmus Sosicles [i.e., the Traveler],
Messenio his servant, and some Sailors.*

Menaechmus. Surely, Messenio, I think seafarers never take so comfortable a joy in anything as when they have been long tossed and turmoiled in the wide seas, they hap at last to ken land.

Messenio. I'll be sworn, I should not be gladder to see a whole country of mine own than I have been at such a sight. But, I pray, wherefore are we now come to Epidamnum? Must we needs go to see every town that we hear of?

Menaechmus. Till I find my brother, all towns are alike to me. I must try in all places.

Messenio. Why, then, let's even as long as we live seek your brother. Six years now have we roamed about thus: Istria, Hispania, Massilia, Illyria, all the upper sea, all high Greece, all haven towns in Italy. I think if we had sought a needle all this time, we must needs have found it, had it been above ground. It cannot be that he is alive; and to seek a dead man thus among the living, what folly is it!

Menaechmus. Yea, could I but once find any man that could certainly inform me of his death, I were satisfied; otherwise I can never desist seeking. Little knowest thou, Messenio, how near my heart it goes.

Messenio. This is washing of a blackamore. Faith, let's go home, unless ye mean we should write a story of our travel.

Menaechmus. Sirrah, no more of these saucy speeches! I perceive I must teach ye how to serve me, not to rule me.

Messenio. Aye so, now it appears what it is to be a servant. Well, yet I must speak my conscience. Do ye hear, sir? Faith, I must tell ye one thing: when I look into the lean estate of your purse, and consider advisedly of your decaying stock, I hold it very needful to be drawing homeward, lest in looking your brother, we quite lose ourselves. For this assure yourself: this town, Epidamnum, is a place of outrageous expenses, exceeding in all riot and lasciviousness; and, I hear, as full of ribalds, parasites, drunkards, catchpoles, coney-catchers, and sycophants as it can hold; then for courtesans, why here's the currentest stamp of them in the world. Ye must not think here to scape with as light cost as in other places. The very name shows the nature: no man comes hither *sine damno*.

Menaechmus. Ye say very well indeed. Give me my purse into mine own keeping, because I will so be the safer, *sine damno*.

Messenio. Why, sir?

Menaechmus. Because I fear you will be busy among the courtesans, and so be cozened of it. Then should I take great pains in belaboring your shoulders; so, to avoid both these harms, I'll keep it myself.

Messenio. I pray do so, sir; all the better.

Enter Cylindrus.

[*Cylindrus.*] I have tickling gear here, i' faith, for their dinners. It grieves me to the heart to think how that cormorant knave, Peniculus, must have his share in these dainty morsels. But what? Is Menaechmus come already, before I could come from the market? Menaechmus, how do ye, sir? How haps it ye come so soon?

Menaechmus. Godamercy, my good friend, dost thou know me?

Cylindrus. Know ye? No, not I. Where's Mouldy-chaps that must dine with ye? A murrain on his manners!

Menaechmus. Whom meanest thou, good fellow?

Cylindrus. Why, Peniculus, worship, that whoreson lick-trencher, your parasitical attendant.

Menaechmus. What Peniculus? What attendant? My attendant? Surely this fellow is mad.

Messenio. Did I not tell ye what coney-catching villains ye should find here?

Cylindrus. Menaechmus, hark ye sir, ye come too soon back again to dinner; I am but returned from the market.

Menaechmus. Fellow, here thou shalt have money of me. Go, get the priest to sacrifice for thee. I know thou art mad, else thou wouldst never use a stranger thus.

Cylindrus. Alas, sir, Cylindrus was wont to be no stranger to you. Know ye not Cylindrus?

Menaechmus. Cylindrus or Coliendrus or what the devil thou art, I know not, neither do I care to know.

Cylindrus. I know you to be Menaechmus.

Menaechmus. Thou shouldst be in thy wits, in that thou namest me so right; but tell me, where hast thou known me?

Cylindrus. Where? Even here, where ye first fell in love with my mistress, Erotium.

Menaechmus. I neither have lover, neither know I who thou art.

Cylindrus. Know ye not who I am? Who fills your cup and dresses your meat at our house?

Messenio. What a slave is this? That I had somewhat to break the rascal's pate withal!

Menaechmus. At your house, whenas I never came in Epidamnum till this day!

Cylindrus. Oh, that's true. Do ye not dwell in yonder house?

Menaechmus. Foul shame light upon them that dwell there, for my part!

Cylindrus. Questionless, he is mad indeed, to curse himself thus. Hark ye, Menaechmus.

Menaechmus. What sayest thou?

Cylindrus. If I may advise ye, ye shall bestow this money, which ye offered me, upon a sacrifice for yourself; for, out of doubt, you are mad that curse yourself.

Messenio. What a varlet art thou to trouble us thus!

Cylindrus. Tush, he will many times jest with me thus. Yet when his wife is not by, 'tis a ridiculous jest.

Menaechmus. What's that?

Cylindrus. This I say: think ye I have brought meat enough for three of you? If not, I'll fetch more for you and your wench and Snatchcrust, your parasite.

Menaechmus. What wenches? What parasites?

Messenio. Villain, I'll make thee tell me what thou meanest by all this talk!

Cylindrus. Away, jackanapes! I say nothing to thee, for I know thee not; I speak to him that I know.

Menaechmus. Out, drunken fool! Without doubt thou art out of thy wits.

Cylindrus. That you shall see by the dressing of your meat. Go, go, ye were better to go in and find somewhat to do there, whiles your dinner is making ready. I'll tell my mistress ye be here.

Menaechmus. Is he gone? Messenio, I think upon thy words already.

Messenio. Tush, mark, I pray, I'll lay forty pound here dwells some courtesan to whom this fellow belongs.

Menaechmus. But I wonder how he knows my name.

Messenio. Oh, I'll tell ye. These courtesans, as soon as any strange ship arriveth at the haven, they send a boy or a wench to inquire what they be, what their names be, whence they come, wherefore they come, etcetera. If they can by any means strike acquaintance with him or allure him to their houses, he is their own. We are here in a tickle place, master; 'tis best to be circumspect.

Menaechmus. I mislike not thy counsel, Messenio.

Messenio. Aye, but follow it, then. Soft, here comes somebody forth. Here, sirs, mariners, keep this same among you.

[*Erotium.*] Let the door stand so, away; it shall not be shut. Make haste within there, ho! Maids, look that all things be ready. Cover the board; put fire under the perfuming pans; let all things be very handsome. Where is he, that Cylindrus said stood without here? Oh, what mean you, sweetheart, that ye come not in? I trust you think yourself more welcome to this house than to your own, and great reason why you should do so. Your dinner and all things are ready, as you willed. Will ye go sit down?

Menaechmus. Whom doth this woman speak to?

Erotium. Even to you, sir; to whom else should I speak?

Menaechmus. Gentlewoman, ye are a stranger to me, and I marvel at your speeches.

Erotium. Yea, sir, but such a stranger as I acknowledge ye for my best and dearest friend, and well you have deserved it.

Menaechmus. Surely, Messenio, this woman is also mad or drunk, that useth all this kindness to me upon so small acquaintance.

Messenio. Tush, did I not tell ye right? These be but leaves which fall upon you now, in comparison of trees that will tumble on your neck shortly. I told ye, here were silver-tongued hacksters. But let me talk with her a little. Gentlewoman, what acquaintance have you with this man? Where have you seen him?

Erotium. Where he saw me, here in Epidamnum.

Messenio. In Epidamnum, who never till this day set his foot within the town?

Erotium. Go, go, flouting jack! Menaechmus, what need all this? I pray go in.

Menaechmus. She also calls me by my name.

Messenio. She smells your purse.

Menaechmus. Messenio, come hither, here take my purse. I'll know whether she aim at me or my purse ere I go.

Erotium. Will ye go in to dinner, sir?

Menaechmus. A good notion, yea, and thanks with all my heart.

Erotium. Never thank me for that which you commanded to be provided for yourself.

Menaechmus. That I commanded?

Erotium. Yea, for you and your parasite.

Menaechmus. My parasite?

Erotium. Peniculus, who came with you this morning when you brought me the cloak which you got from your wife.

Menaechmus. A cloak that I brought you, which I got from my wife?

Erotium. Tush, what needeth all this jesting? Pray leave off.

Menaechmus. Jest or earnest, this I tell ye for a truth. I never had wife, neither have I, nor never was in this place till this instant; for only thus far am I come, since I break my fast in the ship.

Erotium. What ship do ye tell me of?

Messenio. Marry, I'll tell ye, an old rotten weather-beaten ship, that we have sailed up and down in this six years. Is't not time to be going homewards, think ye?

Erotium. Come, come, Menaechmus, I pray leave this sporting and go in.

Menaechmus. Well, gentlewoman, the truth is you mistake my person; it is some other that you look for.

Erotium. Why, think ye I know ye not to be Menaechmus, the son of Moschus, and have heard ye say ye were born at Syracuse, where Agathocles did reign, then Phintia, then Liparo, and now Hiero?

Menaechmus. All this is true.

Messenio. Either she is a witch, or else she hath dwelt there and knew ye there.

Menaechmus. I'll go in with her, Messenio; I'll see further of this matter.

Messenio. Ye are cast away, then.

Menaechmus. Why so? I warrant thee, I can lose nothing; somewhat I shall gain, perhaps a good lodging during my abode here. I'll dissemble with her another while. Now, when you please, let us go in; I made strange with you because of this fellow here, lest he should tell my wife of the cloak which I gave you.

Erotium. Will ye stay any longer for your Peniculus, your parasite?

Menaechmus. Not I, I'll neither stay for him nor have him let come in, if he do come.

Erotium. All the better. But sir, will ye do one thing for me?

Menaechmus. What is that?

Erotium. To bear that cloak which you gave me to the dyer's, to have it new trimmed and altered.

Menaechmus. Yea, that will be well, so my wife shall not know it. Let me have it with me after dinner. I will but speak a word or two with this fellow, then I'll follow ye in. Ho, Messenio, come aside. Go and provide for thyself and these ship-boys in some inn; then look that, after dinner, you come hither for me.

Messenio. Ah, master, will ye be coney-catched thus willfully?

Menaechmus. Peace, foolish knave, seest thou not what a sot she is? I shall cozen her, I warrant thee.

Messenio. Ay, master.

Menaechmus. Wilt thou be gone?

Messenio. See, see, she hath him safe enough now. Thus he hath escaped a hundred pirates' hands at sea, and now one land-rover hath boarded him at first encounter. Come away, fellows.

Act 3. Scene 1.

Enter Peniculus.

[*Peniculus.*] Twenty years, I think, and more have I played the knave; yet never played I the foolish knave as I have done this morning. I follow Menaechmus, and he goes to the hall where now the sessions are holden. There, thrusting ourselves into the press of people when I was in midst of all the throng, he gave me the slip, that I could never more set eye on him, and, I dare swear, came directly to dinner. That I would he that first devised these sessions were hanged, and all that ever came of him! 'Tis such a hindrance to men that have belly-business in hand. If a man be not there at his call, they amerce him with a vengeance. Men that have nothing else to do, that do neither bid any man nor are themselves bidden to dinner, such should come to sessions; not we that have these matters to look to. If it were so, I had not thus lost my dinner this day; which I think, in my conscience, he did even purposely cozen me of. Yet I mean to go see. If I can but light upon the reversion, I may perhaps get my pennyworth. But how now? Is this Menaechmus coming away from thence, dinner done, and all dispatched? What execrable luck have I!

Enter Menaechmus the Traveler.

[*Menaechmus Traveler.*] Tush, I warrant ye, it shall be done as ye would wish. I'll have it so altered and trimmed anew, that it shall by no means be known again.

Peniculus. He carries the cloak to the dyer's, dinner done, the wine drunk up, the parasite shut out of doors. Well, let me live no longer, but I'll revenge this injurious mockery. But first I'll harken awhile what he saith.

Menaechmus. Good gods, who ever had such luck as I? Such cheer, such a dinner, such kind entertainment! And for a farewell, this cloak, which I mean shall go with me.

Peniculus. He speaks so softly, I cannot hear what he saith; I am sure he is now flouting at me for the loss of my dinner.

Menaechmus. She tells me how I gave it her, and stole it from my wife. When I perceived she was in an error, though I knew not how, I began to soothe her and to say everything as she said. Meanwhile I fared well, and that a-free-cost.

Peniculus. Well, I'll go talk with him.

Menaechmus. Who is this same that comes to me?

Peniculus. O well met, fickle-brain, false and treacherous dealer, crafty and unjust promise-breaker! How have I deserved you should so give me the slip, come before and dispatch the dinner, deal so badly with him that hath reverenced ye like a son?

Menaechmus. Good fellow, what meanest thou by these speeches? Rail not on me, unless thou intendest to receive a railer's hire.

Peniculus. I have received the injury, sure I am already.

Menaechmus. Prithee tell me, what is thy name?

Peniculus. Well, well, mock on, sir, mock on; do ye not know my name?

Menaechmus. In troth, I never saw thee in all my life, much less do I know thee.

Peniculus. Fie, awake, Menaechmus, awake, ye oversleep yourself.

Menaechmus. I am awake; I know what I say.

Peniculus. Know you not Peniculus?

Menaechmus. Peniculus or Pediculus, I know thee not.

Peniculus. Did ye filch a cloak from your wife this morning and bring it hither to Erotium?

Menaechmus. Neither have I wife, neither gave I any cloak to Erotium, neither filched I any from anybody.

Peniculus. Will ye deny that which you did in my company?

Menaechmus. Wilt thou say I have done this in thy company?

Peniculus. Will I say it? Yea, I will stand to it.

Menaechmus. Away, filthy mad drivel, away! I will talk no longer with thee.

Peniculus. Not a world of men shall stay me, but I'll go tell his wife of all the whole matter, sith he is at this point with me. I will make this same as unblest a dinner as ever he eat.

Menaechmus. It makes me wonder to see how everyone that meets me cavils thus with me. Wherefore comes forth the maid now?

Enter Ancilla, Erotium's maid.

Ancilla. Menaechmus, my mistress commends her heartily to you; and, seeing you go that way to the dyer's, she also desireth you to take this chain with you and put it to mending at the goldsmith's; she would have two or three ounces of gold more in it, and the fashion amended.

Menaechmus. Either this or anything else within my power, tell her, I am ready to accomplish.

Ancilla. Do ye know this chain, sir?

Menaechmus. Yea, I know it to be gold.

Ancilla. This is the same you once took out of your wife's casket.

Menaechmus. Who, did I?

Ancilla. Have you forgotten?

Menaechmus. I never did it.

Ancilla. Give it me again, then.

Menaechmus. Tarry; yes, I remember it; 'tis it I gave your mistress.

Ancilla. Oh, are ye advised?

Menaechmus. Where are the bracelets that I gave her likewise?

Ancilla. I never knew of any.

Menaechmus. Faith, when I gave this, I gave them too.

Ancilla. Well, sir, I'll tell her this shall be done?

Menaechmus. Ay, ay, tell her so; she shall have the cloak and this both together.

Ancilla. I pray, Menaechmus, put a little jewel for my ear to making for me; ye know I am always ready to pleasure you.

Menaechmus. I will. Give me the gold; I'll pay for the workmanship.

Ancilla. Lay out for me; I'll pay it ye again.

Menaechmus. Alas, I have none now.

Ancilla. When you have, will ye?

Menaechmus. I will. Go bid your mistress make no doubt of these; I warrant her, I'll make the best hand I can of them. Is she gone? Do not all the gods conspire to load me with good luck? Well, I see 'tis high time to get me out of these coats, lest all these matters should be lewd devices to draw me into some snare. There shall my garland lie, because if they seek me, they may think I am gone that way. I will now go see if I can find my man Messenio, that I may tell him how I have sped.

Act 4. Scene 1.

*Enter Mulier, the Wife of Menaechmus the Citizen,
and Peniculus.*

Mulier. Thinks he I will be made such a sot, and to be still his drudge, while he prowls and purloins all that I have to give his trulls?

Peniculus. Nay, hold your peace; we'll catch him in the nick. This way he came, in his garland forsooth, bearing the cloak to the dyer's. And see, I pray, where the garland lies; this way he is gone. See, see, where he comes again now without the cloak.

Mulier. What shall I now do?

Peniculus. What? That which ye ever do, bait him for life.

Mulier. Surely I think it best so.

Peniculus. Stay, we will stand aside a little; ye shall catch him unawares.

Enter Menaechmus the Citizen.

Menaechmus. It would make a man at his wit's end to see how brabbling causes are handled yonder at the court. If a poor man, never so honest, have a matter come to be scanned, there is he outfaced and overlaid with countenance. If a rich man, never so vile a wretch, come to speak, there they are all ready to favor his cause. What with facing out bad causes for the oppressors and patronizing some just actions for the wronged, the lawyers they pocket up all the gains. For mine own part, I come not away empty, though I have been kept long against my will. For taking in hand to dispatch a matter this morning for one of my acquaintance, I was no sooner entered into it, but his adversaries laid so hard unto his charge and brought such matter against him that, do what I could, I could not wind myself out till now. I am sore afraid Erotium thinks much unkindness in me that I stayed so long; yet she will not be angry, considering the gift I gave her today.

Peniculus. How think ye by that?

Mulier. I think him a most vile wretch thus to abuse me.

Menaechmus. I will hie me thither.

Mulier. Yea, go, pilferer, go with shame enough; nobody sees your lewd dealings and vile thievery.

Menaechmus. How now, wife, what ail ye? What is the matter?

Mulier. Ask ye me what's the matter? Fie upon thee!

Peniculus. Are ye not in a fit of an ague, your pulses beat so sore? To him, I say!

Menaechmus. Pray, wife, why are ye so angry with me?

Mulier. Oh, you know not?

Peniculus. He knows, but he would dissemble it.

Menaechmus. What is it?

Mulier. My cloak.

Menaechmus. Your cloak?

Mulier. My cloak, man, why do ye blush?

Peniculus. He cannot cloak his blushing. Nay, I might not go to dinner with you, do ye remember? To him, I say!

Menaechmus. Hold thy peace, Peniculus.

Peniculus. Ha, hold my peace! Look ye, he beckons on me to hold my peace.

Menaechmus. I neither beckon nor wink on him.

Mulier. Out, out, what a wretched life is this that I live!

Menaechmus. Why, what ail ye, woman?

Mulier. Are ye not ashamed to deny so confidently that which is apparent?

Menaechmus. I protest unto you before all the gods—is not this enough?—that I beckon not on him.

Peniculus. Oh, sir, this is another matter; touch him in the former cause.

Menaechmus. What former cause?

Peniculus. The cloak, man, the cloak; fetch the cloak again from the dyer's.

Menaechmus. What cloak?

Mulier. Nay, I'll say no more, with ye know nothing of your own doings.

Menaechmus. Tell me, wife, hath any of your servants abused you? Let me know.

Mulier. Tush, tush!

Menaechmus. I would not have you to be thus disquieted.

Mulier. Tush, tush!

Menaechmus. You are fallen out with some of your friends.

Mulier. Tush, tush!

Menaechmus. Sure I am I have not offended you.

Mulier. No, you have dealt very honestly.

Menaechmus. Indeed, wife, I have deserved none of these words. Tell me, are ye not well?

Peniculus. What, shall he flatter ye now?

Menaechmus. I speak not to thee, knave. Good wife, come hither.

Mulier. Away, away, keep your hands off!

Peniculus. So, bid me to dinner with you again; then slip away from me; when you have done, come forth bravely in your garland to flout me. Alas, you knew not me even now.

Menaechmus. Why, ass, I neither have yet dined, nor came I there since we were there together.

Peniculus. Who ever heard one so impudent? Did ye not meet me here even now, and would make me believe I was mad, and said ye were a stranger and ye knew me not?

Menaechmus. Of a truth, since we went together to the sessions hall, I never returned till this very instant as you two met me.

Peniculus. Go to, go to, I know ye well enough. Did ye think I would not cry quittance with you? Yes, faith, I have told your wife all.

Menaechmus. What hast thou told her?

Peniculus. I cannot tell, ask her.

Menaechmus. Tell me, wife, what hath he told ye of me? Tell me, I say, what was it?

Mulier. As though you knew not! My cloak is stolen from me.

Menaechmus. Is your cloak stolen from ye?

Mulier. Do ye ask me?

Menaechmus. If I knew, I would not ask.

Peniculus. O crafty companion, how he would shift the matter! Come, come, deny it not; I tell ye, I have bewrayed all.

Menaechmus. What hast thou bewrayed?

Mulier. Seeing ye will yield to nothing be it never so manifest. Hear me, and ye shall know in few words both the cause of my grief and what he hath told me. I say, my cloak is stolen from me.

Menaechmus. My cloak is stolen from me?

Peniculus. Look how he cavils; she saith it is stolen from her.

Menaechmus. I have nothing to say to thee. I say, wife, tell me.

Mulier. I tell ye, my cloak is stolen out of my house.

Menaechmus. Who stole it?

Mulier. He knows best that carried it away.

Menaechmus. Who was that?

Mulier. Menaechmus.

Menaechmus. 'Twas very ill done of him. What Menaechmus was that?

Mulier. You.

Menaechmus. I? Who will say so?

Mulier. I will.

Peniculus. And I; and that you gave it to Erotium.

Menaechmus. I gave it?

Mulier. You.

Peniculus. You, you, you! Shall we fetch a kennel of beagles that may cry nothing but "you," "you," "you," "you"? For we are weary of it.

Menaechmus. Hear me one word, wife. I protest unto you by all the gods, I gave it her not; indeed, I lent it her to use a while.

Mulier. Faith, sir, I never give nor lend you apparel out of doors; methinks ye might let me dispose of mine own garments, as you do of yours. I pray then fetch it me home again.

Menaechmus. You shall have it again without fail.

Mulier. 'Tis best for you that I have; otherwise think not to roost within these doors again.

Peniculus. Hark ye, what say ye to me now for bringing these matters to your knowledge?

Mulier. I say when thou hast anything stolen from thee, come to me and I will help thee to seek it. And so farewell.

Peniculus. God-a-mercy for nothing, that can never be; for I have nothing in the world worth the stealing. So now with husband and wife and all, I am clean out of favor. A mischief on ye all!   *Exit.*

Menaechmus. My wife thinks she is notably revenged on me, now she shuts me out of doors, as though I had not a better place to be welcome to. If she shut me out, I know who will shut me in. Now will I entreat Erotium to let me have the cloak again to stop my wife's mouth withal, and then will I provide a better for her. Ho, who is within there? Somebody tell Erotium I must speak with her.

Enter Erotium.

Erotium. Who calls?

Menaechmus. Your friend, more than his own.

Erotium. O Menaechmus, why stand ye here? Pray come in.

Menaechmus. Tarry, I must speak with ye here.

Erotium. Say your mind.

Menaechmus. Wot ye what? My wife knows all the matter now, and my coming is to request you that I may have again the cloak which I brought you, that so I may appease her; and I promise you, I'll give you another worth two of it.

Erotium. Why, I gave it you to carry to your dyer's and my chain likewise, to have it altered.

Menaechmus. Gave me the cloak and your chain? In truth, I never saw ye since I left it here with you and so went to the sessions, from whence I am but now returned.

Erotium. Ah, then, sir, I see you wrought a device to defraud me of them both. Did I therefore put ye in trust? Well, well!

Menaechmus. To defraud ye? No, but I say my wife hath intelligence of the matter.

Erotium. Why, sir, I asked them not; ye brought them me of your own free motion. Now ye require them again, take them, make fops of them. You and your wife together, think ye I esteem them or you either? Go, come to me again when I send for you.

Menaechmus. What, so angry with me, sweet Erotium? Stay, I pray, stay.

Erotium. Stay? Faith, sir, no. Think ye I will stay at your request?

Menaechmus. What, gone in chafing, and clapped to the doors? Now I am every way shut out for a very bench-whistler; neither shall I have entertainment here nor at home. I were best go try some other friends, and ask counsel what to do.

Act 5. Scene 1.

Enter Menaechmus the Traveler, Mulier.

[*Menaechmus Traveler.*] Most foolishly was I overseen in giving my purse and money to Messenio, whom I can nowhere find. I fear he is fallen into some lewd company.

Mulier. I marvel that my husband comes not yet. But see where he is now, and brings my cloak with him.

Menaechmus. I muse where the knave should be.

Mulier. I will go ring a peal through both his ears for this his dishonest behavior. Oh, sir, ye are welcome home with your thievery on your shoulders. Are ye not ashamed to let all the world see and speak of your lewdness?

Menaechmus. How now? What lacks this woman?

Mulier. Impudent beast, stand ye to question about it? For shame, hold thy peace.

Menaechmus. What offense have I done, woman, that I should not speak to you?

Mulier. Asketh thou what offense? O shameless boldness!

Menaechmus. Good woman, did ye never hear why the Grecians termed Hecuba to be a bitch?

Mulier. Never.

Menaechmus. Because she did as you do now: on whomsoever she met withal she railed, and therefore well deserved that dogged name.

Mulier. These foul abuses and contumelies I can never endure; nay, rather will I live a widow's life to my dying day.

Menaechmus. What care I whether thou livest as a widow or as a wife? This passeth, that I meet with none but thus they vex me with strange speeches.

Mulier. What strange speeches? I say I will surely live a widow's life rather than suffer thy vile dealings.

Menaechmus. Prithee, for my part, live a widow till the world's end, if thou wilt.

Mulier. Even now thou deniedst that thou stolest it from me, and now thou bringest it home openly in my sight. Art not ashamed?

Menaechmus. Woman, you are greatly to blame to charge me with stealing of this cloak, which this day another gave me to carry to be trimmed.

Mulier. Well, I will first complain to my father. Ho, boy, who is within there? Decio, go run quickly to my father; desire him of all love to come over quickly to my house. I'll tell him first of your pranks. I hope he will not see me thus handled.

Menaechmus. What, a God's name, meaneth this mad-woman thus to vex me?

Mulier. I am mad because I tell ye of your vile actions and lewd pilfering away of my apparel and my jewels to carry to your filthy drabs.

Menaechmus. For whom this woman taketh me I know not; I know her as much as I know Hercules' wife's father.

Mulier. Do ye not know me? That's well, I hope ye know my father. Here he comes. Look, do ye know him?

Menaechmus. As much as I know Calchas of Troy. Even him and thee I know both alike.

Mulier. Dost know neither of us both, me nor my father?

Menaechmus. Faith, nor thy grandfather neither.

Mulier. This is like the rest of your behavior.

Enter Senex.

[*Senex.*] Though bearing so great a burden as old age, I can make no great haste; yet as I can I will go to my daughter, who I know hath some earnest business with me, that she sends in such haste, not telling the cause why I should come. But I durst lay a wager, I can guess near the matter: I suppose it is some brabble between her husband and her. These

young women that bring great dowries to their husbands are
so masterful and obstinate that they will have their own
wills in everything, and make men servants to their weak
affections. And young men too, I must needs say, be naught
nowadays. Well I'll go see; but yonder, methinks, stands
my daughter and her husband too. Oh, 'tis even as I
guessed.

Mulier. Father, ye are welcome.

Senex. How now, daughter? What, is all well? Why is your
husband so sad? Have ye been chiding? Tell me, which of
you is in the fault?

Mulier. First, father, know that I have not any way misbehaved
myself; but the truth is, I can by no means endure this bad
man, to die for it; and therefore desire you to take me home
to you again.

Senex. What is the matter?

Mulier. He makes me a stale and a laughingstock to all the
world.

Senex. Who doth?

Mulier. This good husband here, to whom you married me.

Senex. See, see, how oft have I warned you of falling out with
your husband!

Mulier. I cannot avoid it, if he doth so foully abuse me.

Senex. I always told ye, you must bear with him; ye must let
him alone; ye must not watch him nor dog him nor meddle
with his courses in any sort.

Mulier. He haunts naughty harlots under my nose.

Senex. He is the wiser, because he cannot be quiet at home.

Mulier. There he feasts and banquets, and spends and spoils.

Senex. Would ye have your husband serve ye as your drudge?
Ye will not let him make merry nor entertain his friends
at home.

Mulier. Father, will ye take his part in these abuses, and forsake me?

Senex. Not so, daughter; but if I see cause, I will as well tell him of his duty.

Menaechmus. I would I were gone from this prating father and daughter.

Senex. Hitherto I see not but he keeps ye well; ye want nothing, apparel, money, servants, meat, drink, all things necessary. I fear there is fault in you.

Mulier. But he filcheth away my apparel and my jewels to give to his trulls.

Senex. If he doth so, 'tis very ill done; if not, you do ill to say so.

Mulier. You may believe me, father; for there you may see my cloak which now he hath fetched home again, and my chain which he stole from me.

Senex. Now will I go talk with him to know the truth. Tell me, Menaechmus, how is it that I hear such disorder in your life? Why are ye so sad, man? Wherein hath your wife offended you?

Menaechmus. Old man—what to call ye I know not—by high Jove and by all the gods I swear unto you, whatsoever this woman here accuseth me to have stolen from her, it is utterly false and untrue; and if I ever set foot within her doors, I wish the greatest misery in the world to light upon me.

Senex. Why, fond man, art thou mad to deny that thou ever setst foot within thine own house where thou dwellest?

Menaechmus. Do I dwell in that house?

Senex. Dost thou deny it?

Menaechmus. I do.

Senex. Hark ye, daughter, are ye removed out of your house?

Mulier. Father, he useth you as he doth me, this life I have with him.

Senex. Menaechmus, I pray leave this fondness; ye jest too perversely with your friends.

Menaechmus. Good old father, what, I pray, have you to do with me? Or why should this woman thus trouble me, with whom I have no dealings in the world?

Mulier. Father, mark, I pray, how his eyes sparkle! They roll in his head; his color goes and comes; he looks wildly. See, see!

Menaechmus. What! they say now I am mad; the best way for me is to feign myself mad indeed, so I shall be rid of them.

Mulier. Look how he stares about! Now he gapes.

Senex. Come away, daughter, come from him.

Menaechmus. Bacchus, Apollo, Phoebus, do ye call me to come hunt in the woods with you? I see, I hear, I come, I fly, but I cannot get out of these fields. Here is an old mastiff bitch stands barking at me, and by her stands an old goat that bears false witness against many a poor man.

Senex. Out upon him, Bedlam fool!

Menaechmus. Hark, Apollo commands me that I should rend out her eyes with a burning lamp!

Mulier. O father, he threatens to pull out mine eyes!

Menaechmus. Good gods, these folk say I am mad, and doubtless they are mad themselves.

Senex. Daughter!

Mulier. Here, father, what shall we do?

Senex. What if I fetch my folks hither, and have him carried in before he do any harm?

Menaechmus. How now! They will carry me in, if I look not to myself. I were best to scare them better yet. Dost thou bid me, Phoebus, to tear this dog in pieces with my nails? If I lay hold on him, I will do thy commandment.

Senex. Get thee into thy house, daughter; away quickly!

Menaechmus. She is gone. Yea, Apollo, I will sacrifice this old beast unto thee; and if thou commandest me, I will cut his throat with that dagger that hangs at his girdle.

Senex. Come not near me, sirrah!

Menaechmus. Yea, I will quarter him, and pull all the bones out of his flesh; then will I barrel up his bowels.

Senex. Sure, I am sore afraid he will do some hurt.

Menaechmus. Many things thou commandest me, Apollo. Wouldst thou have me harness up these wild horses, and then climb up into the chariot, and so override this old stinking toothless lion? So now I am in the chariot, and I have hold on the reins; here is my whip. Hait! Come ye wild jades, make a hideous noise with your stamping; hait, I say, will ye not go?

Senex. What! Doth he threaten me with his horses?

Menaechmus. Hark, now Apollo bids me ride over him that stands there and kill him. How now? Who pulls me down from my chariot by the hairs of my head? Oh, shall I not fulfill Apollo's commandment?

Senex. See, see, what a sharp disease this is, and how well he was even now! I will fetch a physician straight, before he grow too far into this rage. *Exit.*

Menaechmus. Are they both gone now? I'll then hie me away to my ship; 'tis time to be gone from hence. *Exit.*

Enter Senex and Medicus.

Senex. My loins ache with sitting, and mine eyes with looking, while I stay for yonder lazy physician. See now where the creeping draw-latch comes.

Medicus. What disease hath he said you? Is it a lethargy or a lunacy or melancholy or dropsy?

Senex. Wherefore, I pray, do I bring you but that you should tell me what it is, and cure him of it?

Medicus. Fie, make no question of that; I'll cure him, I warrant ye. Oh, here he comes; stay, let us mark what he doth.

Enter Menaechmus the Citizen.

Menaechmus. Never in my life had I more overthwart fortune
  in one day, and all by the villainy of this false knave, the
  parasite, my Ulysses that works such mischiefs against me,
  his king. But let me live no longer, but I'll be revenged upon
  the life of him. His life? Nay, 'tis my life; for he lives by my
  meat and drink. I'll utterly withdraw the slave's life from
  him. And Erotium she showeth plainly what she is, who,
  because I require the cloak again to carry to my wife, saith
  I gave it her and flatly falls out with me. How unfortunate
  am I!

Senex. Do ye hear him?

Medicus. He complains of his fortune.

Senex. Go to him.

Medicus. Menaechmus, how do ye, man? Why keep you not
  your cloak over your arm? It is very hurtful to your disease.
  Keep ye warm, I pray.

Menaechmus. Why, hang thyself, what carest thou?

Medicus. Sir, can you smell anything?

Menaechmus. I smell a prating dolt of thee.

Medicus. Oh, I will have your head throughly purged. Pray tell
  me, Menaechmus, what use you to drink? White wine or
  claret?

Menaechmus. What the devil carest thou?

Senex. Look, his fit now begins.

Menaechmus. Why dost not as well ask me whether I eat
  bread, or cheese, or beef, or porridge, or birds that bear
  feathers, or fishes that have fins?

Senex. See, what idle talk he falleth into!

Medicus. Tarry, I will ask him further. Menaechmus, tell me,
  be not your eyes heavy and dull sometimes?

Menaechmus. What dost think I am, an owl?

Medicus. Do not your guts gripe ye and croak in your belly?

Menaechmus. When I am hungry they do, else not.

Medicus. He speaks not like a madman in that. Sleep ye soundly all night?

Menaechmus. When I have paid my debts I do. The mischief light on thee, with all thy frivolous questions!

Medicus. Oh, now he rageth upon those words; take heed.

Senex. Oh, this is nothing to the rage he was in even now. He called his wife bitch, and all to naught.

Menaechmus. Did I?

Senex. Thou didst, mad fellow, and threatened to ride over me here with a chariot and horses, and to kill me, and tear me to pieces. This thou didst; I know what I say.

Menaechmus. I say thou stolest Jupiter's crown from his head and thou wert whipped through the town for it, and that thou hast killed thy father and beaten thy mother. Do ye think I am so mad that I cannot devise as notable lies of you as you do of me?

Senex. Master doctor, pray heartily make speed to cure him; see ye not how mad he waxeth?

Medicus. I'll tell ye, he shall be brought over to my house, and there will I cure him.

Senex. Is that best?

Medicus. What else? There I can order him as I list.

Senex. Well, it shall be so.

Medicus. Oh sir, I will make ye take [s]neezing powder this twenty days.

Menaechmus. I'll beat ye first with a bastinado this thirty days.

Medicus. Fetch men to carry him to my house.

Senex. How many will serve the turn?

Medicus. Being no madder than he is now, four will serve.

Senex. I'll fetch them. Stay you with him, master doctor.

Medicus. No, by my faith, I'll go home to make ready all things needful. Let your men bring him thither.

Senex. I go.   *Exeunt.*

Menaechmus. Are they both gone? Good gods, what meaneth this? These men say I am mad, who without doubt are mad themselves. I stir not, I fight not, I am not sick. I speak to them, I know them. Well, what were I now best to do? I would go home, but my wife shuts me forth a-doors. Erotium is as far out with me too. Even here I will rest me till the evening; I hope by that time they will take pity on me.

Enter Messenio, the Traveler's servant.

[*Messenio.*] The proof of a good servant is to regard his master's business as well in his absence as in his presence; and I think him a very fool that is not careful as well for his ribs and shoulders as for his belly and throat. When I think upon the rewards of a sluggard, I am ever pricked with a careful regard of my back and shoulders; for, in truth, I have no fancy to these blows, as many a one hath. Methinks it is no pleasure to a man to be basted with a rope's end two or three hours together. I have provided yonder in the town for all our mariners, and safely bestowed all my master's trunks and fardels; and am now coming to see if he be yet got forth of this dangerous gulf, where I fear me [he] is over-plunged—pray God he be not overwhelmed and past help ere I come!

Enter Senex, with four Lorarii [porters].

[*Senex.*] Before gods and men, I charge and command you, sirs, to execute with great care that which I appoint you. If ye love the safety of your own ribs and shoulders, then go take me up my son-in-law, lay all hands upon him. Why stand ye still? What do ye doubt? I say, care not for his threatenings, nor for any of his words. Take him up and bring him to the physician's house. I will go thither before.
                                                        Exit.

Menaechmus. What news? How now, masters! What will ye
do with me? Why do ye thus beset me? Whither carry ye
me? Help, help, neighbors, friends, citizens!

Messenio. O Jupiter, what do I see? My master abused by a
company of varlets.

Menaechmus. Is there no good man will help me?

Messenio. Help ye, master? Yes, the villains shall have my life
before they shall thus wrong ye. 'Tis more fit I should be
killed than you thus handled. Pull out that rascal's eye that
holds ye about the neck there! I'll clout these peasants. Out,
ye rogue! Let go, ye varlet!

Menaechmus. I have hold of this villain's eye.

Messenio. Pull it out and let the place appear in his head!
Away, ye cutthroat thieves, ye murderers!

Lorarii Omnes. O, o! Aye, aye!   [*Cry pitifully.*]

Messenio. Away, get ye hence, ye mongrels, ye dogs! Will ye
be gone? Thou rascal behind there, I'll give thee somewhat
more; take that! It was time to come, master; you had been
in good case if I had not been here now! I told you what
would come of it.

Menaechmus. Now, as the gods love me, my good friend, I
thank thee. Thou hast done that for me which I shall never
be able to requite.

Messenio. I'll tell ye how, sir: give me my freedom.

Menaechmus. Should I give it thee?

Messenio. Seeing you cannot requite my good turn.

Menaechmus. Thou art deceived, man.

Messenio. Wherein?

Menaechmus. On mine honesty, I am none of thy master; I had
never yet any servant would do so much for me.

Messenio. Why, then bid me be free; will you?

Menaechmus. Yea, surely, be free, for my part.

Messenio. O sweetly spoken! Thanks, my good master.

Servus alius. Messenio, we are all glad of your good fortune.

Messenio. O master, I'll call ye master still; I pray, use me in any service as ye did before; I'll dwell with you still, and when ye go home I'll wait upon you.

Menaechmus. Nay, nay, it shall not need.

Messenio. I'll go straight to the inn and deliver up my accounts and all your stuff. Your purse is locked up safely sealed in the casket, as you gave it me. I will go fetch it to you.

Menaechmus. Do, fetch it.

Messenio. I will.

Menaechmus. I was never thus perplexed. Some deny me to be him that I am and shut me out of their doors. This fellow saith he is my bondman, and of me he begs his freedom. He will fetch my purse and money. Well, if he bring it, I will receive it, and let him free. I would he would so go his way. My old father-in-law and the doctor say I am mad. Who ever saw such strange demeanors? Well, though Erotium be never so angry, yet once again I'll go see if by entreaty I can get the cloak on her to carry to my wife. *Exit.*

Enter Menaechmus the Traveler and Messenio.

Menaechmus. Impudent knave, wilt thou say that I ever saw thee since I sent thee away today and bade thee come for me after dinner?

Messenio. Ye make me stark mad. I took ye away and rescued ye from four great big-boned villains, that were carrying ye away even here in this place. Here they had ye up; and cried, "Help, help!" I came running to you; you and I together beat them away by main force. Then, for thy good turn and faithful service, ye gave me my freedom. I told ye I would go fetch your casket; now, in the mean time, you ran some other way to get before me; and so you deny it all again.

Menaechmus. I gave thee thy freedom?

Messenio. You did.

Menaechmus. When I give thee thy freedom, I'll be a bondman myself. Go thy ways.

Enter Menaechmus the Citizen.

[*Menaechmus Citizen.*] Forsworn queans, swear till your hearts ache and your eyes fall out, ye shall never make me believe that I carried hence either cloak or chain.

Messenio. O heavens, master, what do I see?

Menaechmus Traveler. What?

Messenio. Your ghost.

Menaechmus Traveler. What ghost?

Messenio. Your image, as like you as can be possible.

Menaechmus Traveler. Surely not much unlike me as I think.

Menaechmus Citizen. O my good friend and helper, well me! Thanks for thy late good help.

Messenio. Sir, may I crave to know your name?

Menaechmus Citizen. I were to blame if I should not tell thee anything; my name is Menaechmus.

Menaechmus Traveler. Nay, my friend, that is my name.

Menaechmus Citizen. I am of Syracuse in Sicilia.

Menaechmus Traveler. So am I.

Messenio. Are you a Syracusan?

Menaechmus Citizen. I am.

Messenio. O ho, I know ye! This is my master; I thought he there had been my master, and was proffering my service to him; pray pardon me, sir, if I said anything I should not.

Menaechmus Traveler. Why, doting patch, didst thou not come with me this morning from the ship?

Messenio. My faith, he says true, this is my master; you may go look ye a man. God save ye, master. You, sir, farewell. This is Menaechmus.

Menaechmus Citizen. I say that I am Menaechmus.

Messenio. What a jest is this? Are you Menaechmus?

Menaechmus Citizen. Even Menaechmus, the son of Moschus.

Menaechmus Traveler. My father's son?

Menaechmus Citizen. Friend, I go about neither to take your father nor your country from you.

Messenio. O immortal gods, let it fall out as I hope, and for my life these are two twins; all things agree so jump together. I will speak to my master. Menaechmus?

Both. What wilt thou?

Messenio. I call ye not both; but which of you came with me from the ship?

Menaechmus Citizen. Not I.

Menaechmus Traveler. I did.

Messenio. Then I call you. Come hither.

Menaechmus Traveler. What's the matter?

Messenio. This same is either some notable cozening juggler or else it is your brother whom we seek. I never saw one man so like another; water to water, nor milk to milk, is not liker than he is to you.

Menaechmus Traveler. Indeed, I think thou sayest true. Find it that he is my brother, and I here promise thee thy freedom.

Messenio. Well, let me about it. Hear ye, sir, ye say your name is Menaechmus?

Menaechmus Citizen. I do.

Messenio. So is this man's. You are of Syracuse?

Menaechmus Citizen. True.

Messenio. So is he. Moschus was your father?

Menaechmus Citizen. He was.

Messenio. So was his. What will you say if I find that ye are brethren and twins?

Menaechmus Citizen. I would think it happy news.

Messenio. Nay, stay, masters both, I mean to have the honor of this exploit. Answer me: your name is Menaechmus?

Menaechmus Citizen. Yea.

Messenio. And yours?

Menaechmus Traveler. And mine.

Messenio. You are of Syracuse?

Menaechmus Citizen. I am.

Menaechmus Traveler. And I.

Messenio. Well, this goeth right thus far. What is the farthest thing that you remember there?

Menaechmus Citizen. How I went with my father to Tarentum, to a great mart, and there in the press I was stolen from him.

Menaechmus Traveler. O Jupiter!

Messenio. Peace, what exclaiming is this? How old were ye then?

Menaechmus Citizen. About seven year old; for even then I shed teeth; and since that time, I never heard of any of my kindred.

Messenio. Had ye never a brother?

Menaechmus Citizen. Yes, as I remember, I heard them say we were two twins.

Menaechmus Traveler. O fortune!

Messenio. Tush, can ye not be quiet? Were ye both of one name?

Menaechmus Citizen. Nay, as I think, they called my brother Sosicles.

Menaechmus Traveler. It is he; what need farther proof? O brother, brother, let me embrace thee!

Menaechmus Citizen. Sir, if this be true, I am wonderfully glad; but how is it, that ye are called Menaechmus?

Menaechmus Traveler. When it was told us that you and our father were both dead, our grandsire, in memory of my father's name, changed mine to Menaechmus.

Menaechmus Citizen. 'Tis very like he would do so, indeed. But let me ask ye one question more: what was our mother's name?

Menaechmus Traveler. Teuximarcha.

Menaechmus Citizen. Brother, the most welcome man to me, that the world holdeth.

Menaechmus Traveler. I joy, and ten thousand joys the more, having taken so long travail and huge pains to seek you.

Messenio. See now, how all this matter comes about. This it was, that the gentlewoman had ye in to dinner, thinking it had been he.

Menaechmus Citizen. True it is. I willed a dinner to be provided for me here this morning, and I also brought hither closely a cloak of my wife's, and gave it to this woman.

Menaechmus Traveler. Is not this the same, brother?

Menaechmus Citizen. How came you by this?

Menaechmus Traveler. This woman met me, had me in to dinner, entertained me most kindly, and gave me this cloak and this chain.

Menaechmus Citizen. Indeed, she took ye for me; and I believe I have been as strangely handled by occasion of your coming.

Messenio. You shall have time enough to laugh at all these matters hereafter. Do ye remember, master, what ye promised me?

Menaechmus Citizen. Brother, I will entreat you to perform your promise to Messenio; he is worthy of it.

Menaechmus Traveler. I am content.

Messenio. "Io triumphe!"

Menaechmus Traveler. Brother, will ye now go with me to Syracuse?

Menaechmus Citizen. So soon as I can sell away such goods as I possess here in Epidamnum, I will go with you.

Menaechmus Traveler. Thanks, my good brother.

Menaechmus Citizen. Messenio, play thou the crier for me, and make a proclamation.

Messenio. A fit office. Come on. Oyez! What day shall your sale be?

Menaechmus Citizen. This day se'nnight.

Messenio. All men, women, and children in Epidamnum or elsewhere that will repair to Menaechmus' house this day se'nnight shall there find all manner of things to sell: servants, household stuff, house, ground, and all, so they bring ready money. Will ye sell your wife too, sir?

Menaechmus Citizen. Yea, but I think nobody will bid money for her.

Messenio. Thus, gentlemen, we take our leaves; and if we have pleased, we require a *plaudite*.

FINIS

Commentaries

AUGUST WILHELM SCHLEGEL

From Lectures on Dramatic Art and Literature

The Comedy of Errors is the subject of the *Menaechmi* of Plautus, entirely recast and enriched with new developments: of all the works of Shakespeare this is the only example of imitation of, or borrowing from, the ancients. To the two twin brothers of the same name are added two slaves, also twins, impossible to be distinguished from each other, and of the same name. The improbability becomes by this means doubled: but when once we have lent ourselves to the first, which certainly borders on the incredible, we shall not perhaps be disposed to cavil at the second; and if the spectator is to be entertained by mere perplexities they cannot be too varied. In such pieces we must, to give the senses at least an appearance of truth, always presuppose that the parts by which the misunderstandings are occasioned are played with masks, and this the poet no doubt observed. I cannot acquiesce in the censure that the discovery is too long deferred: so long as

From *Lectures on Dramatic Art and Literature* by August Wilhelm Schlegel, translated by John Black (London: George Bell & Sons, 1889). Schlegel's lectures, delivered at Vienna in 1808, and amplified in the German text of 1811, were translated by Black in 1815. The translation underwent slight revision in subsequent printings.

novelty and interest are possessed by the perplexing incidents there is no need to be in dread of wearisomeness.
And this is really the case here: matters are carried so far
that one of the two brothers is first arrested for debt, then
confined as a lunatic, and the other is forced to take refuge
in a sanctuary to save his life. In a subject of this description it is impossible to steer clear of all sorts of low circumstances, abusive language, and blows; Shakespeare has
however endeavored to ennoble it in every possible way.
A couple of scenes, dedicated to jealousy and love, inter-
rupt the course of perplexities which are solely occasioned
by the illusion of the external senses. A greater solemnity
is given to the discovery, from the Prince presiding, and
from the reunion of the long-separated parents of the twins
who are still alive. The exposition, by which the spectators
are previously instructed while the characters themselves
are still involved in ignorance, and which Plautus artlessly
conveys in a prologue, is here masterly introduced in an
affecting narrative by the father. In short, this is perhaps
the best of all written or possible *Menaechmi;* and if the
piece be inferior in worth to other pieces of Shakespeare,
it is merely because nothing more could be made of the
materials.

SAMUEL TAYLOR COLERIDGE

From Shakespearean Criticism

The myriad-minded man, our, and all men's, Shakespeare, has in this piece presented us with a legitimate farce in exactest consonance with the philosophical principles and character of farce, as distinguished from comedy and from entertainments. A proper farce is mainly distinguished from comedy by the license allowed, and even required, in the fable, in order to produce strange and laughable situations. The story need not be probable, it is enough that it is possible. A comedy would scarcely allow even the two Antipholuses; because, although there have been instances of almost indistinguishable likeness in two persons, yet these are mere individual accidents, *casus ludentis naturae,* and the *verum* will not excuse the *inverisimile.* But farce dares add the two Dromios, and is justified in so doing by the laws of its end and constitution. In a word, farces commence in a postulate, which must be granted.

* * *

. . . remarkable as being the only specimen of *poetical farce* in our language, that is, intentionally such. . . .

From *Shakespearean Criticism* by Samuel Taylor Coleridge (2nd ed., edited by Thomas Middleton Raysor. 2 vols. New York: E. P. Dutton and Company, Inc., 1960; London: J. M. Dent & Sons, Ltd., 1961).

WILLIAM HAZLITT

From Characters of Shakespear's Plays

This comedy is taken very much from the *Menaechmi* of Plautus, and is not an improvement on it. Shakespear appears to have bestowed no great pains on it, and there are but a few passages which bear the decided stamp of his genius. He seems to have relied on his author, and on the interest arising out of the intricacy of the plot. The curiosity excited is certainly very considerable, though not of the most pleasing kind. We are teased as with a riddle, which notwithstanding we try to solve. In reading the play, from the sameness of the names of the two Antipholuses and the two Dromios, as well from their being constantly taken for each other by those who see them, it is difficult, without a painful effort of attention, to keep the characters distinct in the mind. And again, on the stage, either the complete similarity of their persons and dress must produce the same perplexity whenever they first enter, or the identity of appearance which the story supposes, will be destroyed. We still, however, having a clue to the difficulty, can tell which is which, merely from the practical contradictions which arise, as soon as the different parties begin to speak; and we are indemnified for the perplexity and blunders into which we are thrown by seeing others thrown into greater and almost inextricable ones.—This play (among other considerations) leads us not to feel much regret that Shakespear was not what is called a classical scholar. We do not think his *forte* would ever have lain in imitating or improving on what others

From *Characters of Shakespear's Plays* by William Hazlitt (2nd ed. London: Taylor & Hessey, 1818).

invented, so much as in inventing for himself, and per-fecting what he invented—not perhaps by the omission of faults, but by the addition of the highest excellencies. His own genius was strong enough to bear him up, and he soared longest and best on unborrowed plumes.

ETIENNE SOURIAU

From The Two Hundred Thousand Dramatic Situations

You may say that the comedy of errors—the mixed-up Menaechmuses in Plautus; Dromio of Ephesus taken for Dromio of Syracuse in Shakespeare; Zerbinetta revealed as the daughter of Argante in *The Tricks of Scapin;* Valère thinking he has secretly married Lucile while marrying Ascagne, actually a girl disguised as a boy, in *The Loving Spite;* Silvia dressed as Lisette in *The Game of Love and Chance;* the confusions under the chestnut trees in *The Marriage of Figaro;* or Gennaro unaware that Lucrezia Borgia is his mother—how worn-out it all seems! Stratagems of comedy or melodrama, not serious dramaturgy!

I should answer: first remember *Oedipus the King*. The gradual removal of the veils that conceal the true situation, actually present from the beginning, constitutes the very action that brings about all the successive theatrical situations in fatal and terrible sequence: Oedipus, king of a people which suffers without knowing why; Oedipus knowing that some criminal is responsible for this misfortune, yet unaware of his identity and seeking him out; Oedipus identified as that criminal without knowing why; Oedipus aware that he is a foundling, etc., etc. . . .

One of the greatest practical and technical difficulties in the artistic handling of these elements is, of course, that the author, who is in on the secret, and the spectator, who sees and hears whatever is shown to him, must, on the one

From *Les Deux Cent Mille Situations Dramatiques* by Etienne Souriau (Paris: Librairie Ernest Flammarion, 1950). Reprinted by permission of Librairie Ernest Flammarion. Translated by the editor.

hand, arrange and, on the other, experience that artistic treatment of ignorances and errors, through a series of imponderables or clever calculations. But these are, or should be, essentially inherent in the situation, as it is lived through by the characters.

How can it be doubted that such a "comedy of errors" or of ignorances is inherent in the internal organization of the life of the human microcosm as presented to us? Theatrical effect, convention, melodramatic device? Certainly not. In any case, who will deny that the condition of human beings, morally speaking, leads them to grope among the shadows and to play blindman's buff with their souls. The danger, in the theater, is to show those souls as too lucid and too sure of themselves, of what they are doing, and of their situation, rather than to show them as too wild and uncertain, proceeding by trials and errors. It is for the demiurge of this little world to be certain of what he is doing and of where he is going or taking us—and not for those who are going along.

BERTRAND EVANS

From Shakespeare's Comedies

To describe the creation, maintenance, and exploitation of the gaps that separate the participants' awarenesses and ours in *The Comedy of Errors* is almost to describe the entire play, for in his first comedy Shakespeare came nearer than ever afterward to placing his whole reliance upon an arrangement of discrepant awarenesses. This comedy has no Falstaff, Toby Belch, Dogberry—not even an Armado. Comic effect emerges not once from character as such. If the Dromios prove laughable, it is not in themselves but in the incompleteness of their vision of situation that they prove so. Language, which regularly afterwards is squeezed for its comic potential, here serves chiefly to keep us advised of situation. Here are no malapropisms, dialectal oddities, few quirks and twists of phrase: the very pun, hereafter ubiquitous, is scanted. With neither character nor language making notable comic contribution, then, the great resource of laughter is the exploitable gulf spread between the participants' understanding and ours.

This gap is held open from beginning to end: it is available for exploitation and is exploited during ten of the eleven scenes. In the course of the action we hold an advantage in awareness over fifteen of the sixteen persons—Aemilia alone never being exhibited on a level beneath ours. Not until *The Tempest* (in the comedies) did Shakespeare again hold one gap open so long for exploitation; never again did he place so great a responsibility on a single gap.

From *Shakespeare's Comedies* by Bertrand Evans (Oxford: The Clarendon Press, 1960). Reprinted by permission of The Clarendon Press.

As in most later plays, Shakespeare here opens the gap—that is to say, raises our vantage point above that of the participants—as soon as possible. After forty lines in Scene 2 (at the entrance of Dromio of Ephesus) the facts of the enveloping situation are fixed in our minds: a father, facing death unless he can raise money by sunset, his twin sons, long separated, and their twin servants are all in the city of Ephesus. But the key fact that is quickly revealed to us is denied them: they are ignorant that all are in the same city. On our side, thus, is complete vision, and on theirs none at all. This condition, kept essentially unchanged, is made to yield virtually all of the comic effects during ten scenes.

In that the secret committed to our keeping is both simple and single, *The Comedy of Errors* is unique among the comedies. In later ones our awareness is packed, often even burdened, with multiple, complex, interrelated secrets, and the many circles of individual participants' visions, though they cross and recross one another, do not wholly coincide. In *Twelfth Night,* thus, certain but not all facts of the intricate situation are known to both Sir Toby and Sir Andrew, and some are known to Sir Toby but not to Sir Andrew; a few, but only a few are shared by Viola and Sir Toby; some are known to Viola alone of the participants; and one fact of enormous significance, known to us alone, is hidden even from Viola. In *The Comedy of Errors* only a single great secret exists, which is ours alone; the participants, therefore, stand all on one footing of ignorance. Shakespeare never again used so simple an arrangement of the awarenesses.

The enveloping situation which makes both action and comic effects possible is itself static; it remains unchanged, until the last 100 lines, by the bustling incidents that fill up the scenes between beginning and end. Between the point midway in the second scene, at which all relevant facts have been put into our minds, and the ending, we neither need nor get additional information in order to hold our one great advantage over the participants. The many expository devices by which Shakespeare was later to sustain the advantage given us in the initial exposition—as soliloquies and asides strategically placed, scene introductions which shed special light on following action, confidential dialogue of persons perpetrating some "practice" on their unwitting fellows—are here absent because they would be superfluous. For whereas in later comedies situations emerge, swell, and multiply, generating new ones to replace the old, so that repeated injections of fact are needed to keep our vision clearer and wider than the participants', in *The Comedy of Errors* the first situation holds firm, unaffected by the frantic activity which it contains. The play has not one "aside," and though there are brief soliloquies they exist not to advise us of what we had been ignorant but to exploit the speaker's ignorance of what we already know.

The Comedy of Errors is unique also in that its exploitable gap between awarenesses is created and sustained throughout the play without the use of a "practicer." No one here willfully deceives another or even passively withholds a secret—for none here knows enough of the situation to deceive others about it, and none has a secret to withhold. In later comedies, some "practice," some form of deliberate deception, is foremost among the means by which Shakespeare creates discrepancies in awareness and is prominent also among the means by which he maintains or widens these. Moreover, in all the later plays in which exploitation of discrepancies is of primary importance, the role of the deceiver is also of primary importance; that is to say, in plays that show a high proportion of scenes in which most participants perceive the situation less clearly than we do, this high proportion is typically the result of the presence and activity of one or more willful practicers. Many of these practicers—in the histories and the tragedies especially—are of a villainous turn, or are outright villains, whose practices on their fellows are wicked. In *Richard III* the huge proportion of scenes which exploit participants' ignorance of their situations owes largely to Richard's secret machinations; in *Titus Andronicus,* to those of Aaron and Tamora; in *Othello,* to those of Iago; in *Much Ado About Nothing,* to those of Don John; in *Cymbeline,* to those of Iachimo. But not all the practicers who serve the dramatist well by opening exploitable gaps between the awarenesses of participants and audience are vicious. There are far, far more "good" than "bad" practicers in Shakespeare's plays, and accordingly more scenes of unawareness are acted under a benign light than under a sinister shadow. For Rosalind is no less a "practicer" than Iago; and Bassanio's Portia, Viola, Helena, and Imogen deceive even as do Edmund and Iachimo, and by deceiving open gaps between other participants' awarenesses and ours. Hamlet stands high among the notable benevolent practicers, along with Oberon, Duke Vincentio, and many others, all looking ultimately to Prospero.

With the roles of "practicers" it will be necessary to be much concerned hereafter—and with the differences in dramatic effect when, on the one hand, the highest point of awareness among the participants is occupied by a benevolent or, at worst, a sportive practicer and, on the other, when it is held by a vicious one. Frequently the truth that is hidden from the persons of a scene is worse than they suspect; often it is better than they dream. Nearly always, it is the nature of the practicer that determines. Nevertheless, though his role is conspicuous in most plays, the practicer is but one of several means used by the dramatist to create differences between awarenesses. And the fullest evidence that a play can rely for its effects almost exclusively on exploitation of such differences and yet get along without any deceiver, either benevolent or wicked, is presented by *The Comedy of Errors.* If Antipholus of Syracuse deceives Adriana by looking like his brother, yet he does not do so deliberately, and he is himself deceived by Dromio of Ephesus, who looks like Dromio of Syracuse. And if Dromio of Syracuse deceives by resembling his brother, yet he is simultaneously deceived because Antipholus of Ephesus looks like Antipholus of Syracuse. None who deceives in this play is aware that he deceives. None perceives the truth clearly enough to try to deceive another about it.

In fact, none sees the truth at all, or guesses anywhere near it. The third distinguishing mark of *The Comedy of Errors,* seen from the point of view of its uses of awareness, is the universal depth of the participants' ignorance. In later plays persons ignorant of a situation occasionally glimpse the truth, even though dimly and obliquely, and the effect is an instant flash of irony. So, for example, in *Twelfth Night,* the Duke at once sees and sees not when, speaking to the loving "Cesario," he asserts that "thine eye/Hath stay'd upon some favor that it loves." And, in tragedy, Romeo, entering the Capulet house, expresses misgivings of "some consequence yet hanging in the stars"—and his hit on the truth told us in the Prologue is recorded by a flash. But no person in *The Comedy of Errors* ever rises enough from the bottom of oblivion to glimpse the truth that we see steadily. In the first lines of Scene ii, the First Merchant mentions a fact which— if he but knew—would be enormously significant to Antipholus of Syracuse: "This very day a Syracusian merchant/Is apprehended for arrival here." And he goes on:

> And not being able to buy out his life,
> According to the statute of the town,
> Dies ere the weary sun set in the west.
> There is your money that I had to keep.   (1.2.5–8)

Without a word about the plight of the "Syracusian merchant," Antipholus takes the money—the very sum that would buy his father's life—and turns to instruct his servant. The intellectual remoteness of Antipholus from a truth that physically brushes against him at the outset of the action is matched constantly thereafter by the remoteness of other participants from truth that assaults their eyes and ears, and escapes detection. In his first use of the method, Shakespeare risks no dialogue that strikes the unsuspected truth. Nor, certainly, does he allow any participant to come close to guessing the truth. In *Twelfth Night,* after her encounter with the officers taking Antonio to jail, Viola's quick mind accurately interprets the incident: "Prove true, imagination, O, prove true, / That I, dear brother, be now ta'en for you!" There are no such moments in *The Comedy of Errors;* here Shakespeare keeps all persons safely oblivious. Though truth beats at them incessantly, it beats in vain.

C. L. BARBER

From Shakespearian Comedy in *The Comedy of Errors*

Shakespeare's sense of comedy as a moment in a larger cycle leads him to go out of his way, even in this early play, to frame farce with action which presents the weight of age and the threat of death, and to make the comic resolution a renewal of life, indeed explicitly a rebirth. One must admit, however, that he does rather go out of his way to do it: Egeon and Emilia are offstage and almost entirely out of mind in all but the first and last scenes. We can notice, however, that the bonds of marriage, broken in their case by romantic accident, are also very much at issue in the intervening scenes, where marriage is subjected to the very unromantic strains of temperament grinding on temperament in the setting of daily life. Moreover, Adriana and her Antipholus are both *in* their marriage (as wooing couples are in love); its hold on them comes out under the special stress of the presence of the twin doubles. The seriousness of the marriage, however trying, appears in Adriana's long speech rebuking and pleading with her husband when he seems at last to have come home to dinner (it is, of course, the wrong brother):

> Ah, do not tear away thyself from me;
> For know, my love, as easy mayst thou fall
> A drop of water in the breaking gulf,
> And take unmingled thence that drop again . . .

From "Shakespearian Comedy in *The Comedy of Errors*," by C. L. Barber. *College English,* 25 (April, 1964): 493–97. Reprinted by permission of the National Council of Teachers of English and C. L. Barber.

> As take from me thyself and not me too.
> How dearly would it touch thee to the quick,
> Shouldst thou but hear I were licentious . . .   (2.2.125–32)

That for her husband home and wife are really primary is made explicit even when he is most angry:

> Since mine own doors refuse to entertain me,
> I'll knock elsewhere, to see if they'll disdain me.
>
> (3.1.120–21)

Shakespeare nowhere else deals with the daily substance of marriage, its irritations and its strong holding power (*The Merry Wives of Windsor* touches some of this, at a later stage of married life; the rest of the comedies are wooing and wedding). There *is* a deep logic, therefore, to merging, in the ending, the fulfillment of a long-stretched, romantic longing of husband and wife with the conclusion, in the household of Antipholus, of domestic peace after domestic frenzy. No doubt their peace is temporary, but for the moment all vexation is spent; and Adriana *may* have learned something from the Abbess' lecture, even though the Abbess turns out to be her mother-in-law!

LOUISE GEORGE CLUBB

Italian Comedy and *The Comedy of Errors*

T. W. Baldwin's latest word on the compositional genetics of *The Comedy of Errors* accounts exhaustively for every single gene, and not one is Italian. Nevertheless, Professor Baldwin states that Shakespeare's comedy is "probably the most fundamentally Italianate play of the English lot, and yet there is not a specific element which can be traced to direct borrowing from the Italian," adding in a note:

> It must be evident to anyone who has grasped this development of the type in England that so skillfully complicated a play as *Errors* could not have been constructed before the end of the 'eighties. Even so, it is as remarkable a personal accomplishment for the late 'eighties as Udall's *Ralph Roister Doister* was for the early 'fifties. I have the impression that this point of evolution would be stronger if it were put on the background of the development in Italy of this more complicated form from the simpler form of Plautus and Terence.[1]

Whether this impression, with its apparently subversive effect on the rest of the book, is inserted merely as a protective clause to appease Italianists, only Professor Baldwin can say. But his suggestion is very much worth taking, though it touches on the sore old question of whether or not Italian Renaissance comedy exercised any significant influence on the Elizabethan drama, especially Shakespeare's.

We reprint a portion of an essay originally published in *Comparative Literature,* 19 (1967): 240–51.

[1] *On the Compositional Genetics of The Comedy of Errors* (Urbana, 1965), p. 208.

There are only a few proved connections to support Stephen Gosson's famous complaint that Italian comedies were "ransackt to furnish the Playe houses in London." Some comedies of Ariosto, Grazzini, Aretino, the Intronati, Salviati, Piccolomini, Pasqualigo, Della Porta, and Oddi were translated or adapted in England. From the late 1570s, Italian comedy was decidedly chic at Cambridge, where Latin versions were frequently performed. Both of Machiavelli's and four of Aretino's comedies were printed in London in 1588. Royal interest in "Comedia Italiana" is proved by Queen Elizabeth's request that her courtiers organize a performance of one. There are records of seven visits to England of Italian players between 1546 and 1578, and by 1591 the traffic seems to have been brisk enough to make disguise as Italian entertainers desirable to foreign spies.[2]

But despite the handful of undisputed facts, as despite the analogues recorded by several generations of scholars, the investigation of the Elizabethan debt to Italian comedy has been stymied by the scarcity of documentary proof of physical contact or direct borrowing, and by the distractions of the common raw materials, notably Latin comedy and *novelle*.

With regard to Shakespeare the question is especially tantalizing, for half his plays smack of Italian drama, none more than *The Comedy of Errors*. It is generally agreed that the sources of *The Comedy of Errors* are a combination of *Menaechmi* and *Amphitruo,* Gower's version of Apollonius of Tyre, and the account of St. Paul's travels in The Acts of the Apostles, that Shakespeare's handling is more complex than Plautus', and that the whole is given a serious turn, a touch of spirituality and of horror. It is customary to add that Shakespeare raised the moral tone, cleaned up the meretrix, introduced topics of marriage, courtship, and providence, and developed the themes of madness and sorcery—indeed, Professor Baldwin calls the latter the "chief structural thread."

The Italianate quality of *The Comedy of Errors* has

---

[2] K. M. Lea, *Italian Popular Comedy, II* (Oxford, 1934), pp. 362–63 and 352 ff.

never been met head on. K. M. Lea will not commit herself beyond the suggestion that Shakespeare "seems to have been acquainted with the way the comedy of mistaken identity was exploited on the Italian stage" and points to parallels between the devices for moving and complicating action in *The Comedy of Errors* and those in *commedia dell'arte* scenarios. Other scholars consider the style of *The Comedy of Errors* a derivation of Gascoigne's and Lyly's ventures into Italianate comedy, attributing the leftover differences to Shakespeare's desire to outcomplicate *Mother Bombie*. Even M. C. Bradbrook, who distinguishes between the "English Plautine" *Mother Bombie* and the "Italian Plautine" *Comedy of Errors*, does not come to grips with the Italian tradition or with the way in which *The Comedy of Errors* is linked to it.[3]

*   *   *

It will be noticed that except for certain commonplaces of situation, the plots of the plays used as examples of *commedia grave* do not resemble that of *The Comedy of Errors*. The time of searching for Shakespeare's immediate sources is past. There are many Italian regular comedies based on *Menaechmi,* but there is no reason to suppose that Shakespeare used any of them or to doubt that his sources were Plautus, Gower, and St. Paul. His choice of elements and his way of blending them, however, give pause. The addition of pathos and hint of tragedy; the moral de-emphasizing of the courtesan's role to play up the wife Adriana and her nubile sister; the dialogue of these two on the topos of jealousy in marriage; the weaving of multiple sources into a newly complicated pattern of errors with something like a unifying theme in the thread of feared madness and sorcery; Aegeon's evaluation of "the gods" at the beginning, proved false at the end, when the maddening errors and nearly fatal sentence become instruments to reunite families and confirm loves: the combination of these elements, characteristic of *commedia grave,* could not have been suggested by Lyly or Gascoigne, for both *Mother Bombie* and *Supposes* belong to the earlier type of regular comedy.

[3] *The Growth and Structure of Elizabethan Comedy* (London, 1955), p. 66.

While Geoffrey Bullough recognizes that Shakespeare's addition of pathos and tragic import to his source was anticipated by "some of the Italians," he still accepts E. K. Chambers' statement that Shakespeare was "consciously experimenting with an archaistic form," and he adds, "the remarkable thing is the complexity he wove within the simple outline provided by Plautus' *Menaechmi*."[4] But examining *The Comedy of Errors* against the background of Italian tradition, as Baldwin suggests, reveals that the form is anything but archaistic. The complexity answers the demands of Italian regular comedy in general, and the character of its unity reflects the *commedia grave* in particular. As for the pathos and tragic import, they are not fortuitously anticipated by "some" Italians, but were deliberately developed by a sizable group of conscious artists representing the avant-garde of the day.

It cannot be proved that Shakespeare read Italian plays, or saw *commedia dell'arte* troupes or Italian amateurs at Elizabeth's court perform *commedie gravi*, or heard about them from a friend. Nor can *The Comedy of Errors* be labelled *commedia grave*, for Shakespeare's most Italianate play is still not an Italian one. It is next to certain, however, that the brilliant young upstart crow knew something about the latest Continental fashion in comedy.

[4] *Narrative and Dramatic Sources of Shakespeare* (London, 1957), pp. 3, 5, 10.

COPPÉLIA KAHN

Identity in *The Comedy of Errors*

Now, the twin-sibling plays, *Errors* and *Twelfth Night*. In each, the protagonist feels an intense affection for his twin that inspires his crucial actions, and the confusion caused by being mistaken for his twin leads ultimately not only to the desired reunion with the twin, but to a previously unsought union with a marriage partner. The double of these plays, the beloved twin, brings with him not just the morbid anxieties Freud and Rank find, but also an ultimately benign confusion that catalyzes reunion, rebirth, and fulfillment. The twin is a compromise figure, a projection of contending desires; it is through the twin that the protagonist retains ties with the filial past, but also through the twin that he finds a mate and breaks with that past to create his own future. Searching for his twin and mistaken for him, Antipholus of Syracuse meets Luciana and falls in love; grieving for her twin and disguised as him, Viola meets Orsino and falls in love.

But in their searching and grieving, Antipholus S. and Viola are both regressing to the earliest stage of identity formation, identification with one perceived as the same as oneself, which is distinct from object choice, love for someone distinct from and outside the self, predicated on an already formed ego. Identification is first experienced at the mother's breast, when the infant fuses with one who is not yet perceived as not-me. It is also in infancy that the mother's face mirrors the child to himself, confirming his existence through her response to him before he has an

From Coppélia Kahn, *Man's Estate: Masculine Identity in Shakespeare* (University of California Press, 1981), pp. 199–205. The footnotes have been renumbered.

inner sense of his separateness and permanence.[1] Thus the twin, as narcissistic mirror, represents the mother as the earliest, most rudimentary confirmation of the self.

In *Errors,* the twins' very names stress the idea behind the whole action, that identity is formed in relationship to significant others. Shakespeare changed the names from Menaechmus (in his source, Plautus's *Menaechmi*) to Antipholus, from the Greek *anti + philos:* love against or opposed to. The entire family, we realize as the play proceeds, has landed in Ephesus as either the direct or indirect result of storm, shipwreck, and separation. As each character is introduced, we see that he feels uprooted and alienated from himself because he has lost that other closest to him. The dominant metaphor for this collective psychic state is being lost in or on the sea—precisely the event that caused the state. Shakespeare thus internalizes the external and conventional events of the romance plot.

Psychological interest focuses on Antipholus of Syracuse, the melancholy, questing brother who comes to Ephesus in search of a self as well as a family. His first soliloquy crystallizes the interior action of the family romance:

> He that commends me to mine own content
> Commends me to the thing I cannot get.
> I to the world am like a drop of water
> That in the ocean seeks another drop,
> Who, falling there to find his fellow forth,
> Unseen, inquisitive, confounds himself.

[1] See D. W. Winnicott's description of this process, "Mirror Role of Mother and Family in Child Development," in his *Playing and Reality* (New York: Basic Books, 1971), pp. 111–118; also Paula Elkisch, "The Psychological Significance of the Mirror," *Journal of the American Psychoanalytic Association* 5 (1965): 235–244, relates the need to see oneself in a mirror to narcissistic crises of identity; one who fears ego loss turns to the mirror for protection against it, trying to retrieve in the mirrored image his self, his boundaries. Morris W. Brody, "The Symbolic Significance of Twins in Dreams," *Psychoanalytic Quarterly* 21 (1952): 172–180, claims that twins in dream and folklore, whether of the same or opposite sexes, represent the dreamer and his or her mother in the fusion of the womb or of nursing; they symbolize the ambivalent wish to maintain union with the mother but at the same time not to be swallowed up in her, maintaining both separation through duplication of the self and union through sameness.

> So I, to find a mother and a brother,
> In quest of them, unhappy, lose myself.   (1.2.33–40)

One might argue that Antipholus seeks to repeat an oedipal triangle, with his brother taking his father's place. But as the action focuses exclusively on his relationship to his brother, it seems, rather, that he wants to make a mirroring mother of his brother. He envisions extinction— total merger with an undifferentiated mass—as the result of his search. The image of a drop of water seeking another drop stresses his need for his identical twin, but also suggests the futility of this means of self-definition. As one half of a single drop of water, will Antipholus be more "content" or have more of a self? And the image of that one drop falling into a whole ocean conveys the terror of failing to find identity: irretrievable ego loss.

We cannot place much weight on Antipholus S. himself as a character with a complex inner world. Rather, his speech adds a powerful psychological dimension to the farcical action as a whole: it encourages us to see the incipient confusion and the ensuing descent into madness as fantasies of identity confusion and ego loss in adolescence, attendant on the break away from filial identifications and into adult identity. Erikson notes that when "identity hunger" is extreme, young people

> are apt to attach themselves to one brother or sister in a way resembling that of twins. . . . They seem apt to surrender to a total identification with at least one sibling . . . in the hope of regaining a bigger and better one by some act of merging. For periods they succeed, but the letdown which must follow the loss of artificial twinship is only the more traumatic. Rage and paralysis follow the sudden insight—also possible in one of a pair of twins—that there is enough identity only for one, and that the other seems to have made off with it.[2]

The irony for Erikson's adolescent and for Shakespeare's character is that seeking identity by narcissistic mirror-

---

[2] *Identity: Youth and Crisis,* p. 178.

ing leads only to the obliteration, not the discovery, of the self.

That obliteration takes the form of the "errors," the comic confusions of identity, which provide the mirth of the play. The metaphorical and dramatic forms the errors take, however—metamorphosis, engulfment, and enchantment—allow for a psychological reading along with a farcical one and continue the theme of identity confusion and ego loss. Shakespeare shifts the scene of Plautus's comedy from Epidamnum to Ephesus in order to call on all the associations of that city with magic and witchcraft (well known to his audiences through St. Paul's visit to Ephesus) and gains a language in which he can express that theme.

Metamorphosis is first hinted at when Antipholus S., quite naturally fearing he has been robbed, voices deeper anxieties about the robbery of his very identity, by "dark-working sorcerers that change the mind, / Soul-killing witches that deform the body" (1.2.99–100). When at first he accedes, dazed and passive, to the new identity rather harshly attributed to him by his brother's wife, his response is parodied by that of his servant, who feels that he is being "transformed . . . both in mind and in my shape" to an ape; to one who only plays a part, who isn't really who he seems to be. Then, falling in love with Luciana when she persuades him more tenderly that he is someone else, Antipholus S. envisions her as a god, who would "create" him anew.

Calling her a mermaid and a siren, he picks up the oceanic imagery of his earlier soliloquy, and at this point the idea of metamorphosis shades into that of engulfment. Her sister would drown him, but she will rescue him; metaphorically, save him from that obliteration of self, that inauthentic metamorphosis into another person, which her sister promised:

> O, train me not, sweet mermaid, with thy note,
> To drown me in thy sister's flood of tears.
> Sing, siren, for thyself, and I will dote;
> Spread o'er the silver waves thy golden hairs;
> And as a bed I'll take them, and there lie . . .

>   (3.2.45–49)

In raptures he continues, while she protests that he, as her sister's husband, ought to be saying such things to her sister, Adriana. Identifying himself ever more closely with Luciana, as "mine own self's better part, / Mine eye's clear eye, my dear heart's dearer heart," (3.2.61–62) even saying, "I am thee," he asks her to marry him. But again parody questions this instant surrender of self to another, when Dromio of Syracuse wails, "I am an ass, I am a woman's man, and besides myself." He equates metamorphosis with possession by a woman, and possession by a woman with loss of self in the form of engulfment. In a hilariously disgusting blazon of the fat cook Luce, he identifies parts of her body with countries and continents; "spherical, like a globe," she gushes grease, sweat, and rheum, and "lays claim" to Dromio, believing he is his twin. Woman becomes identified with those engulfing waters in which Antipholus S. feared to "confound" himself in act 2. Dromio's fears of being lost in Luce prove contagious; by the end of act 3, Antipholus S. regards Luciana as a mermaid luring him to death by drowning and hastens to leave on the next ship.

The play now takes up a third metaphor for ego loss: possession by spirits. Antipholus of Ephesus's mistaken arrest for debt is described as seizure by "a devil," "a fiend, a fury," and the Courtesan is called "the devil's dam" who appears, like Satan, as "an angel of light" to gain men's souls. Metaphor becomes dramatic reality when the conjurer Dr. Pinch arrives to exorcise Antipholus E. But his efforts, of course, are vain. The real deliverance from the bonds of error is by angelic power. Pauline wordplay runs through the scenes focusing on Antipholus E.'s arrest; mistakenly and to no avail, he seeks deliverance from the sergeant's bonds with the coins—angels—which will pay his debt.[3] These echoes of Paul's miraculous deliverance from prison prepare us for the denouement at the abbey, wherein the evil powers of

---

[3] Antipholus S.'s hoped-for redemption from arrest by money in the form of angels parodies the liberation of Peter from prison in *Acts* 12:1–11, and adds a spiritual dimension to the subsequent liberation of Antipholus from the errors of mistaken identity and domestic dissension plaguing him.

Lapland sorcerers and Circe's cup show themselves to be providence in disguise.

Counterpointing this series of metaphorical and dramatic projections of what it is like to lose or "confound" one's identity, one's relationship to others, and one's grasp of reality in general, are two other senses of reality. Both involve a sense of time. As an aspect of its concern with the development of identity as process rather than fixed state, *Errors* fittingly stresses the importance of time in two ways. First, from the beginning of the play, it is the means by which the network of obligations and relations in ordinary life is maintained, allowing people to experience and reaffirm their identities constantly. When the twins are mistaken for each other, appointments are broken, people are late, and the network breaks down. Much of the comic action depends on this precise and mundane sense of time. Contrasted with it is the idea that time is an organic process analogous to conception, birth, and growth; it proceeds at a proper pace toward a destined goal, can neither be hurried nor stopped, and is controlled by God, like the tempest itself. Emilia's final lines firmly link this sense of time with a sense of identity as growth in time—the serious and realistic theme underlying the farce:

> Thirty-three years have I but gone in travail
> Of you, my sons, and till this present hour
> My heavy burden ne'er delivered.   (5.1.401–403)

Identity grows through time, and through loss, confusion, and challenge. Errors are part of a process whereby youth grows into and out of the family to find itself.

The Comedy of Errors on Stage and Screen

This may seem the slightest of Shakespeare's plays; certainly it is the very shortest, with no more than 1,787 lines. Yet it has enjoyed "a considerable life on the stage," as one of its many adapters, Thomas Hull, attested in 1764; and the continuing history of its performance has been at least as rich and eventful as that of those first 170 years. Its relative slightness seems, increasingly, to have invited elaboration. Its modest and marginal place in the Shakespearean canon stimulated ingenuity and licensed innovation on the part of its successive producers. Here was "a play which blushes at no experiment," in the words of the actor-director-critic, Robert Speaight. Paradoxically, it was also Shakespeare at his most traditional, since it had retained close ties with its Latin sources and had paid its respects to the classical unities, though the jocose Plautine model had been far from constraining. In keeping with that tradition, it has a long record of amateur presentation under more or less academic auspices. But, given the rapidity of its timing, the neatness of its dialogue, and the agility of its twists and turns, *The Comedy of Errors* has never ceased to attract the most professional talents.

Its *donnée,* the gimmick of the identical twins, would have been much easier to present in the Roman theater, where the actors wore masks. Unmasked actors, only roughly resembling each other in physique and physiognomy, had to rely as best they could on costume and makeup, plus a willing suspension of disbelief. Shakespeare had compounded the mixups of the *Menaechmi* by redoubling his doubles, but his pair of twins held a compensating advantage for their audience: while it would be less plausible to confuse them, it would be less difficult to tell them apart. It was an exceptional circumstance that could recruit two comedians who were brothers, Charles and Henry Webb, to play the complementary Dromios during the mid-nineteenth century. Certain modern productions, like the one at Stratford, Connecticut, in 1963, have sought to resolve the dilemma by casting dual roles, with a single actor as the two Antipholi and another as both Dromios. This is an expedient which ends by creating as many dilemmas as it resolves, since direct confrontation must be avoided and stand-in mutes employed to blunt the recognition scene. Needless to say, the technique of double exposure can effectually eliminate such problems, when the medium is film.

Farce derives its name from a French word for stuffing; literally it welcomes the gags and the knockabout business that fill in its contours *ad libitum*. More broadly speaking, it is structured by surprises, which in turn depend upon improbable situations, all too frequently upon coincidence. Spectators need not worry too much about what goes on, if events move fast and emotions do not go very deep. Accordingly, plot flourishes at the expense of characterization, more than elsewhere in Shakespearean drama, since the precondition for the two main sets of characters is that they should be nearly indistinguishable. Such reduplication does nothing to bolster leading roles, and it is not surprising that actor-managers tended on the whole to stay away. John Philip Kemble included the play in his repertory during the early years of the nineteenth century, and emphasized its more sentimental discomfitures—those glimpses of later Shakespeare through Egeon and Adriana—but without much popular success. Sybil Thorndike would make her debut at the Old Vic as Adriana in the Ben Greet production of 1915. Alfred Lunt, starting out at the age of twenty with Boston's Castle Square stock company in 1913, was not above appearing as the Second Officer.

With so short and unified a script, the staging could be basic in its simplicity, and conveniently suited to courtyards and refectories. The characters keep moving back and forth along a city street, the classic ambience for comedy, which could have been conventionally denoted by the ancient proscenium (a façade with several doorways) or by the multiple scene of the Middle Ages (a progression from one *domus,* or symbolic "mansion," to the next). Shakespeare's Folio text sets the scenes by repeated reference to specific locations: the Phoenix (home of the Ephesian Antipholus), the Porpentine (abode of the Courtesan), and the Priory (rallying point for the grand finale). This could have been stylized, and even signalized by placards, at three entrances to the Elizabethan stage. The text in *Bell's British Theatre,* used by Kemble, specified an integrated background, "A public place," while some productions made the most of unlocalized screens or curtains. If place can be unitary, time is continuous, covering about six hours—from mid-morning to mid-afternoon—of one busy day. The concise dramatic action has occasionally suffered further abridgment to fit in with double bills. Thus it counterbalanced Milton's *Comus* on an outdoor program at Regent's Park in 1934.

Our earliest recorded mention of *The Comedy of Errors* occurs in the *Gesta Grayorum,* a vivid first-hand account of the festivities at Gray's Inn during the Christmas season of 1594. Lawyers' headquarters, the Inns of Court were the cultural centers of London; they prided themselves on their courtly entertainments, and had been the formative sponsors of English tragedy a generation before. Now, after three or four years when the plague had shut down their annual celebration, the members of Gray's Inn had invited their legal colleagues from the Inner Temple to a grandiose sequence of nightly revels: feasting and dancing, allegorical pageantry, Latin orations written by Francis Bacon. On Innocents' Night (December 28) their great hall became so crowded and tumultuous, that the official ceremony was broken off, the Templarian guests went home, the scheduled "inventions" by the hosts were called off, and Shakespeare's company was called in to furnish the evening's entertainment. ". . . And after such sports," writes the chronicler, "a Comedy of Errors (like to *Plautus* his *Menaechmi*) was played by the Players. So that Night was begun, and continued to the end, in nothing but Confusion and Errors, whereupon it was ever afterwards called *The Night of Errors.*"

We do not know whether that was the play's premiere, or whether it had been publicly produced during the previous year or so; but it seems well chosen to embellish a special occasion under private auspices, and has been generally counted as Shakespeare's initial comedy: Its broad title, which so soon became a proverbial phrase for confusions or mistakes of any kind, might—like *As You Like It* or *All's Well That Ends Well*—have been affixed to virtually any comic plot. Later adaptations likewise seem to have opted for generalizing titles: *Every Body Mistaken* (1716), *See If You Like It* (1734), *In Such a World* (1935). Gray's Inn was to witness a tercentenary revival in 1895 by the Elizabethan Stage Society under the direction of William Poel, an effective part of his campaigns for a return to the original conditions of Shakespeare's staging. Arnold Dolmetsch furnished an appropriate consort of Renaissance music. Bernard Shaw, who consistently supported Poel's amateur group as part of his own campaigns against histrionic professionals like Sir Henry Irving, wrote a strongly enthusiastic review. This production should win "the palm of the season," he pointedly declared. It was "a delightful, as distinguished from a commercially promising, first night."

The play had celebrated a much earlier anniversary when, just ten years after that bewildering "night of errors" at Gray's Inn, it was presented at court before the new king, James I, on Innocents' Day, 1604. We know that it continued to be in the active repertory during the Restoration, since a promptbook has survived that once belonged to what was then called "the Nursery," a recruiting ground and training school for the two licensed theatrical companies:

> Where unfledged Actors learn to laugh and cry,
> Where infant Punks their tender voices try—

so Dryden would rather harshly sum up their apprentice efforts. There was, moreover, an acting version among the archives of the Smock Alley Theatre in Dublin during the last years of the seventeenth century, though we have no record of its performance. A transcript of "The Famous

Comedy of Errors," dating from 1694 and preserved in the French library at Douai, which was an expatriate center for English Catholics during their years of persecution at home, would seem to suggest that the famous comedy had been locally revived by students at the English-speaking college. It was represented less faithfully in England, during the early eighteenth century, by adaptations heavily reworked.

But Shakespeare's own version (more or less) reentered the repertory at Drury Lane in 1741, and figured as a staple at Covent Garden from 1770 onward. This does not mean that the play no longer posed its standing invitation to would-be adapters with minds of their own. A highly farcical three-act *rifacimento* by William Woods, *The Twins, or Which is Which?*, introduced at the Theatre Royal in Edinburgh, was published in London in 1780 and ran in the provinces through the following generation. As interest in Shakespearean drama spread to the Continent, further modulations and extensions could be looked for. In 1786, shortly after the world premiere of Mozart's *Marriage of Figaro* in Vienna, the Austrian court could listen to another new opera entitled *Gli Equivoci* (a sophisticated Italian rendering of "the errors"). Both works had the same accomplished librettist, Lorenzo da Ponte, who had read *The Comedy of Errors* in a recent French translation. The new composer, designated in German as *"ein Engländer,"* was Stephen Storace, youthful scion of an Anglo-Italian musical family. It almost seems inevitable that a scenario with such symmetrical rhythms and choric climaxes, such potential duets and vocal ensembles, should sooner or later be set to music.

An elaborate musical version in English was mounted at Covent Garden in 1819, composed by Sir Henry Bishop to a libretto by Frederick Reynolds. The original occupied a fairly unusual position among Shakespeare's comedies, in that it had contained no lyrics whatsoever. The prolific Bishop, who was to turn out about seventy works for the stage, including other operas of Shakespearean inspiration, is chiefly remembered today for a single song: "Home, Sweet Home." His *Comedy of Errors* is really a kind of ballad-opera, augmented not only with his melodies but with tunes from Mozart, Thomas Arne, and still others. In order to draw upon these contributions Reynolds had spun out the story line, and more than made up for its absence of musical interludes, by somehow working in the drinking scene from *Antony and Cleopatra* and such other numbers as the willow song from *Othello,* "When Icicles Hang by the Wall" from *Love's Labor's Lost,* "Tell Me Where Is Fancy Bred" from *The Merchant of Venice,* and even excerpts from the *Sonnets.* Contemporaries seem to have admired this olio for its songs, score, and spectacle—admired it in spite of the plot, which "was of course absurd, but . . . was borne by the audience for the sake of the music."

Succeeding generations of producers seem to have oscillated between imposing radical alterations, on the one hand, and reverting to something like the playwright's intentions on the other. By 1855 the actor-manager Samuel Phelps was seeking to redeem the Shakespearean text, when he staged it among his revivals at Sadler's Wells. Benjamin Webster, who produced it several times through those middle years, took a straightforward approach, playing out the continuities in a curtained space without interruption. He himself played Antipholus of Syracuse; but if there was an increasing tendency to build up a stellar part, it was that of the Syracusian Dromio. Stuart Robson came to star in the comedy during that period, repeating his lines with a habitual squeak but renewing his twin-partners, while enlarging his American productions on a more and more spectacular scale. Picturesque tableaux were interpolated; the narrated shipwreck was dramatized as a prologue; Amazons joined Bacchantes in a *corps de ballet;* a procession for the tutelary goddess, Diana, recreated her second-century Ephesus in archeological detail. Alfred Thompson, the scenic artist of Irving's Lyceum, had been specially commissioned to design the settings and to sketch the more than two hundred costumes requisitioned for the cast.

Influenced perhaps by the development of the cinema, where so many different components—both artistic and technical—must be brought together and synthesized by one responsible individual, our century has seen the emergence of a director's theater. *The Comedy of Errors,* which is not dominated by any actor but requires the coordination of many within some sort of integrating conception, lends itself to this method of stagecraft with particular adaptability. Thus Max Reinhardt was compared to a puppet master for his Berlin production of 1911, where the stage consisted largely of a bridge, with ships on one side, houses on the other, and puppetlike actors rushing up and down. Theatrical traditions, which had crystallized with the touring companies in Britain and other English-speaking countries, were centralized at Stratford-on-Avon under the leadership of F. R. Benson and subsequently William Bridges-Adams. After the old Victorian playhouse had burned down, the present Memorial Theatre was built and inaugurated, looming above its riverside gardens vast and nondescript, yet open to directorial and scenic experimentation. An important transition was marked in the nineteen thirties, when the innovative Russian director, Theodore Komisarjevsky, was entrusted with the reinterpretation of six plays.

Never having directed Shakespeare before, Komisarjevsky could announce to the press, "I am not in the least traditional." His scenery, an Italianate or Mediterranean "toytown," was in itself by no means unconventional; yet it centered upon a clock tower that burlesqued the temporal theme by chiming the wrong hours and whirling its hands at irregular intervals. "Time itself joined in the sport," commented one reviewer. There was a pantomime by way of induction, with a hurdy-gurdy to supply the sound effects. Dialogue was vocally orchestrated; some of the speeches were broken up and passed from mouth to mouth, while others were pronounced by several speakers in choral unison. Costumes varied widely in colors, styles, and periods, though most of the men wore Chaplinesque bowler hats. Amid a welter of contemporary allusion, the actress portraying the Courtesan was costumed and made up to resemble Mae West. In undertaking to deconstruct the standardized treatment of Shakespeare, it was shrewd of Komisarjevsky to pick *The Comedy of Errors* as a test case; for there were not many critics who would insist upon a strict construction or be put off by high-spirited improprieties. That constituted, for better and for worse, a breakthrough.

Its date, 1938, proved to be an *annus mirabilis,* since the most popular adaptation, *The Boys from Syracuse,* burst forth upon Broadway in that same year. This musical comedy, one of the happiest collaborations between the vibrant scores of Richard Rodgers and the colloquial lyrics of Lorenz Hart, was paced by the assured direction of George Abbott and enhanced by the brilliant choreography of George Balanchine. Its outstanding mime was the wistful Jimmy Savo, paired with the lyricist's brother Teddy as his fellow Dromio, while Eddie Albert and Ronald Graham carried on tunefully at the more debonaire level of the Antipholi. Songs like "This Can't Be Love" and "Sing for Your Supper" still resonate with nostalgic echoes for many. One of these collaborators justified the distance from Shakespeare's language on the grounds that it permitted them to escape the puns. Of all the elements in their joint concoction, their title was the last and hardest to pick out. At length they offered a prize for the best suggestion. Among the also-ran alternatives were *The Shakespeare Follies, The Bard's Last Stand, It's About Time, The Face Is Familiar,* and—not excluding puns—*Twin Feature, Double Trouble, Two to Go,* and *Wherefore Art Thou Dromio?*

The selected title must have evoked an extra reverberation in New York ears: the slightly condescending awareness that newcomers from upstate had recently arrived in the big town. This reverses the Shakespearean situation, where Syracuse is the offstage metropolis and Ephesus the exotic outpost. But it may help to explain why *The Boys from Syracuse* met with so indifferent a reception at Drury Lane in 1962—all the more indifferent because it had been preceded there by the pseudo-Shavian evocation of London in *My Fair Lady.* As for *The Comedy of Errors* itself, Komisarjevsky's was a hard act to follow, and it would not be restaged at Stratford for twenty-four years. In the meantime (1957), cut down to one fast-talking hour, it divided the billing with *Titus Andronicus* at the Old Vic. These two plays made an extreme but interrelated contrast; both were thinly rooted in the early classicism that would be guiding Shakespeare from apprenticeship toward mastery: "Seneca cannot be too heavy, nor Plautus too light." Tragedy and comedy were both set in an Elizabethan inn yard and performed, as it were, by a troupe of strolling players. The most notable performer was the dancer Robert Helpmann as Doctor Pinch, one of those bit parts which expands into comical flourishes.

The first post-Komisarjevsky production at Stratford-on-Avon happened through a lucky accident. What was now the Royal Shakespeare Theatre had scheduled *King Lear*, a more traditionally Stratfordian vehicle, when its principal actor became indisposed. At the last moment Clifford Williams "knocked together" a *Comedy of Errors* which was adjudged to be surprisingly "solid and intricate," which would go on to re-create for London viewers "a Pirandello world of masquerade," and which would culminate in a command performance before the royal family at Windsor. More precisely, the Italian atmosphere was that of the commedia dell'arte; on a bare stage the cast appeared in black tights for an introductory parade, and those who were not directly involved would wander in and out of the dramatic action. At the British Stratford there have been subsequent revivals. Trevor Nunn's, a decade later (1972), reached the widest audience after it had been filmed and televised. John Napier's (1976), coming so soon afterward, tried hard to divagate: with a fragmented text, a contemporary setting, a middle eastern dictator as duke, and a courtroom scene for the resolution. Adrian Noble (1982), dressing most of his characters as clowns, seems to have turned back to the harlequinade.

When Shakespearean themes could be reanimated with such far-out variations in the mother country, it could be expected that they would be pressed even farther in North America, through a series of cultural syntheses which blended the indigenous with the imported. First brought to the New York theater by a traveling English company in 1804, the play reappeared very frequently throughout the nineteenth century. A pioneering black group, The Ethiopian Art Theater, took it from Chicago and Washington to Broadway for two precarious weeks (1923) in an updated production *"à la jazz"*—according to W. E. B. Du Bois, whose article protested against the snobbery that was keeping his fellow blacks away from the classics. Ideological tensions between the rival towns became a major issue with Players, Inc., a group of strollers whose version featured crowds with signs reading "Ephesus for Ephesians" and "Syracusans Go Home" (1959). *The Comedy of Errors* has been a regular favorite in the alfresco program of the New York Shakespeare Festival in Central Park. In its most striking incarnation (1975), Italy was noisily projected as it might have been in the far-from-romantic nineteen thirties; the Duke was a Mafioso, guns went off, and actors spoke with Italian-American accents.

Meanwhile (again in 1975), Elizabethan affairs were conveyed much closer to home by the Canadian Shakespeare Festival in Stratford, Ontario. Robin Phillips' musicalized rendition was relocated in the American West during the latter nineteenth century. The Duke—in order to meet that contingency—was a rancher, surrounded by cowboys and adept at presiding over square dances. The *decor* was a farmyard, complete with drying laundry and clucking chickens, and centering on a prairie schooner. At this juncture we have come a long way; we are closer to *Oklahoma!* here than to the urban conventions of ancient comedy. If the aims were modernization and naturalization, it would have been more appropriate to transmute the *dramatis personae* into types encountered along the midway of a carnival. Consequently, in the Shakespeare Festival in Ashland, Oregon (1976), the Antipholi were enacted as animal tamers, the Dromios as a team of clowns, and Doctor Pinch as a medicine man, while the Priory was reduced to a funhouse. Under the same sponsorship six years later, a renovated *Comedy of Errors* added a Harpo Marx personage known as "the Kid"—as if there were not enough interlopers already. The critics' complaint, that too many pies were thrown, might apply more widely.

When each revision strives to outdo the very latest, there can be no limits. To date the uttermost endeavor has been that of five acrobatic zanies who—traducing Dostoyevsky along with Shakespeare—bill themselves as the

Flying Karamazovs (originally at Chicago's Goodman Theater in 1983, then in New York and on television in 1987). Four of them accounted for the dual twins; the fifth personified Shakespeare himself, not speaking but laughing continually at his own jokes; a sixth comedian supplemented their muggings as an eccentric janitor; and Adriana twirled the baton of a drum majorette. Ephesus, reconceived this time as the winter quarters of a circus ("three-ring Shakespeare"), could thus play host to an uproarious vaudeville of acts on stilts, trapezes, and tightropes, of tap dancing and belly dancing, of unexpected incursions by unicycles and kiddy cars. A program note explained: "The plot has something to do with twins and jugglers," evidently taking off from the Shakespearean warning against "nimble jugglers that deceive the eye." But juggling, for Shakespeare, did not necessarily mean tossing tenpins into the air; it was a byword for trickery in a more general sense, with overtones of deception, and was etymologically connected with joking.

Latitude had to be broadened even further, when Shakespeare's dramas were transposed to the audiovisual media, but if this raised technological complications, it opened up fresh possibilities. It was all too obvious that *The Comedy of Errors,* "because of its reliance upon intractably visual material," was uniquely unsuited to aural dramatization via the radio. Yet its peculiar visual requirements, at best imperfectly realized on the stage, were readily adaptable to the film through the use of composite shots. Both Dromios could look just like Joe Penner, and both Antipholi like Allan Jones, with the Courtesan looking like no one but Martha Raye, when *The Boys from Syracuse* was screened in 1940. The play itself, not reaching the cinema houses except through its musical popularization, would be repeatedly filmed for the television screens. It was rather gradual in adjusting to, and expanding with, the new medium. The main concern was for the Royal Shakespeare Company to be televised by the British Broadcasting Corporation. There would be unquestionable value in recording, disseminating widely, and ultimately preserving such interpretations, notably that of Clifford Williams. But the effect on home viewers could be too "stagey"; some of them felt that Trevor Nunn's production was "overdirected" (1976).

Conversely and more lately, when the BBC undertook to range through the whole Shakespearean sequence, it was ready to reconsider the drama in terms of the camera; and its *Comedy of Errors* (1984), as directed by James Cellan Jones, with Cyril Cusack as Egeon and Wendy Hiller as Emilia, turned out to be one of its most suggestive reenactments. Freed from platform or proscenium, the photographer made the most of spaciousness and mobility; a map of the Mediterranean was laid out underfoot in mosaic as a dancing-place for the players, a counterpart of the Greek *orchestra*. But the observer's vision could move, in a flash, from the distancing of a long shot to the intimacy of a close-up: a pair of clasped hands, a pack of Tarot cards. Monologues could begin full-face and proceed through a *montage* of associations. Whereas the inherited convention had dwelt upon externals, the streets and the façades, there was now a psychological impulse to penetrate interiors. When visualization can be linked with characterization, and characters can be regarded through one another's eyes, their blunders and their bafflements assume a deeper dimension. A brittle farce, modulated by shifting viewpoints, takes on the characteristics of a novel.

It could scarcely have been predicted that so comparatively slight a play, so limited and formalized at its beginnings, would have so colorful a history and so worldwide a diffusion. Not only did it have a place in the universal adoption of Shakespeare's works into other languages and cultures, but it more than held its ground among them. Mikhail Morozov designates fourteen Shakespearean plays that currently belong to "the basic repertory" of the Russian theater; his list includes *The Comedy of Errors*, though it omits *Macbeth, Julius Caesar,* and *The Tempest.* Naturally, performance in distant regions was bound to be colored by native tastes and customs. We have had occasion to notice several instances of high-pressured Americanization. Comparably a Swahili rendering, performed by the National Theater of Kenya (1955), was enlivened by African folk-dances. It seems clear enough that we are dealing with a thematic structure which, while lending itself to all kinds of incidental embellishment, firmly persists across regional and historical change. This principle was already established when Shakespeare found stimulus in Plautus, who had hit upon an important archetype: the question of identity and otherness, the self and the *alter ego,* the haunting apparition of the Double.

Plautus had dashed off the outlines lightly and brightly. Shakespeare would not have been himself, even in the course of his earliest comic undertaking, if he had not darkened the Roman picture with Elizabethan touches of *chiaroscuro:* the overarching suspense of Egeon's plight, the feminine pathos of Adriana's dilemma—not to mention the providential resurgence of Emilia as *dea ex machina.* The resultant mingle-mangle has allowed great leeway to its dramatic interpreters, who may choose to stress the more serious aspects or else to fall back upon the farcical substructure. That ambivalence, reinforcing the plotted ambiguities, made it easier to interpolate more freely. There have been frequent reactions in favor of Shakespeare's well-made script; hence this brief chronicle has had to veer between the minimalist presentation and the jazzed-up extravaganza. It has been a long time now since critics objected to the play on grounds of improbability; doubtless their afterthoughts reflect a shift from presumptions of stability and rationalism toward a state of mind where confusion comes closer to social norms. At all events, it is heartening that Shakespeare can still speak to an age of existential absurdity, and that his comedy of errors can vie with those of Beckett and Ionesco for distinction in the Theater of the Absurd.

Postscript by the General Editor

The last decade of the twentieth century saw a few especially interesting productions, including Ian Judge's modern-dress version performed by the Royal Shakespeare Company at Stratford-upon-Avon in 1990. The play began on a somber stage, with black, white, and gray,

but when this episode with Egeon and the Duke was over,
the prison walls vanished and the stage was flooded with
color. What made the production especially notable, however, was the use of one actor to play the two Antipholus
brothers, and another actor to play the two Dromio
brothers. In fact, this device of using one actor for each
pair of brothers was not new; it had been used a number of
times, perhaps most notably in 1963 at Stratford, Connecticut, in a production directed by Douglas Seale; in
1983 in a Swedish production directed by Lief Söder-
ström; in 1988 at Santa Cruz, in a production directed by
Danny Scheie; in 1989 at Stratford, Ontario, in a production directed by Richard Monette; and also in the 1984
BBC television production, where editing allows the
viewers to see a single actor in two roles simultaneously.
(By means of the split-screen technique, in which two
shots are shown on the screen at the same time, television
can simultaneously show one performer in two roles, but
the live theater cannot, and thus in the stage productions
doubles had to be used in the final scene, when the two
Antipholus brothers and the two Dromio brothers confront
each other.)

The question is: Does it make sense for one actor to play
the two brothers? Directors who think that the play cannot
be convincing unless the two Dromios look alike and the
two Antipholus brothers look alike cannot find two pairs
of twins to perform the roles, so they perhaps are tempted
to use one performer for each set of twins. But in fact, who
demands this sort of realism in any play, much less in this
play? If two actors have pretty much the same build, costumes and makeup can surely do the trick of creating close
resemblances. Further, the point is not, of course, to confuse the audience by having characters who look alike; it
is the characters in the play who are baffled, not we—we
are securely in the know—and if *they* say they are confused, that is surely good enough for us as spectators. And
still further, if we are already familiar with the play, when
it is performed with two actors taking the four roles we
will probably be distracted by wondering how the director
will handle the final confrontation. And surely we will be
disappointed—annoyed—when doubles are brought in,

and their backs are kept to the audience as much as is possible. The final grand recognition scene, which ought to be lyrical and wonderful, becomes in this sort of production a shabby thing, diminished by clumsy artifice. In short, the gimmick doesn't work, and indeed it has a blighting effect. Even in the television versions where this device is used, it seems unsatisfactory; we in the audience, secure in our knowledge that two sets of twins are now in Ephesus, ought to enjoy the confusion of the other characters who mistakenly think if they see a Dromio that he is the only Dromio, or an Antipholus is the only Antipholus. The joke is rather spoiled if indeed there is, so to speak, only one Antipholus and one Dromio, i.e., one actor playing the roles of two brothers.

Probably the most successful production in the last decade of the twentieth century—it goes without saying that the four brothers were played by four actors, not two—was Tim Supple's modern-dress production at the Other Place, in Stratford-upon-Avon, in 1996. Duke Solinus was a black man in a military uniform, the Antipholuses wore light-colored linen suits, and the Dromios wore baggy black shorts and T-shirts. It was funny without being rowdy, and the serious elements coexisted effectively, as they do not when the director gets it into his head that because the play has affinities with the *commedia dell'arte,* clowns should clutter the stage, miming the other players. At the end of Supple's production the Abbess, Emelia, maintained her dignity. She blessed the group, but she did not embrace her long-lost husband, Egeon; she was now a nun, and too many years had separated them. This scene is rich in reconciliations—not only the obvious reconciliations of brothers to each other and to their parents, and of Emelia and Egeon, but also of Antipholus of Ephesus to his wife and to his status as a respectable citizen—but in Supple's production the joy was suffused by wonder, by awe. And the audience was not concerned with *how* the reunion of the brothers would be handled on the stage (as the audience would be if twins were played by one actor); rather, the audience could enjoy seeing the fulfillment of what it had long anticipated.

It is not a matter of neglecting the comedy but of recognizing that, for all of its farcical scenes, *The Comedy of Errors* also includes a good deal of serious material, notably of course the plight of Egeon. Some productions spoof Egeon's long tale of woe, often by having *commedia dell'arte* characters clown during the delivery—a sure sign that the director does not trust the play—but in fact if the speech is spoken well it is moving, and when Solinus, Duke of Ephesus, responds to Egeon, the audience shares the Duke's emotion:

> Hapless Egeon, whom the fates have marked
> To bear the extremity of dire mishap!
> Now trust me, were it not against our laws,
> Against my crown, my oath, my dignity,
> Which princes, would they, may not disannul,
> My soul should sue as advocate for thee.   (1.1.140–45)

But seriousness is not confined to the opening scene. Throughout the play the issue of identity is treated not only comically but also seriously, as in the early passage when Antipholus of Syracuse responds to a merchant who cautions Antipholus not to reveal that he is a Syracusan. The friendly merchant takes his leave of Antipholus with a conventional phrase, "Sir, I commend you to your own content," and Antipholus, alone on the stage, soliloquizes:

> *S. Antipholus.* He that commends me to mine own content
> Commends me to the thing I cannot get.
> I to the world am like a drop of water
> That in the ocean seeks another drop,
> Who, falling there to find his fellow forth,
> Unseen, inquisitive, confounds himself.
> So I, to find a mother and a brother,
> In quest of them, unhappy, lose myself.   (1.2.32–40)

A moment later Dromio of Ephesus appears, initiating the confusion that is the main stuff of the play, but, again, under all of the comedy is the serious motif of identity, a theme that Shakespeare returns to again and again, not only in comedy but also in the major tragedies and in the late romances. It is this complexity that Tim Supple's production captured, and that most productions miss, especially productions that use one actor to play two brothers.

—Sylvan Barnet

Suggested References

The number of possible references is vast and grows alarmingly. (The *Shakespeare Quarterly* devotes one issue each year to a list of the previous year's work, and *Shakespeare Survey*—an annual publication—includes a substantial review of biographical, critical, and textual studies, as well as a survey of performances.) The vast bibliography is best approached through James Harner, *The World Shakespeare Bibliography on CD-Rom: 1900–Present.* The first release, in 1996, included more than 12,000 annotated items from 1990–93, plus references to several thousand book reviews, productions, films, and audio recordings. The plan is to update the publication annually, moving forward one year and backward three years. Thus, the second issue (1997), with 24,700 entries, and another 35,000 or so references to reviews, newspaper pieces, and so on, covered 1987–94.

Though no works are indispensable, those listed below have been found especially helpful. The arrangement is as follows:

1. Shakespeare's Times
2. Shakespeare's Life
3. Shakespeare's Theater
4. Shakespeare on Stage and Screen
5. Miscellaneous Reference Works
6. Shakespeare's Plays: General Studies
7. The Comedies
8. The Romances
9. The Tragedies
10. The Histories
11. *The Comedy of Errors*

The titles in the first five sections are accompanied by brief explanatory annotations.

1. Shakespeare's Times

Andrews, John F., ed. *William Shakespeare: His World, His Work, His Influence,* 3 vols. (1985). Sixty articles, dealing not only with such subjects as "The State," "The Church," "Law," "Science, Magic, and Folklore," but also with the plays and poems themselves and Shakespeare's influence (e.g., translations, films, reputation)

Byrne, Muriel St. Clare. *Elizabethan Life in Town and Country* (8th ed., 1970). Chapters on manners, beliefs, education, etc., with illustrations.

Dollimore, John, and Alan Sinfield, eds. *Political Shakespeare: New Essays in Cultural Materialism* (1985). Essays on such topics as the subordination of women and colonialism, presented in connection with some of Shakespeare's plays.

Greenblatt, Stephen. *Representing the English Renaissance* (1988). New Historicist essays, especially on connections between political and aesthetic matters, statecraft and stagecraft.

Joseph, B. L. *Shakespeare's Eden: The Commonwealth of England 1558–1629* (1971). An account of the social, political, economic, and cultural life of England.

Kernan, Alvin. *Shakespeare, the King's Playwright: Theater in the Stuart Court 1603–1613* (1995). The social setting and the politics of the court of James I, in relation to *Hamlet, Measure for Measure, Macbeth, King Lear, Antony and Cleopatra, Coriolanus,* and *The Tempest.*

Montrose, Louis. *The Purpose of Playing: Shakespeare and the Cultural Politics of the Elizabethan Theatre* (1996). A poststructuralist view, discussing the professional theater "within the ideological and material frameworks of Elizabethan culture and society," with an extended analysis of *A Midsummer Night's Dream.*

Mullaney, Steven. *The Place of the Stage: License, Play, and Power in Renaissance England* (1988). New Historicist analysis, arguing that popular drama became a cultural institution "only by . . . taking up a place on the margins of society."

Schoenbaum, S. *Shakespeare: The Globe and the World*

(1979). A readable, abundantly illustrated introductory book on the world of the Elizabethans.

Shakespeare's England, 2 vols. (1916). A large collection of scholarly essays on a wide variety of topics, e.g., astrology, costume, gardening, horsemanship, with special attention to Shakespeare's references to these topics.

2. Shakespeare's Life

Andrews, John F., ed. *William Shakespeare: His World, His Work, His Influence,* 3 vols. (1985). See the description above.

Bentley, Gerald E. *Shakespeare: A Biographical Handbook* (1961). The facts about Shakespeare, with virtually no conjecture intermingled.

Chambers, E. K. *William Shakespeare: A Study of Facts and Problems,* 2 vols. (1930). The fullest collection of data.

Fraser, Russell. *Young Shakespeare* (1988). A highly readable account that simultaneously considers Shakespeare's life and Shakespeare's art.

———. *Shakespeare: The Later Years* (1992).

Schoenbaum, S. *Shakespeare's Lives* (1970). A review of the evidence and an examination of many biographies, including those of Baconians and other heretics.

———. *William Shakespeare: A Compact Documentary Life* (1977). An abbreviated version, in a smaller format, of the next title. The compact version reproduces some fifty documents in reduced form. A readable presentation of all that the documents tell us about Shakespeare.

———. *William Shakespeare: A Documentary Life* (1975). A large-format book setting forth the biography with facsimiles of more than two hundred documents, and with transcriptions and commentaries.

3. Shakespeare's Theater

Astington, John H., ed. *The Development of Shakespeare's Theater* (1992). Eight specialized essays on theatrical companies, playing spaces, and performance.

Beckerman, Bernard. *Shakespeare at the Globe, 1599–1609* (1962). On the playhouse and on Elizabethan dramaturgy, acting, and staging.

Bentley, Gerald E. *The Profession of Dramatist in Shakespeare's Time* (1971). An account of the dramatist's status in the Elizabethan period.

———. *The Profession of Player in Shakespeare's Time, 1590–1642* (1984). An account of the status of members of London companies (sharers, hired men, apprentices, managers) and a discussion of conditions when they toured.

Berry, Herbert. *Shakespeare's Playhouses* (1987). Usefully emphasizes how little we know about the construction of Elizabethan theaters.

Brown, John Russell. *Shakespeare's Plays in Performance* (1966). A speculative and practical analysis relevant to all of the plays, but with emphasis on *The Merchant of Venice*, *Richard II*, *Hamlet*, *Romeo and Juliet*, and *Twelfth Night*.

———. *William Shakespeare: Writing for Performance* (1996). A discussion aimed at helping readers to develop theatrically conscious habits of reading.

Chambers, E. K. *The Elizabethan Stage*, 4 vols. (1945). A major reference work on theaters, theatrical companies, and staging at court.

Cook, Ann Jennalie. *The Privileged Playgoers of Shakespeare's London, 1576–1642* (1981). Sees Shakespeare's audience as wealthier, more middle-class, and more intellectual than Harbage (below) does.

Dessen, Alan C. *Elizabethan Drama and the Viewer's Eye* (1977). On how certain scenes may have looked to spectators in an Elizabethan theater.

Gurr, Andrew. *Playgoing in Shakespeare's London* (1987). Something of a middle ground between Cook (above) and Harbage (below).

———. *The Shakespearean Stage, 1579–1642* (2nd ed., 1980). On the acting companies, the actors, the playhouses, the stages, and the audiences.

Harbage, Alfred. *Shakespeare's Audience* (1941). A study of the size and nature of the theatrical public, emphasizing the representativeness of its working class and middle-class audience.

Hodges, C. Walter. *The Globe Restored* (1968). A conjectural restoration, with lucid drawings.

Hosley, Richard. "The Playhouses," in *The Revels History of Drama in English*, vol. 3, general editors Clifford Leech and T. W. Craik (1975). An essay of a hundred pages on the physical aspects of the playhouses.

Howard, Jane E. "Crossdressing, the Theatre, and Gender Struggle in Early Modern England," *Shakespeare Quarterly* 39 (1988): 418–40. Judicious comments on the effects of boys playing female roles.

Orrell, John. *The Human Stage: English Theatre Design, 1567–1640* (1988). Argues that the public, private, and court playhouses are less indebted to popular structures (e.g., innyards and bear-baiting pits) than to banqueting halls and to Renaissance conceptions of Roman amphitheaters.

Slater, Ann Pasternak. *Shakespeare the Director* (1982). An analysis of theatrical effects (e.g., kissing, kneeling) in stage directions and dialogue.

Styan, J. L. *Shakespeare's Stagecraft* (1967). An introduction to Shakespeare's visual and aural stagecraft, with chapters on such topics as acting conventions, stage groupings, and speech.

Thompson, Peter. *Shakespeare's Professional Career* (1992). An examination of patronage and related theatrical conditions.

———. *Shakespeare's Theatre* (1983). A discussion of how plays were staged in Shakespeare's time.

4. Shakespeare on Stage and Screen

Bate, Jonathan, and Russell Jackson, eds. *Shakespeare: An Illustrated Stage History* (1996). Highly readable essays on stage productions from the Renaissance to the present.

Berry, Ralph. *Changing Styles in Shakespeare* (1981). Discusses productions of six plays (*Coriolanus*, *Hamlet*, *Henry V*, *Measure for Measure*, *The Tempest*, and *Twelfth Night*) on the English stage, chiefly 1950–1980.

————. *On Directing Shakespeare: Interviews with Contemporary Directors* (1989). An enlarged edition of a book first published in 1977, this version includes the seven interviews from the early 1970s and adds five interviews conducted in 1988.

Brockbank, Philip, ed. *Players of Shakespeare: Essays in Shakespearean Performance* (1985). Comments by twelve actors, reporting their experiences with roles. See also the entry for Russell Jackson (below).

Bulman, J. C., and H. R. Coursen, eds. *Shakespeare on Television* (1988). An anthology of general and theoretical essays, essays on individual productions, and shorter reviews, with a bibliography and a videography listing cassettes that may be rented.

Coursen, H. P. *Watching Shakespeare on Television* (1993). Analyses not only of TV versions but also of films and videotapes of stage presentations that are shown on television.

Davies, Anthony, and Stanley Wells, eds. *Shakespeare and the Moving Image: The Plays on Film and Television* (1994). General essays (e.g., on the comedies) as well as essays devoted entirely to *Hamlet*, *King Lear*, and *Macbeth*.

Dawson, Anthony B. *Watching Shakespeare: A Playgoer's Guide* (1988). About half of the plays are discussed, chiefly in terms of decisions that actors and directors make in putting the works onto the stage.

Dessen, Alan. *Elizabethan Stage Conventions and Modern Interpretations* (1984). On interpreting conventions such as the representation of light and darkness and stage violence (duels, battles).

Donaldson, Peter. *Shakespearean Films/Shakespearean Directors* (1990). Postmodernist analyses, drawing on Freudianism, Feminism, Deconstruction, and Queer Theory.

Jackson, Russell, and Robert Smallwood, eds. *Players of Shakespeare 2: Further Essays in Shakespearean Performance by Players with the Royal Shakespeare Company* (1988). Fourteen actors discuss their roles in productions between 1982 and 1987.

————. *Players of Shakespeare 3: Further Essays in Shake-

spearean Performance by Players with the Royal Shakespeare Company (1993). Comments by thirteen performers.

Jorgens, Jack. *Shakespeare on Film* (1977). Fairly detailed studies of eighteen films, preceded by an introductory chapter addressing such issues as music, and whether to "open" the play by including scenes of landscape.

Kennedy, Dennis. *Looking at Shakespeare: A Visual History of Twentieth-Century Performance* (1993). Lucid descriptions (with 170 photographs) of European, British, and American performances.

Leiter, Samuel L. *Shakespeare Around the Globe: A Guide to Notable Postwar Revivals* (1986). For each play there are about two pages of introductory comments, then discussions (about five hundred words per production) of ten or so productions, and finally bibliographic references.

McMurty, Jo. *Shakespeare Films in the Classroom* (1994). Useful evaluations of the chief films most likely to be shown in undergraduate courses.

Rothwell, Kenneth, and Annabelle Henkin Melzer. *Shakespeare on Screen: An International Filmography and Videography* (1990). A reference guide to several hundred films and videos produced between 1899 and 1989, including spinoffs such as musicals and dance versions.

Sprague, Arthur Colby. *Shakespeare and the Actors* (1944). Detailed discussions of stage business (gestures, etc.) over the years.

Willis, Susan. *The BBC Shakespeare Plays: Making the Televised Canon* (1991). A history of the series, with interviews and production diaries for some plays.

5. Miscellaneous Reference Works

Abbott, E. A. *A Shakespearean Grammar* (new edition, 1877). An examination of differences between Elizabethan and modern grammar.

Allen, Michael J. B., and Kenneth Muir, eds. *Shakespeare's Plays in Quarto* (1981). One volume containing facsimiles of the plays issued in small format before they were collected in the First Folio of 1623.

Bevington, David. *Shakespeare* (1978). A short guide to hundreds of important writings on the subject.

Blake, Norman. *Shakespeare's Language: An Introduction* (1983). On vocabulary, parts of speech, and word order.

Bullough, Geoffrey. *Narrative and Dramatic Sources of Shakespeare*, 8 vols. (1957–75). A collection of many of the books Shakespeare drew on, with judicious comments.

Campbell, Oscar James, and Edward G. Quinn, eds. *The Reader's Encyclopedia of Shakespeare* (1966). Old, but still the most useful single reference work on Shakespeare.

Cercignani, Fausto. *Shakespeare's Works and Elizabethan Pronunciation* (1981). Considered the best work on the topic, but remains controversial.

Dent, R. W. *Shakespeare's Proverbial Language: An Index* (1981). An index of proverbs, with an introduction concerning a form Shakespeare frequently drew on.

Greg, W. W. *The Shakespeare First Folio* (1955). A detailed yet readable history of the first collection (1623) of Shakespeare's plays.

Harner, James. *The World Shakespeare Bibliography*. See headnote to Suggested References.

Hosley, Richard. *Shakespeare's Holinshed* (1968). Valuable presentation of one of Shakespeare's major sources.

Kökeritz, Helge. *Shakespeare's Names* (1959). A guide to pronouncing some 1,800 names appearing in Shakespeare.

———. *Shakespeare's Pronunciation* (1953). Contains much information about puns and rhymes, but see Cercignani (above).

Muir, Kenneth. *The Sources of Shakespeare's Plays* (1978). An account of Shakespeare's use of his reading. It covers all the plays, in chronological order.

Miriam Joseph, Sister. *Shakespeare's Use of the Arts of Language* (1947). A study of Shakespeare's use of rhetorical devices, reprinted in part as *Rhetoric in Shakespeare's Time* (1962).

The Norton Facsimile: The First Folio of Shakespeare's Plays (1968). A handsome and accurate facsimile of the first collection (1623) of Shakespeare's plays, with a valuable introduction by Charlton Hinman.

Onions, C. T. *A Shakespeare Glossary*, rev. and enlarged by

R. D. Eagleson (1986). Definitions of words (or senses of words) now obsolete.

Partridge, Eric. *Shakespeare's Bawdy*, rev. ed. (1955). Relatively brief dictionary of bawdy words; useful, but see Williams, below.

Shakespeare Quarterly. See headnote to Suggested References.

Shakespeare Survey. See headnote to Suggested References.

Spevack, Marvin. *The Harvard Concordance to Shakespeare* (1973). An index to Shakespeare's words.

Vickers, Brian. *Appropriating Shakespeare: Contemporary Critical Quarrels* (1993). A survey—chiefly hostile—of recent schools of criticism.

Wells, Stanley, ed. *Shakespeare: A Bibliographical Guide* (new edition, 1990). Nineteen chapters (some devoted to single plays, others devoted to groups of related plays) on recent scholarship on the life and all of the works.

Williams, Gordon. *A Dictionary of Sexual Language and Imagery in Shakespearean and Stuart Literature*, 3 vols. (1994). Extended discussions of words and passages; much fuller than Partridge, cited above.

6. Shakespeare's Plays: General Studies

Bamber, Linda. *Comic Women, Tragic Men: A Study of Gender and Genre in Shakespeare* (1982).

Barnet, Sylvan. *A Short Guide to Shakespeare* (1974).

Callaghan, Dympna, Lorraine Helms, and Jyotsna Singh. *The Weyward Sisters: Shakespeare and Feminist Politics* (1994).

Clemen, Wolfgang H. *The Development of Shakespeare's Imagery* (1951).

Cook, Ann Jennalie. *Making a Match: Courtship in Shakespeare and His Society* (1991).

Dollimore, Jonathan, and Alan Sinfield. *Political Shakespeare: New Essays in Cultural Materialism* (1985).

Dusinberre, Juliet. *Shakespeare and the Nature of Women* (1975).

Granville-Barker, Harley. *Prefaces to Shakespeare*, 2 vols. (1946–47; volume 1 contains essays on *Hamlet*, *King*

Lear, Merchant of Venice, Antony and Cleopatra, and *Cymbeline*; volume 2 contains essays on *Othello, Coriolanus, Julius Caesar, Romeo and Juliet, Love's Labor's Lost*).

———. *More Prefaces to Shakespeare* (1974; essays on *Twelfth Night, A Midsummer Night's Dream, The Winter's Tale, Macbeth*).

Harbage, Alfred. *William Shakespeare: A Reader's Guide* (1963).

Howard, Jean E. *Shakespeare's Art of Orchestration: Stage Technique and Audience Response* (1984).

Jones, Emrys. *Scenic Form in Shakespeare* (1971).

Lenz, Carolyn Ruth Swift, Gayle Greene, and Carol Thomas Neely, eds. *The Woman's Part: Feminist Criticism of Shakespeare* (1980).

Novy, Marianne. *Love's Argument: Gender Relations in Shakespeare* (1984).

Rose, Mark. *Shakespearean Design* (1972).

Scragg, Leah. *Discovering Shakespeare's Meaning* (1994).

———. *Shakespeare's "Mouldy Tales": Recurrent Plot Motifs in Shakespearean Drama* (1992).

Traub, Valerie. *Desire and Anxiety: Circulations of Sexuality in Shakespearean Drama* (1992).

Traversi, D. A. *An Approach to Shakespeare,* 2 vols. (3rd rev. ed, 1968–69).

Vickers, Brian. *The Artistry of Shakespeare's Prose* (1968).

Wells, Stanley. *Shakespeare: A Dramatic Life* (1994).

Wright, George T. *Shakespeare's Metrical Art* (1988).

7. The Comedies

Barber, C. L. *Shakespeare's Festive Comedy* (1959; discusses *Love's Labor's Lost, A Midsummer Night's Dream, The Merchant of Venice, As You Like It, Twelfth Night*).

Barton, Anne. *The Names of Comedy* (1990).

Berry, Ralph. *Shakespeare's Comedy: Explorations in Form* (1972).

Bradbury, Malcolm, and David Palmer, eds. *Shakespearean Comedy* (1972).

Bryant, J. A., Jr. *Shakespeare and the Uses of Comedy* (1986).

Carroll, William. *The Metamorphoses of Shakespearean Comedy* (1985).

Champion, Larry S. *The Evolution of Shakespeare's Comedy* (1970).

Evans, Bertrand. *Shakespeare's Comedies* (1960).

Frye, Northrop. *Shakespearean Comedy and Romance* (1965).

Leggatt, Alexander. *Shakespeare's Comedy of Love* (1974).

Miola, Robert S. *Shakespeare and Classical Comedy: The Influence of Plautus and Terence* (1994).

Nevo, Ruth. *Comic Transformations in Shakespeare* (1980).

Ornstein, Robert. *Shakespeare's Comedies: From Roman Farce to Romantic Mystery* (1986).

Richman, David. *Laughter, Pain, and Wonder: Shakespeare's Comedies and the Audience in the Theater* (1990).

Salingar, Leo. *Shakespeare and the Traditions of Comedy* (1974).

Slights, Camille Wells. *Shakespeare's Comic Commonwealths* (1993).

Waller, Gary, ed. *Shakespeare's Comedies* (1991).

Westlund, Joseph. *Shakespeare's Reparative Comedies: A Psychoanalytic View of the Middle Plays* (1984).

Williamson, Marilyn. *The Patriarchy of Shakespeare's Comedies* (1986).

8. The Romances (*Pericles, Cymbeline, The Winter's Tale, The Tempest, The Two Noble Kinsmen*)

Adams, Robert M. *Shakespeare: The Four Romances* (1989).

Felperin, Howard. *Shakespearean Romance* (1972).

Frye, Northrop. *A Natural Perspective: The Development of Shakespearean Comedy and Romance* (1965).

Mowat, Barbara. *The Dramaturgy of Shakespeare's Romances* (1976).

Warren, Roger. *Staging Shakespeare's Late Plays* (1990).

Young, David. *The Heart's Forest: A Study of Shakespeare's Pastoral Plays* (1972).

9. The Tragedies

Bradley, A. C. *Shakespearean Tragedy* (1904).

Brooke, Nicholas. *Shakespeare's Early Tragedies* (1968).

Champion, Larry. *Shakespeare's Tragic Perspective* (1976).

Drakakis, John, ed. *Shakespearean Tragedy* (1992).

Evans, Bertrand. *Shakespeare's Tragic Practice* (1979).

Everett, Barbara. *Young Hamlet: Essays on Shakespeare's Tragedies* (1989).

Foakes, R. A. *Hamlet versus Lear: Cultural Politics and Shakespeare's Art* (1993).

Frye, Northrop. *Fools of Time: Studies in Shakespearean Tragedy* (1967).

Harbage, Alfred, ed. *Shakespeare: The Tragedies* (1964).

Mack, Maynard. *Everybody's Shakespeare: Reflections Chiefly on the Tragedies* (1993).

McAlindon, T. *Shakespeare's Tragic Cosmos* (1991).

Miola, Robert S. *Shakespeare and Classical Tragedy: The Influence of Seneca* (1992).

——. *Shakespeare's Rome* (1983).

Nevo, Ruth. *Tragic Form in Shakespeare* (1972).

Rackin, Phyllis. *Shakespeare's Tragedies* (1978).

Rose, Mark, ed. *Shakespeare's Early Tragedies: A Collection of Critical Essays* (1995).

Rosen, William. *Shakespeare and the Craft of Tragedy* (1960).

Snyder, Susan. *The Comic Matrix of Shakespeare's Tragedies* (1979).

Wofford, Susanne. *Shakespeare's Late Tragedies: A Collection of Critical Essays* (1996).

Young, David. *The Action to the Word: Structure and Style in Shakespearean Tragedy* (1990).

——. *Shakespeare's Middle Tragedies: A Collection of Critical Essays* (1993).

10. The Histories

Blanpied, John W. *Time and the Artist in Shakespeare's English Histories* (1983).

Campbell, Lily B. *Shakespeare's "Histories": Mirrors of Elizabethan Policy* (1947).

Champion, Larry S. *Perspective in Shakespeare's English Histories* (1980).

Hodgdon, Barbara. *The End Crowns All: Closure and Contradiction in Shakespeare's History* (1991).

Holderness, Graham. *Shakespeare Recycled: The Making of Historical Drama* (1992).

————, ed. *Shakespeare's History Plays: "Richard II" to "Henry V"* (1992).

Leggatt, Alexander. *Shakespeare's Political Drama: The History Plays and the Roman Plays* (1988).

Ornstein, Robert. *A Kingdom for a Stage: The Achievement of Shakespeare's History Plays* (1972).

Rackin, Phyllis. *Stages of History: Shakespeare's English Chronicles* (1990).

Saccio, Peter. *Shakespeare's English Kings: History, Chronicle, and Drama* (1977).

Tillyard, E. M. W. *Shakespeare's History Plays* (1944).

Velz, John W., ed. *Shakespeare's English Histories: A Quest for Form and Genre* (1996).

11. *The Comedy of Errors*

In addition to the items listed in Section 7, The Comedies, consult the following titles. Note especially the volume edited by Robert S. Miola, which collects some twenty reviews of productions as well as much of the best criticism.

Bishop, T. G. *Shakespeare and the Theatre of Wonder* (1996).

Brooks, Harold F. "Themes and Structure in *The Comedy of Errors*." In *Early Shakespeare: Stratford-upon-Avon Studies 3* (1961).

Brown, John Russell. *Shakespeare and His Comedies* (1957).

Charney, Maurice, ed. *Shakespearean Comedy* (1980).

Fergusson, Francis. "Two Comedies." In *The Human Image in Dramatic Literature* (1957).

Foakes, R. A., ed. *The Comedy of Errors. The Arden Edition of the Works of William Shakespeare* (1962).

Freedman, Barbara. *Staging the Gaze: Postmodernism, Psychoanalysis, and Shakespearean Comedy* (1991).

Grivelet, Michel. "Shakespeare, Molière, and the Comedy of Antiquity." In *Shakespeare Survey* 22 (1969).

Kinney, Arthur F. "Shakespeare's *Comedy of Errors* and the Nature of Kinds." *Studies in Philology* 85 (1988): 29–52.

Lanier, Douglas. " 'Stigmatical in Making': The Material Character of *The Comedy of Errors*." *English Literary Renaissance* 23 (1993): 81–112.

Miola, Robert S., ed. *The Comedy of Errors: Critical Essays* (1997).

Salgãldo, Gãmini. " 'Time's Deformed Hand': Sequence, Consequence, and Inconsequence in *The Comedy of Errors*." In *Shakespeare Survey* 25 (1972).

Salingar, Leo. *Shakespeare and the Traditions of Comedy* (1974).

Smith, Bruce R. "A Night of Errors and the Dawn of Empire: Male Enterprise in *The Comedy of Errors*." In *Shakespeare's Sweet Thunder*. Ed. Michael J. Collins (1997), pp. 102–25.

Tetzeli von Rosador, Kurt. "Plotting the Early Comedies: *The Comedy of Errors, Love's Labour's Lost, Two Gentlemen of Verona*." In *Shakespeare Survey* 37 (1984).

Thompson, Ann. " 'Errors' and 'Labors': Feminism and Early Shakespearean Comedy." In *Shakespeare's Sweet Thunder*. Ed. Michael J. Collins (1997), pp. 90–101.

Williams, Gwyn. "*The Comedy of Errors* Rescued from Tragedy." *A Review of English Literature,* 5 (October 1964): 63–71.

The Signet Classic Shakespeare Series:

The Comedies

*extensively revised and updated to provide more
enjoyment through a greater understanding of the texts*

READ THE TOP 25 SIGNET CLASSICS

To order call: 1-800-788-6262

S324